WHAT'S UP, DOC?

WHAT'S UP, DOC?

Psychology On the Rocks

David Begelman Ph.D.

Copyright © 2019 by David Begelman Ph.D.

ISBN: Softcover   978-1-7960-2591-0
              eBook   978-1-7960-2590-3

Print information available on the last page.

Rev. date: 04/15/2019

To order additional copies of this book, contact:
Xlibris
1-888-795-4274
www.Xlibris.com
Orders@Xlibris.com
794815

CONTENTS

Dedication

To Micah, Alec and Luca

Les enfants du paradis

Author Biography

David Begelman, Ph.D. is a practicing clinical psychologist and neuropsychologist with offices in New Milford and Litchfield, Connecticut. He is a graduate of the High School of Music and Art in New York City, and studied art with Mark Rothko. He has degrees in psychology and philosophy from Brooklyn College, New York University, and Yeshiva University. He was research assistant to Professor Irvin Rock in the Department of Experimental and Clinical Psychology of Yeshiva University, and has held administrative positions in a variety of clinical and academic settings. He was Assistant Professor of Psychiatry at Yale University and held consultant or staff positions in a variety of hospitals and clinics as well as being in private practice. In addition to these professional positions, Dr. Begelman has a theater background. Aside from appearing in many plays across the years, He was a past member of the Connecticut Critics Circle and was drama critic for the Danbury News-Times of Danbury, Connecticut and film and theater critic for the Citizen News of New Fairfield, Connecticut. As an actor, he performed many roles, including five Shakespearean leads: Shylock, King Lear, Prospero, Petruchio and Oberon/Theseus in the Connecticut Stage production of Midsummer Night's Dream. Currently, he is a board member of a non-profit production company, Love/Art/Play, dedicated to mounting projects for the support of needy women and children. He has been married to his wife, Arlene, for over sixty years and is the proud father of two children and three grandchildren.

Book Description

Psychology on the Rocks: What's Up Doc? Surveys the systems of a group of well known theorists, including Sigmund Freud, Carl Jung, B. F. Skinner, Paul McHugh, Søren Kierkegaard, Thomas Szasz, M. Scott Peck, Bernie Siegel, Thomas Nagel, Freeman Dyson and Oliver Sacks. Essays included explore the seminal works of these thinkers from a critical standpoint, viewing their writings as subject to the limitations of outlook that exceed the legitimate boundaries of what we presently know in social science or philosophical fields of inquiry. In his book, the author draws upon his background as a working clinician of many years with two offices in Connecticut, professional appointments in the past at clinics, hospitals, and academia as well as in private practice. He has advanced degrees in both psychology and philosophy.

Freud as Degenerate: Psychoanalysis, the Seduction Papers, and Racial Theory

A neglected but important aspect of Freud's formulations during what Young-Bruel (1994) has termed the originary decade of psychoanalytic theory, from 1890 to 1900, has already been dealt with to some extent by others (Stewart, 1976; Sulloway, 1992; Gilman, 1993a, 1993b). Essentially, it is a subtext of theorizing involving the notion of *degeneration*, a widespread preoccupation within Victorian medical circles. As then understood, degeneration conflated ideas of psychiatric disorder, ethnicity, and the hereditary transmission of traits. It figured negatively[1] in Freud's Seduction Theory (ST), which, while a predominantly environmentalist account of the psychoneuroses, was tacitly wedded to his wish to "dislodge heredity" as a formative factor. He says as much at key junctures in his three seduction papers of 1896: *Heredity and the Etiology of the Neuroses* (Freud, 1896a), *Further Remarks on the Neuro-Psychoses of Defence* (Freud, 1896b), and *The Aetiology of Hysteria* (Freud, 1896c), as well as in his correspondence with Wilhelm Fliess (Masson, 1985, pp. 264-266).

On the first occasion of Freud's public repudiation of the ST, in his *Three Essays On the Theory of Sexuality* (Freud, 1905), we find him still dismissing the role of heredity in explaining sexual inversion. Freud first alluded to the ST in October of 1895, in one of his numerous letters to Wilhelm Fliess. What might be characterized as the "official" story in the minds of many of Freud's followers and biographers has been summarized by Esterson as Freud's reporting that many of his patients in the 1890s reported being sexually abused in childhood and that he became convinced that in eliciting such accounts was the clue to the creation of hysteria he had been seeking. Subsequently, however, he came to realize those reports were fantasized by his patients, leading him to develop a theory of infantile fantasies that became one of the cornerstones of psychoanalysis (Esterson, 1993, p. 11).

Of the three seduction papers, *The Aetiology of Hysteria* focuses primarily on Freud's arguments for the reality of infantile seductions. It has been given the most critical attention in recent years, in part due to Jeffrey Masson's book *The Assault on Truth* (Masson, 1984). Masson argued that Freud's abandonment of the ST, based as it was on the view that his patients' reports of early sexual abuse were fantasies rather than realities, was a mistake. According to Masson, the abuse was real, not imagined. Masson also contends that the switch from reality to fantasy sprang from less than honorable motives on Freud's part. Among these was the need to exonerate his mentor, Wilhelm Fliess, from a charge of medical incompetence in the Emma Eckstein case.

Nineteen months [2] after the delivery of *The Aetiology of Hysteria* to the Viennese Medical Society and in a letter to Fliess dated September 21, 1897, Freud indicated he no longer believed in the ST. The admission is startling for several reasons. First, it drenches in irony Freud's bitterness over what he felt was a hostile reaction to the paper by the medical group to which it was presented. Since Freud himself abandoned the ST months after delivering his paper, what was the justification for his indignation at colleagues who felt the same way a short time earlier?

Second, the actual reasons Freud adduced for abandoning the ST are paradoxical. Among several he enumerated in the letter to Fliess were: (1) he had been unable to bring even one analysis to a successful conclusion, noting an "absence of complete successes" upon which he depended; (2) the fact that his "partial successes" might admit of alternative explanations; (3) that the ST was predicated upon an epidemiological paradox: a prevalence of sexual abuse implausibly high to accept as a true sociological picture, and that (4) he was unable to distinguish truth from fantasy. In the September, 1897 letter to Fliess, Freud stated that because of these four considerations, he was moved to give up his "neurotica" (i.e., the ST), and no longer knew where he stood theoretically. These explanations for his reversal bear further critical scrutiny.

(1) *Incomplete Successes.* This reason for abandonment of the ST seems odd in the light of Freud's obvious enthusiasm about therapeutic successes when he delivered his third seduction paper. Despite this,

his expression of disappointment is difficult to assess in advance of understanding what he meant by "a successful conclusion." As in the case history of Frau P., clinical outcomes routinely counted as "successes" are frequently admixtures of favorable and unfavorable results. Given this, how did the actual course of improvement in such a case bear on any definition of "cure" or "successful conclusion" motivating Freud to rework his etiological formulation in 1897? In other words, if Frau P.'s checkered therapeutic history paralleled those of other patients in Freud's caseload, how did the character of such clinical courses fuel doubts he began to harbor about the ST?

Frau P.'s analysis was reported by Freud to culminate in the remission of psychotic symptoms, maintained up to the authorship of his second seduction paper. In the paper, Freud indicated that an exacerbation of symptomatology all but nullified the gains of treatment, at which point Frau P. was given institutional care. Despite the clinical regression, she rallied and returned home. Improvement lasted another twelve to fifteen years, and she functioned well enough to carry on household responsibilities. The only reported sign of morbidity was her ostensible avoidance of contact with family members. Her symptoms returned once again later on in her life, whereupon she was rehospitalized, only to die of pneumonia in an asylum (Freud, 1896b, pp. 175-183). Since the onset of Frau P.'s problem coincided with a post-partum period, it possible that the psychosis was precipitated by this crucial life phase.

Rosy conceptions of "cure" often enjoy a connotation that fail to match the realities of clinical practice—whatever the condition. Clinicians who pin their hopes on making perfectionist criteria probative of their etiological formulations will frequently have to confront standards of "cure" unworkably stringent as requirements of serviceable theories. Accordingly, a question arises over whether Freud's 1897 standard of "success" involved an overly idealistic one. Did "cure" for him mean complete remission of symptoms with no possibility of relapse? Some salient symptoms? Most symptoms? If the first of these possibilities, it is doubtful whether *any* post-1897 adjustments of theoretical perspective would meet the demands of such idealistic criteria of treatment "success." The idea of fantasies of seduction as pathogenic would also appear to have been no more consistent with therapeutic results than the ST discarded for this reason.

The issue of therapeutic success is important in another respect. It bears on a larger and more contentious issue of the relationship between Freud's theories and the efficacy of psychoanalytic treatment procedures [3]. Whatever his later convictions, there is ample indication that in 1896 Freud relied heavily on therapeutic outcome as probative of theory confirmation. In *The Aetiology of Hysteria*, for example, he avers that in eighteen cases, his theory was confirmed by "therapeutic success" in every single case (Freud, 1896c, p. 199). At least his self-professed reasons for giving up his "neurotica" imply the same standard. In *Further Remarks on the Neuro-Psychoses of Defence*, Freud avers that when repressions of memories of early seduction scenes are lifted, patients' problems are "resolved" (Freud, 1896b, p. 174).

Elsewhere, Freud laments the therapeutic upshot of analyses lagging behind if one has not penetrated earliest sexual trauma, implying that desired results are contingent upon unearthing such memories. Here, his conviction about the connection between correct interpretation and treatment cure is obvious, although one may raise a question about the logical status of the linkage. If Freud held to conceptually independent criteria of "cure" and "correct analysis," his 1897 contention that the majority of his unresolved cases represented "incomplete analyses" was an empirical one. On the other hand, it is possible Freud may have fudged the point for the purposes of making forays into fresh theoretical territory. This would have been the case had he married the correctness of a theoretical formulation to beneficial results obtained in the consulting room. Whatever the case, there can be little doubt that in 1896 Freud was depending in large measure on therapeutic success as a yardstick of theoretical legitimacy.

In *Heredity and the Aetiology of the Neuroses*, Freud declared that even his approach to *stock* or *concurrent* causes, stressors which may enter into the causation of the psychoneuroses, but are not "indispensable for the production of the latter" bore fruit (Freud, 1896a, p. 147). His proviso here, however, was that treatment focusing exclusively upon such factors cannot be shielded from the possibility of relapse. The implication is clear: treatment aimed at causes specific to these disorders, memories of sexual trauma, when "complete," is immunized from relapse. The need to trace associations back to infantile sources in this phase of Freud's theorizing was based upon his assumption that only such a strategy would guarantee permanent cure of the psychoneuroses. Accordingly, in the absence of the presumed connection between his therapeutic strategy and "cure," the approach would be a fruitless one. That is, if in 1896 any technique founded upon alternative etiological assumptions was able to eradicate permanently all signs of neurotic disorder, the need to probe pre-adolescent memories of sexual trauma would be redundant. In such an event, the very basis for suspecting a connection between disorder and early sexual abuse would be weakened or nullified. Lasting symptom removal would then not be the upshot of a "deep analysis" exclusively. Consequently, the latter could not then monopolize the preferred approach or underscore a proper view of etiology.

In fact, Freud thought along roughly similar lines. One of his self-professed reasons for revising his outlook in 1897 was that the clinical course of his treatment cases suggested that the actual pathogen had to be driven back into the head. Actual sexual trauma, while capable of intensifying a clinical disorder—Freud subsequently did not come to deny either its existence or its role in exacerbating symptoms—no longer qualified as the true cause of the psychoneuroses. It was superseded by the unconscious process of organismic and essential, not merely accidentally heightened or externally derived, sexuality. It was Freud's 1896 conviction that durable clinical results were exclusively the upshot of methods wedded to proper interpretations. During that time, he held fast to this belief, as well as its corollary: the failure to eradicate symptoms was a presumptive indication that an analysis had not been "complete," had not dug deeply enough.

(2) *Alternative Explanations.* This reason for abandoning the ST remains a mystery, inasmuch as the possibility of alternative explanation is a theoretical risk of any formulation in the sciences, including those hypothetically associated with producing "complete" cures, however these are defined. It was not the fact that Freud's cures were "incomplete" that increased the likelihood of the possibility of alternative explanations

to the ST, since the same possibility existed had Freud produced the type of cure he sought in every case.

Vacillating emphases on the "completeness" or "incompleteness" of his cures in the originary canon seems to have kept pace with Freud's shifting enthusiasms for particular theories. When promoting the ST in 1896, he proclaimed "complete cure," using methods that owed allegiance to this theory, whereas in 1897 and thereafter he complained that the curative picture was grimmer than he had earlier indicated. In *Heredity and the Aetiology of the Neuroses,* and contrary to his 1897 pronouncements, Freud asserts that the symptoms of hysteria [4] can only be understood if they are traced back to traumatic sexual experiences. How can hysteria *only* be understood as the delayed effect of sexual trauma when alternatives to such a formulation exist—and indeed existed by Freud's own 1897 admission? Was Freud unaware of the possibility of alternative explanation in 1896, or did his enthusiasm for the ST at that time drown out the promptings of theoretical open-mindedness?

One of Freud's specific examples of an alternative to the ST during the originary period was masturbation. Long held to be a chief cause of neurotic disturbance by Victorian medicine generally—atavisms of its dire consequences on development still resound in corridors of sensibility resistant to disengaging religious dogma from scientific knowledge—it was dismissed by Freud in *Further remarks On the Neuro-Psychoses of Defence* as the true basis for the psychoneuroses. Although found "side by side with hysteria, this is due to the circumstance that masturbation itself is a much more frequent consequence of abuse or seduction than is supposed" (Freud, 1896b, p.165). The argument begs the question, since its conclusion is arbitrarily selective about causality when the factors under consideration covary with each other. Another instance of *petitio principii* appears in the very next paragraph where Freud assures us that the traumatic underpinnings of hysteria are proved by the development of the disorder. Here, precisely the theory Freud attempts to prove is used as evidence for itself.

(3) *The Prevalence of Childhood Sexual Abuse.* Freud's 1897 reservations about the prevalence of childhood sexual abuse is in

blatant contradiction to statements about it in the seduction papers. In *The Aetiology of Hysteria* he avers that certain children were more exposed to sexual assault that previous commentators had suspected. Consequently, he felt that other investigators would eventually uncover a greater frequency of "sexual experiences" and "sexual activity" during childhood (Freud 1896c, p. 207). [5]

Despite these assurances about the widespread reality of the Victorian sexual abuse of children, we are asked by Freud nineteen months later to believe his doubts about the ST were in part triggered by his realization that such abuse was not all that prevalent. Even modern critics like Grünbaum (1979) have accepted Freud's 1897 reasoning that the "preposterously high" level of sexual trauma required by the ST "over-taxed Freud's own belief in his seduction etiology" (Grünbaum, 1979, p.135). However, the fancied statistical improbabilities implied by the ST was not the tale told in 1896, and the contrast between the earlier polemic and his remarks in the 1897 Fliess correspondence is noteworthy. Perhaps Freud had good reasons for renouncing a theory he propounded months before; but sudden awareness of epidemiological verities was not one of them. There was nothing new in the sociological picture of infant abuse he could have learned about in the intervening period that would explain his revisionism. He was as sociologically sophisticated about its prevalence in 1896 as he was in 1897. That Freud suddenly realized the lesser extent of the abuse in 1897, but not nineteen months earlier is difficult to swallow. Moreover, it flies in the face of the way he marshaled evidence for the widespread nature of the problem in *The Aetiology of Hysteria.*

(4) *The Inability to Differentiate Between Real and Fantasized Events.* In *The Aetiology of Hysteria,* Freud felt that the reality of early sexual abuse as a causative factor was underscored by the striking similarity of accounts of the eighteen patients who had been in treatment with him up to April of 1896. This, he conjectured, vouched for the reality of infantile experiences unless it was assumed those scenes were a product of shared rumor-mongering by the patients involved (Freud, 1896c, p. 205).

Subsequently, as we have seen, Freud ostensibly felt no need to reconcile the similarity of reports of abuse with the newly hypothesized pathogen, *fantasized* experiences. The basis for the historical reality of seduction, the uniformity of reports from patient to patient, was suddenly forgotten in the flurry of enthusiasm for the power of fantasy. If, after 1897, reported seductions were construed as imagined rather than real, what was to be made of the uniformity of theme in patients' disclosures that Freud leaned on earlier to bolster a case for the actuality of the traumas? How much uniformity of theme is to be expected in fantasized material? Ought it to be more thematically heterogeneous than reports of actual trauma? If so, how much more? If not, how much less?

Perhaps there is no basis for assuming that fantasized events should be less uniform thematically than actual ones. But Freud earlier was insistent on the idea that uniformity confirmed the reality of trauma, whereas when switching to fantasy in 1897 he was apparently not bothered by the issue. This is all the more surprising in the light of Freud's wholesale reliance on the notion of uniformity for other polemical purposes. For example, the lack of uniformity among precipitating events of adolescence or late childhood was used by Freud to dramatize the fact the real pathogen must have lurked farther back in chronology (Schimek, 1987, p. 941).[7]

Preoccupations with the consistency of thematic material is a motif showing up at many historical junctures, and in many guises. In the sixteenth century, Thomas Erastus faulted Johann Weyer's theory of the falsity of witch confessions in the latter's 1563 treatise *De Praestigiis Daemonum* as implausible because their *similarity* from suspect to suspect across numerous witch trials proved they were based upon real events (Monter, 1969, p. 64). In the 1980s and 1990s, similarity of theme in reports of ritual cult abuse became the evidential basis for their reality, even when demons put in appearances at covens (Smith & Pazder, 1980; Stratford, 1988). "Similarity," however, is itself an unexamined concept. When the seventeenth century Spanish inquisitor, Alonso de Salazar y Frías, subjected "similar" reports of satanic cult activity to more exacting scrutiny, he found them to be a mishmash of conflicting testimony, and pronounced the affair a gigantic hoax (Baroja, 1965; Henningsen, 1969, 1980). During the early modern period, witches harbored grandiose goals, such as the destruction of Christendom. Nowadays, the servants of Satan, who enjoy advance billing as engineers of Evil, allegedly sexually molest toddlers in day care establishments. Apparently, latter-day Satanists are either prone to underachievement, or believe in starting small (Ebersole & Ebersole, 1993; Sebald, 1995).

Issues pertaining to the uniformity of clinical material played a decisive role in yet another pre-1896 controversy. This was the wrangle over theories of hypnotism that had been waged between the Salpêtrière School led by Charcot, and the Nancy School of Bernheim. While critical of Charcot, Freud could not go along with Bernheim's stress on a view of hypnotic phenomena as mere effects of suggestibility (Freud, 1888). In his critique of Bernheim, Freud argued that suggestibility could not account for the *uniformity* of particular and stereotyped stages of hypnosis produced by induction procedures. Freud thought that had hypnosis been the effect of suggestion merely, its psychic, motoric, and behavioral sequelae would have been much more varied than the stalwart patterns Charcot reliably produced without any seeming task demands on his subjects. It was only to emerge later that the manifestations *were* varied, and that the stereotypy of Charcot's demonstrations with hysterics were in all likelihood shaped by the implicit task demands of the Salpêtriére context, unknown even to him (Sulloway, 1991).

Textual Inconsistencies

There are other paradoxes in the seduction papers. For example, despite Freud's references to "reports" of early seduction by his hysterical and obsessional patients, the actual character of these disclosures remains unclear. While a question may be raised about the difficulty in discriminating between patient disclosures based upon actual trauma from those based upon fantasy *if* Freud's patients reported memories of being molested as children, whether they did or not is itself a hotly contested issue of modern scholarship. Without belaboring the detailed exegeses of such critics as Cioffi (1972, 1974, 1988); Schimek (1987); Macmillan (1991); Sulloway (1991); Shatzman (1992); Esterson (1993); and Crews (1986; 1995; 1998), suffice it to say that there is ample evidence in the canon to suggest that the founder of psychoanalysis left a rather murky picture of his data-base for the ST. Indeed, and in line with Freud's own statements, what he referred to as patient "memories" of early sexual abuse may have been reconstructions he had himself imposed on the material. Accordingly, conceptions of the data-base on the part of modern commentators have increasingly undergone transformations from the view that Freud's patients recalled intact scenes of sexual assault they disclosed to him (Masson, 1984; Erdylei, 1984) to the view that Freud's method involved purblind inferences to sexual scenarios from a less than suasive trail of symptoms, nodal points, and mental associations.[6]

The Verbal Crucible

In his second seduction paper, *Further Remarks On the Neuro-Psychoses of Defence,* Freud insists that psychoanalysis is the only method that can unearth the true pathogen behind the psychoneuroses (Freud, 1896b, p. 164). The implication is that it is useless to depend upon patient reports outside of psychoanalysis to accomplish the same task. He is less than clear, however, about whether traumas disclosed in therapy are inaccessible to consciousness because they are only inferred from their symptomatic manifestations, or only inaccessible outside of the analytic treatment context. The problem here involves the aforementioned confusion over whether what Freud referred to as "reports" of seductions were just that, or whether they were inferences—tortuous or not—to sexual scenarios which even his patients protested they did not remember. Be that as it may, Freud's distrust of anamnesis—questioning the patient as to events of the past—could hardly be said to spring from a wholesale distrust of verbal behavior as a channel of information. On the contrary, Freud's approach to the latter in the seduction papers exhibited curious levels of selectivity. Reliance on conscious recollections was eschewed as a legitimate route to the reconstruction of the pathogen, whereas the method of free association, while a meandering and laborious one, was nonetheless considered to be a dependable *verbal* conduit to the unconscious. Yet even here the picture is inconsistent. When a reliance on anamnesis served polemical purposes, Freud resorted to it as if its shortcomings suddenly evaporated: "...the aetiological pretensions of the infantile scenes rest not only on the regularity of their appearance in the *anamneses of hysterics* (Italics mine), but, above all, on the evidence of there being associative and logical ties between those scenes and the hysterical symptoms" (Freud, 1896c, p. 210). Ironically, Freud had been definite earlier in the same essay that it was "useless" to depend upon anamnestic material gleaned from outside psychoanalysis, and that it grossly distorts the psychoanalytic procedure to describe it as involved in any such enterprise.

The probative value of free association depends upon more than whether it is immune to the effects of "suggestion." Suggestibility, while a significant issue in its own right, is only one worrisome aspect of the problem. There are several others: (2) the problem of whether a reconstructive method mediated by free association with the effect of suggestion controlled is an epistemologically sound way to identify pathogens, and (3) whether the factors so identified have the causally relevant status to begin with (Grünbaum, 1984; Erwin, 1993). With respect to (2), and even in the absence of practitioner (i. e., Rosenthal) effects, what ensures that free association wends an unerring way to the source of neurotic disorder? Here the risk is not so much contamination by a response-set created by the therapeutic relationship as much as it is a diversion of the investigative process. Columbus might manage to cross the Atlantic with his navigational skills to be sure, but why should he have assumed that where he landed was India? With respect to (3), what, absenting the role of suggestion or derailment from a proper mental spoor, guarantees that the factor unearthed is actually a pathogen at all? Had Columbus landed in India, what made him believe he would find there the gold to enrich Spain's economy? Or if he found it, that there was a sufficient supply to mine? Or, if a sufficient supply, not tucked away in inaccessible hills? (Lourie, 1955).

Doubts about the nature of Freud's data-base in his originally thirteen (and subsequently, eighteen) patient caseload aside, there are other troublesome inconsistencies in the text (Thornton, 1983; Vetter, 1988; Israëls & Schatzman, 1993). For example, after his momentous reversal in 1897 on the reality of the seductions, Freud subsequently reported that one of the reasons for his newer stance on fantasy was that he hadn't realized in 1896 that seduction was only a necessary, not sufficient condition for hysteria. In other words, he later denied that he had been aware of the fact that while all hysterics were sexually abused as infants, not all individuals so abused later developed hysteria. The statement is belied by Freud's comments in *The Aetiology of Hysteria,* where he explicitly takes pains to emphasize his conviction that trauma is not sufficient to produce hysteria. He averred that it does not matter how many persons experienced sexual trauma and do not develop hysteria, unless those who become hysterics all underwent such experiences (Masson, 1984, pp. 269-270).

The Identity of Perpetrators

In his later *Autobiographical Study* (Freud, 1925, pp. 33-35), Freud retrospectively finds support for the so-called "father etiology" in the 1895 cases he treated with Breuer (Breuer & Freud, 1895) as well as the 1896 caseload. The "father etiology" was presumably the pathogenic effect of paternal incest in the creation of hysteria. However, there is little in Freud's identification of perpetrators in his original caseloads to justify such attributions. Accordingly, while Masson's interpretations reflect recent social concerns about paternal incest, no such pattern is referenced in the original three seduction papers. In the thirteen-patient caseload of the first of those papers, over half the perpetrators are brothers. In the last of the papers, most perpetrators are hired servants.

In addition, one stranger and two "close relatives" are cited (Esterson, 1993).

Some critics have insisted that Freud disguised the identity of fathers to protect Victorian family reputations. However, the identification of seven brothers as perpetrators suggests that maintaining veneers of social respectability was not uppermost in Freud's mind. Nor can this hunch explain the formulation of a "father etiology" shortly after he took pains to protect fathers from the calumny such a theory advertises. The "father etiology," after all, surfaces within a year after the delivery of the last seduction paper, as well as in the letters to Fliess. Mention of this theory is contained in the correspondence to Fliess in the 1896 letter of 12/6, and the 1897 letters of 1/3, 1/12, 1/24, 2/8, 4/28,/5/2, 5/31, 6/22, and 12/12 (Masson, 1985). Its introduction may have coincided with the development of alternative theory-driven surmises.

The theory that paternal perpetrators of incest were disguised as servants, uncles, or other relatives has been a popular one with apologists like Gay (1988, pp. 94-95), who favor exegeses diminishing textual inconsistencies or abrupt reversals in the canon. However, contradictions in the Freudian oeuvre are so numerous, retrospective remarks by the founder of psychoanalysis tend to come under a cloud. For example, in a footnote to the 1924 edition of the *Studies in Hysteria*, Freud discloses that two of his patients in the early caseload, Katherina and Rosalia H., had each been assaulted by their fathers—not as he originally reported, by other relatives. Katherina was reported by Freud in 1895 to have been abused by an "uncle." Even taking the correction into account, the sexual episode disclosed by Katherina was not one of infantile molestation, but unsuccessful overtures starting at the age of fourteen by the would-be perpetrator. On one occasion the "uncle" promptly fell asleep after invading the patient's bed. In addition, two years later, when Katherina was about sixteen, she merely witnessed him through a window engaging in coitus with a cousin, Francisca. The sexual provenance of this case is complicated by another component. Katherina's "hallucination" of her uncle's face, coinciding as this did with episodes of hyperventilation, also came after occurrences of threat and rage on the part of her uncle who felt the girl had blown his cover with his wife who subsequently abandoned him because of Katherina's revelations.

Unmasking "uncles" as "fathers" may correct a hitherto bowdlerized record—providing the true identity of the perpetrator is thus revealed. However, the traumatic criteria Freud had outlined as cornerstone assumptions of the ST are not met in Katherina's case, even if the perpetrator was her father. The required pathogenesis, a father who initiates sexually abusive patterns in the years of a patient's life prior to eight to ten is, if anything, insinuated, not documented by Freud. The other possibility is that in 1924 Freud simply forgot what he had said in 1895, putting a later theoretical spin on his earlier discovery. Accordingly, readjustments in the identity of perpetrators alone are not necessarily tantamount to satisfying criteria of pathogenesis. Gay's (1988) exegesis may be a study in irrelevance if it is based upon such cases as Katherina's.

Katherina aside, there is every reason to suppose that early infantile seductions were themselves questionable inferential constructions in Freud's theory that adult hysteria was produced by earlier pathogenic experiences meeting criteria of *traumatic force* and *suitability as determinant* (Freud, 1896c). "Force" and "suitability," nowhere precisely defined by Freud, place constraints on the type of event he was prepared to allow as causal in 1896 although its intended theoretical effect was to dampen explanation based upon heritability or degeneration. In other words, to disallow that a touch, glance, frottage, or otherwise inconsequential adolescent event has "traumatic force" virtually precludes differential response sensitivities based upon inherent biological vulnerability. The latter portends the role of hereditarian blight, whereas Freud's notions of *force* and *suitability* drew the boundaries of what environmental events could be deemed to play a sufficient causal role in hysteria without the complexities and variations introduced by a theory of degeneration.

The spell of Freud's formulations lies in his capacity as rhetorician to convince the reader he is trotting out indisputable clinical truths, when he is only relying on assumptions that conspire to ensure a preordained outcome (Fish, 1986; Wilcocks, 1994). In *The Aetiology of Hysteria*, for example, he refers to the case of a married couple whose "high degree of readiness to feel hurt on one occasion" requires a background of smoldering past resentments or squabbles between them. Freud's reasoning here is erroneous; the sensitivity in question demands no such assumption, since a plausible alternative hypothesis may attribute "readiness to become hurt" to a temperamental factor ungummed from an actual history of squabbling. Be that as it may, Freud then turns to the case of a neurosis produced in a nubile girl by the secret stroke of a boy's hand. Here, he conjectured that while it is possible to declare such a girl "eccentrically disposed" or "over-sensitive," this theory is implausible when analysis shows the touching "reminded her of another, similar touching" in her very early childhood. (Freud, 1896a, p. 279).

The argument is circular if in the absence of robust evidence for the causal role of early seduction, analysis "shows" the necessity for assuming it. Ironically, the reasoning would still be fallacious even if such evidence were forthcoming. The assumptive causal role of early seduction in this case would still have to be weighed against the possibility of inherent temperamental or biogenic vulnerability, especially in light of Freud's assumption that seduction is a necessary, but not sufficient, condition of hysteria. If some individuals do not later develop hysteria despite earlier experiences meeting the "force" and "suitability as determinant" criteria, what accounts for why individuals having similar experiences early in life can be differentiated symptomatically later on?

Definitions of Sexual Abuse

The Freudian notion of childhood sexual abuse itself cries out for definition. Critics have in the main discussed Freud's reliance on reports of early sexual abuse in terms of whether such disclosures could be construed as actual "reports" at all. Many have sidestepped the issue of what sense of the term "abuse" figured as essential to the ST. Masson, in commenting on the specific nature of the sexual scenarios, has referred to them as "aggressive acts against...children—for seduction was an act of violence" (Masson, 1984, p.12). The extreme nature of the acts, Masson feels, justifies designating them as abusive, even in their least brutal form. The abusiveness, Masson insists, is suggested by several of the leading terms Freud used to describe the acts in question: "*Verguwaltigung* (rape), *Musbrauch* (abuse), *Verfuhrung* (seduction), *Angriff* (attack), *Attentat* (assault), *Aggression* (aggression), *Traumen* (traumas)" (Masson, 1984, p. 3). As a general rule, other commentators tend to share Masson's view that the sexual events underscored by the ST were in the category of childhood rape or molestation—with some exceptions.

At other times, Freud seemed to rely upon a somewhat wider notion of sexual trauma than that articulated in Masson's book, or, indeed, in most recent commentary on the subject. This has already been pointed out by Cioffi. This writer insists that the ST did not require any such egregious aspect of "seductions," since the theory is not one involving "child rape," not "even in the broadest sense." He insists that the etiological factor of childhood sexual arousal lies "quite simply in its precocity." This includes such causes as "doctor and nurse games," not assaults by "adult perverts," a theory that such causes are hardly "preposterous" enablers of later hysteria (Cioffi, 1988, p. 62).

Cioffi claims that critics like Masson misconstrue the ST since the theory posits the pathogenic power of sexual arousal in childhood whatever that nature or degree of sexual stimulation (i.e., encompassing sexual acts not unduly aggressive in character). Yet that all or most of the seductions were in the nature of aggressive acts is apparent in several of the descriptions Freud supplies in his eighteen patient caseload. He mentions scenes described, *inter alia*, as those of "brutal assault," "positively revolting," involving "all the abuses known to debauched and impotent persons, among whom the buccal cavity and the rectum are misused for sexual purposes" (Freud, 1896c, p. 214).

Cioffi's minimalist theory of seduction founders on an important point. If such sociological universals as "doctor and nurse games" were for Freud pathogenic, the reasons for his 1897 disavowal of the ST remain incoherent. What sense attaches to having been previously mistaken about a preposterously high level of doctor and nurse games in accounting for hysteria? If brutal assaults—in contrast to *any* kind of sexual stimulation in childhood—were not etiologically necessary to produce later hysteria, what picture of things was Freud repudiating in 1897? Moreover, had sexual precocity been the culprit as Cioffi avers, even innocuous cleansing and toileting rituals might satisfy minimalist requirements for "seduction." Whatever Freud meant by the term, such inconsequential daily routines seemed to be far from what he had in mind—at least in 1896.

Perhaps problems surrounding Freud's definition of sexual abuse can be partially resolved by pointing out that he may have equivocated its meaning, depending on the needs dictated by alternative theoretical perspectives. That is, switching concepts of abuse may explain certain incongruities in the canon. For example, in 1931 in the essay *Female Sexuality,* Freud asserted that all of his earlier hysterical patients revealed that their *mothers* had seduced them in infancy (Freud, 1931, p. 238). Freud characterized this patient allegation as lodged "regularly," although pages before in the same essay he maintains that those accused are mothers and *nurses* (Freud, 1931, p. 232). Far from contradicting the father etiology, or the identity of perpetrators in the seduction papers, the remark may only reflect a later and expanding notion of "infantile seduction" meeting minimalist criteria of sexual abuse. At other junctures in the canon, Freud considered "traumatic" such events as the visual witnessing of primal scenes as in the cases of Katherina (Freud & Breuer, 1895) and the Wolf-Man (Freud, 1918). While in the seduction papers Freud mentions the more gruesome types of sexual attack nowadays documented as all too prevalent, other of his later comments suggest such egregious events were only a subclass of a wider range he later considered pathogenic. Unquestionably, there is a radical transformation in the status of the pathogen after Freud emphasized the role of infantile fantasy, and it may be premature to suppose that the only significant alteration in theory was the switch from reality to fantasy. In fact, the coercive and brutal characteristics of "seduction" cited in *The Aetiology of Hysteria* all but vanished when the sexual episode was transmuted into a figment of childhood imagination.

Even at that, the picture is not always consistent. There seem to be changing definitions of the pathogen even within a single theoretical time frame—and during the originary period. In *Heredity and the*

Aetiology of the Neuroses, there is mention of a pathogen involving "an event of passive sexuality, an experience submitted to with indifference or with a small degree of annoyance or fright" (Freud, 1896a, p. 155). How does such a low-keyed event comport with our idea of infantile rape or molestation? Additionally, how is the event in question experienced with *indifference* unless it instantiates a minimalist, and looser definition of sexual abuse? We are here torn between at least two possibilities: (1) that Freud still clung to the notion of "trauma" as narrowly defined, i.e., a coercive or brutal event, but opining it can on occasion be experienced *indifferently* by the victim, or that (2) that Freud shifted the meaning of "trauma" to cover sexual episodes of a far less dramatic nature. We have, in effect, two substantially different conceptions of the pathogen: a wider one which less often informed speculation in the seduction papers, and a more narrow one prevailing in the seduction papers and adumbrated in, for example, current theories of Dissociative Identity Disorder and sociological concerns about the prevalence of childhood sexual abuse (Lynn & Rhue, 1994; Cohen, Berzoff & Elin, 1995; Hacking, 1995). In the main, critics who have commented on the issue have elected to argue that Freud was adhering exclusively to the narrow (Masson) or wider (Cioffi) definition of sexual trauma. However, there is a third possibility: slippery and alternating reliance on both senses of "trauma," depending upon rhetorical purpose.

Equivocating between the narrow and wider definitions may have had a strategic purpose: permitting Freud to exit the ST in late 1897. In the September 21, 1897 letter to Fliess, one of the reasons Freud gave for abandoning the ST was the unlikelihood of such widespread perversions by fathers—as if fathers had ever originally been cited as predators! Under the looser definition of trauma, of course, such "perversions" need not have been the restricted playing field in establishing ST surmises.

Ironically, suspecting a connection between infantile sexual episodes and later symptoms, far from being a Freudian innovation, was endemic in Victorian medical theorizing.[7] In *Heredity and the Aetiology of the Neuroses*, Freud himself acknowledges that "Sexual disorders have always been admitted among the causes of nervous illness," although "subordinated to heredity" (Freud, 1896a, p. 149). During 1885 and before, fully a decade before Freud's ST, Henoch, Cohn, Schaefer, and Herz all argued that that if infantile sexual episodes caused neurosis, the latter were more widespread than observed (Carter, 1983). This was the very same argument Freud relied on in 1897 when rejecting the ST. Under the looser definition of abuse, however, widespread "trauma" in children is not only not rare, it is virtually inevitable, and authored by a social cast of characters far more varied than fathers. As was mentioned, the wider notion also embraces phenomena we would refrain from classifying as "perverse" or abusive." [8]

Sidestepping Heredity

Returning to the other thematic emphasis in the seduction papers, we note that in *Heredity and the Etiology of the Neuroses,* the term *heredity* or its cognates is referenced about thirty-six times. The invisible grip that the Victorian glossing of this concept had on the founder of psychoanalysis in the originary decade and beyond remains to be clarified. Freud's ST, whatever else it represents as a landmark contribution to trauma theory, was also a cryptic expression of its author's need to circumvent attributing the neuroses to biogenic, particularly hereditarian, factors. The subtext of degeneration in the ST becomes more apparent when we see it as an aspect of Freud's campaign to rescue the psychoneuroses from the aura of immutability cast by hereditarian doctrine.

Far from restricting himself to symptomatic patterns for which the notion of repression played a key role, Freud also supplied environmentalist accounts of the actual neuroses. These were subdivided into neurasthenia and the anxiety neuroses. The former embraced a pattern of debilitation and energy depletion (specifically, "fatigue, intracranial pressure, flatulent dyspepsia, constipation, spinal parasthesias, sexual weakness, etc. (Freud, 1896a, p. 150) traceable to patterns of masturbation, or depletion of the sexual factor. The other was the anxiety neuroses (*Zwangsneurose*), patterns roughly coextensive with what nowadays might be diagnosed as generalized anxiety disorder, panic disorder, simple phobia, post-traumatic stress disorder, or adjustment disorder with anxious mood (for Freud, irritability, states of anxious expectation, phobias, anxiety attacks, complete or rudimentary, attacks of fear and vertigo, tremors, sweating, congestion, dyspnea, tachycardia, etc., chronic diarrhea, chronic locomotor vertigo, hyperaesthesia, insomnia, etc.), the pathogen for which was frustration of the sexual factor, as in *coitus interruptus*, "enforced abstinence, unconsummated genital excitation…sexual efforts which exceed the subject's psychical capacity, etc." (Freud, 1896a, pp. 150-151).

Much is made of the fact that the reception accorded the seduction papers on the part of the medical community was a hostile one—as though Freud delivered his address to a medical community unprepared to receive discoveries in advance of their time. On the contrary, Freud would have never had the temerity to present what in terms of modern medicine constitutes junk science had not his peers been already partially receptive to a linkage between sexuality and neurotic disorder. Kraft-Ebbing's comment about Freud's ST that it "sounded like a scientific fairy-tale" ("*Es klingt wie ein wissenschaftliches Märchen*") was in all likelihood prompted by the convoluted explanations of its author, not by the idea of a connection between sexual events and later neurotic disturbance *simpliciter*, a linkage many Victorian physicians already held as established.

Freud's attitude towards heredity was not always of a piece. It underwent several distinct changes in the originary period. The hereditarian cast to speculation over psychiatric conditions was rife in Victorian academic and medical theorizing, and Freud, like many of his contemporaries, originally endorsed heredity as a primary pathogen. The trend was especially discernable in the early days of his sojourn at Salpêtrière, under Charcot's influence. In 1888 he claimed that hysteria was hereditary, sexual factors being of secondary importance and overrated in clinical practice (Freud, 1888, p. 50).

Freud's earlier endorsement of Charcot's genetic position on the etiology of hysteria was backed up by seemingly persuasive arguments. He stressed the fact that hysteria, while inherited, could not be attributed to anatomical abnormalities of the sexual organs. Here, he countered that the condition occurred in sexually immature individuals, women with a complete lack of genitalia, and women who have diseases of the sexual organs who nonetheless do not suffer from hysteria.

Freud's French Connection

Before his traveling bursary stipend was awarded by the Viennese medical Society, Freud looked forward to his Parisian trip in order to familiarize himself with a broader spectrum of pediatric cerebral pathology (Freud 1886a, p. 8). Attending Charcot's Monday and Tuesday lectures, the *consultation extreme,* he was privy to case presentations of challenging and puzzling clinical phenomena, including hysteria. In his 1886 summary of his experiences, Freud placed double emphasis on Charcot's contribution to the study of hysteria, namely: (1) emphasizing the disorder as a true medical condition, rather than a factitious one, i.e., one that had come to be regarded in traditional medical circles as simulation or malingering; and (2) codifying the somatic signs and stages of hysteria, stigmata that cropped up more frequently than hitherto assumed.

Szasz (1961) has argued that the switch from "malingering" to "hysteria" or "medical disorder" was a conceptual one not based upon purely empirical considerations. True, there were characteristic features of hysterical patterns both Charcot and Freud catalogued, and the decision to classify them as "sickness" rather than "dissembling" or "malingering" may be likened to certain *judicial* rulings in contrast to purely empirical discoveries. Szasz concludes on this basis that the switch was illicit because it was driven by the purchasing of a newer social role commanding sympathetic treatment as "disease" at the expense of a falsehood. However, the sympathetic social role can as readily be seen as a consequence of diagnosing "disorder," rather than as a motivation for engineering the reclassification. Furthermore, saying that hysterics should be accorded a social role more commensurate with "faking" than "being sick" was in the past also a move in a language-game requiring its own validation. (Is the original classification of "typhoid fever, and carcinomas and fractures" as "illnesses" illicit because of the essential dissimilarities among these phenomena?) According to Szsaz, what are the "scientific observations or logical arguments" for categorizing hysteria as *malingering* historically, and prior to Charcot's newfangled reclassification as *disorder*, given the essential differences between ordinary cases of malingering (i.e., without the quasi-neurological overlay) and "hysteria"?

Freud's attitude toward the French neurologist was one of an admiring student. He was enthralled by his instructor's command of the subject matter and his spellbinding lectures. As a result, Freud in 1886 (Freud, 1886b) was inspired to author a German translation of Charcot's work, *Neue Vorlessungen uber die Krankheiten des Nervensystems insbesondre uber Hysterie* (New Lectures On the Diseases of the Nervous System, including Hysteria), not to mention another article appearing in French in *Archives de Neurologie* in 1893. In his Charcot paper of 1893 (Freud, 1893), Freud draws a parallel between hysteria and cases of witchcraft and demon possession during the Middle Ages, phenomena he was later to explore in his 1922 paper *A Seventeenth Century Demonological Neurosis*, as well as in letters to Fliess of January 17 and 24 (Masson, 1985, pp. 224-228).

Nothing in Freud's Paris report of 1886 gives indication that there was more to the panegyric he accorded his teacher than meets the eye—but there was. In August of 1893, well before the publication of the ST, Freud authored another essay, *Charcot*, which diplomatically explored the weaknesses of his former teacher's views on hysteria. While extolling Charcot's restoring "dignity to the topic" (Freud, 1893, p. 19), Freud proceeds to probe the essential weakness of his teacher's position. This for Freud consisted in Charcot's insistence on hysteria being a form of hereditary degeneracy, a subclass of *famille nèvropathique* (Féré, 1884). On this theory, other pathogens are relegated to the minor category of *agents provocateurs*, mere triggering factors atop the real vulnerability.

Freud's objection to Charcot's theory is discernable in the last paragraph of *Charcot*. The formulation informed by genetic taint, Freud declares, "will no doubt require sifting and amending" (Freud, 1893, p.23). the reason for this is that "so greatly did Charcot overestimate heredity as a causative agent that he left no room for the acquisition of nervous illness...nor did he make a sufficiently sharp distinction between organic nervous affections and neuroses, either as regards their etiology or in other aspects" (Freud, 1893, p. 23). Then, as in all elegies in which trotting out the limitations of the deceased requires the expression of compensatory sentiments lest one be perceived as kicking the corpse, Freud appends a diplomatic salute to the value Charcot "taught us," a value that "changing times" could not diminish (Freud, 1893, p. 23).

Charcot's influence on Freud is discernable in the importation of ideas surfacing later in the seduction papers, especially *Heredity and the Aetiology of the Neuroses*. For example, Charcot's distinction between traumatic and organic paralysis was transformed into the Freudian distinction between the origins of hysteria and hereditary disorder. The independence of hysteria from practitioner effects mirrors the position adopted by Charcot in his controversy with Bernheim on the subject of hypnotic induction as a neurological tool versus an effect of suggestibility. Finally, the phrase *agents provocateurs* in *The Aetiology of Hysteria* was not only borrowed from the Charcot lexicon, but given a meaning that clashed with the one honored by the French neurologist. For Charcot, *agents provocateurs* were environmental triggers producing clinical patterns in genetically compromised organisms; for Freud, they became the accidental triggers in later chronological development betraying the existence of precocious sexual experience amounting to environmentally sourced trauma. The appropriation of concepts and terminology from Charcot in the service of a psychological theory wholly contrary to the Frenchman's theoretical intent is not mere speculation; Freud explicitly makes such an attribution (Freud 1896a, p. 155).

In 1888 Freud reserved a minor functional role for sexuality in the origins of hysteria as a concession to the "high psychical significance" of this factor in all kinds of neurosis (Freud, 1888, pp. 50-51; Levin, 1944, pp. 123-124). The second phase of his thinking, beginning with the transitional period of 1892 to 1893, involved recognition of a less dramatic influence of heredity as a contributing factor, as when, in Draft A Freud relegated its influence to the status of a "multiplier" (Stewart,

1976). Freud referenced the potentiating effect of heredity, like that of an electrical circuit, even in the first seduction paper *Heredity and the Problem of the Neuroses* (Freud, 1896a, p. 147). Diminishing its role was more apparent in the last of the three papers, *The Aetiology of Hysteria*. This paper argues that the infantile sexual episode preempted a more dominant role for heritability. However, Freud's final position in this paper equivocated on the issue of just how secondary a factor heredity was. For example, Freud insisted that "pseudo-heredity," a lineage of family neuroses springing from seductions, could get masked as a biogenic transmission of traits. The actual role of the latter variable uncomplicated by psychosocial factors was left indeterminate.

The Medicalization of Race

Freud's sojourn in Paris at the Salpêtrière from October 1885 to February 1886 coincided with a period of anti-Semitic ferment in France (Stewart, 1976; Gilman, 1993a). The failure of the Catholic bank, the *Union Generale* in 1882, was blamed on the Jews in general and Rothschild influence in particular (Stewart, 1976; Weber, 1986). There were several contemporaneous trials of Jews for ritual murder. Edouard Drumont's inflammatory *La France juiv*, a diatribe against Jewish influence on national affairs, enjoyed popularity (Stewart, 1976). The Dreyfus affair, a scandal that drove a deep cleavage between French factions convinced that no less than the honor of the country was at stake, was fulminating. Dreyfusards like Emile Zola began clamoring for redress around the time the ST was formulated and abandoned. French intolerance in this period of ferment had a distinctly racial cast when it came to Jews, although flagrant episodes of open violence against Italian immigrants was sparked by economic motives purely (Weber, 1986, pp. 134-135). The influx of Jewish immigrants from Eastern Europe sparked fears of racial taint and degeneration through intermarriage with them. This social anxiety was expressed indirectly in a British literary metaphor: Bram Stoker's *Dracula*. Its principal character is a scourge from the Slavic (Romanian) East. He turns his victims into one of his own kind by draining their blood or exchanging it with his own.[9]

One year before Freud's stay in Paris, in 1884, Charles Féré had developed the notion of *famille névropathique* (Féré, 1884), underscoring a lineage involving the hereditary predisposition to nervous disease. In 1894, two years before Freud's ST, he traced several cases of hysteria to early sexual molestation, but with a difference: Féré did not feel repression played any role in the etiology of the condition.

The idea of hereditary predisposition in Victorian thinking was linked to the medicalization of race. High on the list of groups vulnerable to the blights of hereditary taint were Jews. Racial theorists of nineteenth century Europe, including Freud's idol Jean-Marie Charcot, considered Jews and Asiatics particularly at risk. Latter day pundits, like Murray and Herrnstein in *The Bell Curve* place them at the top—at least as far as I.Q. is concerned (Murray & Herrnstein, 1994). Consistency was never a strong card in racial theorizing.

Heated debates over degenerative gene pools were quite the rage in Victorian Europe. They captured the imagination of many medical theorists, including Charles Darwin's cousin, Sir Frances Galton, Alsberg, Binswanger, Budul, Siebert, Pilcz, Kirchhof, Buschan, Burgle, Wulfing-Luer, Leroy-Beaulieu, Ziemssen, Löwenfeld, Erb, Krafft-Ebing, Gutmann, Kraepelin, Frigyes, and Charcot (Gilman, 1993a, pp. 93-168). While the rudimentary European sociological literature did not document a relatively greater incidence of brother-sister incest among Jews, the common Victorian assumption was that they were more susceptible to such patterns because of their degenerated blood lines. Alleging brother-sister incest among Jews was ironic. The Aryan crown-prince of racial purity, Siegfried, was himself the product of an incestuous union: Siegmund and Sieglinde. Seven cases of brother-sister incest crop up in Freud's original caseload. Many of these patients were Jewish, while Thomas Mann's novella *Blood of the Walsungs* is the story of a Jewish incestuous pair by the names of Siegmund and Sieglinde (Gilman, 1993b, p. 178).

Freud references hereditarian doctrine many times in the seduction papers of 1896. In *Further Remarks On the Neuro-Psychoses of Defence*, and at the end of its first section, Freud declares; "How greatly the claims of hereditary disposition are diminished by the establishment in this way of [environmental] aetiological factors as a determinant needs no more than a mention" (Freud, 1896b, p. 163). The conclusion is fallacious. Freud's view of the inconsistency between the ST and a theory of genetic predisposition was not only specious; it was promoted on the basis of data he amassed at break-neck speed. The first seduction paper relied on a cohort of thirteen patients. Since it was sent off to the publisher on February fifth, and Freud reported data on eighteen patients on April twenty-first of the same year, it appears he was able to determine the requisite etiology of five new cases in the amazing time of two and a half months, or seventy-five days. Considering the fact that he characterized his procedures as "laborious" on the first occasion he coined the term "psychoanalysis," it is astonishing that five cases yielded up their secrets—if they did this—with such alacrity. The idea that hereditary predisposition as an etiological factor is diminished in likelihood because Freud outlined specific events in the life history of patients to account for later neurosis is a *non sequitur*, especially in light of his insistence that not all sexually abused children become hysterics subsequently. Cannot temperamental differences among individuals with a genetic predisposition also account for the morbidity?

In *Heredity and the Aetiology of the Neuroses*, Freud announces that the ST undercuts the role of heredity by recruiting the notion of "accidental factors" in the life span. By "accidental factors" he means those precocious sexual events that were environmentally induced, not an aspect of native endowment, or traits templated in the germplasm.

Why was Freud so motivated to dispute the hereditarian stance, and so eager to develop a purely psychological theory to explain neuroses? While Sulloway (1992) has argued persuasively that Freud's system was an extension of the nineteenth century biology in which he was trained, there is another side to the story. Moreover, grounding in biological science does not account for Freud's attraction to crackpot theories such as Fliess's biorhythms, nasal determinism, or his preoccupation with numerology (as this relates to the occult significance of addresses and telephone numbers, not to mention intimations of his own death).

Even as staunch a loyalist as Gay felt that Freud should have been more skeptical of Fliess's "dogmatism" and "obsessions," not to mention the latter's "high-flying attempt to ground biology in mathematics" (Gay, 1988, p. 57).

Freud's environmentalism may have been his version of coming to grips with nineteenth century racial theory condemning Jews to degenerative blood lines. In fact, this subtext had personal and specific meaning for him. Shortly after his endorsement of Charcot's views on the genetic basis for hysteria, Freud had occasion to remind himself of the "neuropathic taint" among members of his own family tree, observing that such "stories are very common in Jewish families" (Freud, 1964, p. 203). In his February 11, 1897 letter to Fliess, Freud drew attention to his discovery of hysteria in several of his siblings, and in the letters of August 14 and October 3 of the same year cites the discovery of the condition in himself. To racial theorists, of course, such "discoveries" were hardly revelations when it came to Jews! McGrath notes that the increasingly anti-Semitic ambience of the late nineteenth century European French and German scene may have been the backdrop that motivated Freud to counter with an environmentalist, not hereditarian take on the neuroses (McGrath, 1986, p. 161).

Was Freud's perception of hysteria in his nuclear family for him an alarming confirmation of Victorian racial theory—so alarming it was necessary for him to theorize it away? Some authors (Balmary, 1979; Krüll, 1979) have dwelt on the fate of the ST during the originary period as this relates to the theme of Freud's relationship with his father. What such a focus may ignore, however, is the extent to which Jacob Freud's imputed "perversity" may have been a forced move (and eventually a *reductio ad absurdum*) in a formulation originally framed as an alternative to racial doctrine. In short, an implication of the ST was that if Freud's family members were "hysterics," then their condition was the effect of an older sex abuser in the nuclear family configuration. Why the culprit had to be Jacob (rather than the mother, brothers, servants, or family relatives or nursemaids) probably stems from the vagaries of Freud's finger-pointing.

Victorian theories of Jewish degeneration, as were mentioned, were driven by medical notions of hereditary taint. Considering this, it would have been impossible for Freud to have considered the idea of genetic transmission ungummed from self-incrimination. If, however, heredity was nothing but repressed sexual molestation, then *neuroses were created because of what happened to people, not because of their native endowment.* This theme registered in nineteenth century treatises of European Jewish physicians. In an all too apparent defensive mode, many of them argued that the presumed higher percentage of neurosis among Jews reflected their adverse social circumstances and struggles in prejudiced communities, not the biological consequences of degeneration (Fishberg, 1911).

Politics and Paranoia

The relationship between an enduring, but often "civilized" Viennese anti-Semitism, and Freud's presumed hypersensitivity about this is another intriguing issue. What, it may be asked, is a "normal," not "hypersensitive" response to such a *Weltanschauung*? The force of the term "hypersensitive" smacks of deviancy of reaction, while the assumed boundaries of non-pathological reactivity to racial prejudice remains a murky determination. We know that Freud felt increasingly isolated from the medical establishment. If this was in part sparked by its implicit hostility to Jews, what should the proper Jewish response have been?

A critical consensus has it that despite the intolerance of Viennese society to ethnic difference—an intolerance as instanced by its tacit acceptance of *fin de siecle* racial theories of Jewish degeneration and extended to persons of color and Asiatic descent (Gilman, 1993a)— Freud's personal attitude toward the establishment was uniquely stamped in the form of a personality quirk. Accordingly, critics seek to psychiatricize Freud's attitude toward his social milieu, a textual stance they feel is confirmed by what Esterson has called Freud's "paranoia" (Esterson, 1993, p.130). The problem here is that the trait in question was manifested in a society in which Jews were already derogated. In such an atmosphere, who establishes the permissible boundaries of antipathy or normalcy of response? When one is the target of such pressure, just what attitude is the acceptable one, and according to whose standards?

As a questionable case in point of Freud's "paranoia" (Farrell, 1996), let us consider the 1897 episode of his belated appointment as *Extraordinarius* (i.e., Associate Professor) to the faculty of the University of Vienna. Freud's candidacy was recommended by both Nothnagel and Krafft-Ebing in January of that year, and in June by the academic assembly of the university. Von Hartel, the Minister of Education, temporized on recommending appointment until February 27, 1902. It was finally endorsed by Emperor Franz Joseph on March 11, 1902, fully five years after it was received by the ministry. Moreover, it was not until the intervention of well-placed patients and after the request was renewed by sponsors that it was finally ratified. Freud was also informed by his instructor Sigmund Exner in 1902 that there was a move afoot to abort the nomination. Freud had written Fliess on February 8, 1897 he had been warned by his sponsors that there may be forces at work intent on sabotaging the appointment. The subsequent controversy over whether anti-Semitism played any role in delaying Freud's appointment is perhaps studded with more complexities than recent critics allow.

Ellenberger (1970), Sulloway (1992), and Glicklhorn and Glicklhorn (1960) have insisted that anti-Semitism did not motivate the delay, although this was Freud's perception. Ellenberger feels that Freud was neither "really isolated" nor "ill-treated" by colleagues (Ellenberger, 1970, p.448) while Sulloway argues that seven of the ten 1897 candidates in Freud's group were Jewish and that von Hartel was down on record as denouncing anti-Semitism. However, as McGrath (1986) points out, the administrative quota on promotions might have been put in place explicitly to offset the number of Jews rising through the academic ranks. The possibility of some such tacit policy is suggested by the tumultuous political events occurring during this period of Austrian history. Partial support to Kasimir Badeni's coalition government was given by the anti-Semitic Christian Socials, a party responsible for the 1895 election of the racist demagogue Karl Lueger as mayor of Vienna. It is plausible to suppose that the coalition was perceived as being made more fragile by concessions to Jews at governmental levels. Quotas on academic promotions—especially in cases in which seventy per cent of candidates were Jewish—would have effectively diminished opportunities for anti-Semites to rabble-rouse around local issues.

Whatever the true picture behind Freud's appointment delay, his alleged "paranoia" about the promotion hinges on the outcome of a political analysis of some complexity. Thus, had the quota actually been established on anti-Semitic grounds, Freud's "paranoia" begins to look more like political astuteness. The upshot of another way of looking at such events is to query how much "paranoia" over anti-Semitism is really paranoia in an anti-Semitic environment? This in no way diminishes the possibility of personality factors entering the equation, although separating reality from paranoid distortion may not be as easy as some suppose.

Similar considerations apply to Ellenberger's denial of "ill treatment" of Freud at the hands of his colleagues. A case in point is the Salpêtrière sojourn. Charcot's treatment of Freud was in many respects collegial—even to the point of permitting his student to translate his works. Yet what should have been Freud's attitude toward a mentor who believed on theory his student was at risk for being a racial degenerate? It is, of course, quite in the style of conventional wisdom everywhere to fashion its own criteria of mistreatment—to which those on the receiving end are expected to adhere.

Quashing heredity for Freud took yet another form: construing it as a farrago of fixed and acquired characteristics. Thus, Freud's Lamarckian assumptions concerning inheritance implied that racial characteristics passed along through the germplasm themselves originated in the experiences of one's ancestors. Translated into terms compatible with a doctrine of the susceptibility of Jews to psychological disorder, this meant that what was passed along was still in the nature of what *happened* to people, not what they *were* intrinsically. Freud's forays into the generational transmission of traits, memories, and melodramas, as in *Totem and Taboo* (Freud, 1912-1913, pp. 1-161) were probably partially driven by the need to explain the origins of similar infantile fantasies. For if after 1897 he came to regard seduction fantasies as scenarios ungrounded in reality and springing from the Oedipal conflict, why was the scenario always the same, and what was the provenance of its singular thematic material? Here Lamarckianism also came to the rescue. True, the theme of killing the father and sexually possessing the mother is inherited to be sure, but not from flatfooted chromosomes. It derives from the *experiences* of one's ancestors who in the distant past were caught up in real life Oedipal dramas.

Freud, like so many of his contemporaries, both Jew and Gentile, was so taken with the alleged epidemiological realities upon which racial theory depended, his strategy for self-redemption developed within the constraints it imposed. The strategy became one of rescuing the vulnerability thought to be a statistically high risk for Jews, neurosis, from the purview of genetic blight. Achieving this meant showing how the blight in question was freed from an aura of inevitability by being stamped with environmentally wrought characteristics. The theoretical adjustments necessary to get out from under the depredations of racial theory amounted to quite a two-step by Freud. But his failure to fashion a plausible alternative for self-redemption must be considered in the light of his feeling downgraded.

Unlike contemporary social and biological scientists (Gould, 1981), Freud was in no position to attack racial theory directly. The latter was an intellectual tradition so ingrained in the medical thinking of his era, opposing its statistics on the prevalence of Jewish mental disorder would have been akin to bowdlerizing anatomy or reversing knowledge about infectious diseases. Racial theory had—and still has—another unique characteristic. It tends to color thinking about ethnicity by instilling attitudes that linger long after their open expression has been rendered anachronistic by updated knowledge. When current dictates of diplomacy, manners, or tact forbid the overt expression of racially inspired sentiment, the invisibly harbored doctrines can persevere as strongly as ever.

Endnotes

[1] The British philosopher J. L. Austin (Austin, 1960) undertook to discuss "trouser words." These are words like "real" whose negative usage "not real" or "unreal" give the trouser word its definite sense. It is one of the purposes of this paper to argue that Freud's tacit preoccupation with the idea of degeneration was the trouser aspect of his seduction theory. Infantile sexual abuse, accordingly, was the manifest theme of the seduction papers, but it was *degeneration* that wore the pants.

[2] Esterson (1993, pp. 14-15) and others fix the period at 18 months, one month less than the period between the delivery of *The Aetiology of Hysteria* and the letter to Fliess of September 21, 1897.

[3] By and large, the connection between theory and therapeutic effectiveness is nowadays played down by Freudian loyalists who have sought to unglue the psychoanalytic theoretical edifice from the effectiveness of psychoanalytic therapy. In line with this, Sachs (1989) disputes Grünbaum's contention that "attribution of *therapeutic* success to the undoing of repressions—rather than to mere suggestion—was the foundation, both logically and historically, for the central dynamical significance that unconscious ideation acquired in psychoanalytic theory: without the reliance on the presumed dynamics of *their* therapeutic results, Breuer and Freud could have never propelled clinical data into repression etiologies" (Grünbaum, 1984, p. 182). Sachs faults Grünbaum for ignoring Freud's argument that analytic assumptions are confirmed through parallels between the findings in neuroses and cases of paranoia and *dementia praecox* (schizophrenia), which are untreatable and impervious to the effects of suggestion.

Sachs may be wrong on several counts. First, Grünbaum in due course discusses at least three different senses of "linkage" in which the connection between psychoanalytic theory and therapy come into play (Grünbaum, 1991). Second, when the treatment of paranoia met theoretical needs of the moment in 1896, Freud was far from pessimistic about the therapeutic outlook for psychotic cases. He even produced a paranoid "cure" in the case of Frau P.—subject, of course, to whatever claims of clinical regression in this patient he found it convenient to posit in later revisions of theory. Third, there is an incongruity between there being virtually no psychotic patients in Freud's caseload and his maintaining that the "translation of symbols and the phantasies" of psychosis "coincides faithfully" with the data produced in neurotic cases. This conclusion, derivable only on the basis of the requisite psychoanalytic procedures in the consulting room, was evidently drawn without a sufficient enough number of psychotic patients in the caseload to establish its credibility. Fourth, there is an inconsistency between a dearth of such patients and Freud's pronouncement that such patients are *not* vulnerable to suggestion.

Erwin (1993) has addressed the question of the alleged imperviousness of psychotics to suggestion, arguing that the research literature would seem to indicate otherwise. However, a share of Erwin's evidence involves confirmation of the "suggestibility factor" in operant studies embracing verbal conditioning and instrumental behaviors (Krasner, 1958; Ayllon & Haughton, 1964; Salzinger & Pisoni, 1961). A question arises here about the relevance of operant conditioning studies to Freud's notion of "suggestibility." Thus, to assert that a patient's behavior has been modified by reinforcement does not imply that the resultant patterns have been created through the effect of "suggestion," even if the latter concept is blurry. In the experimental analysis of behavior, suggestion effects may be construed as the by-products of reinforced patterns, but the converse does not hold. A pattern is not indisputably the effect of "suggestion," merely because it was reinforced, just as the tendency for laboratory planaria to turn right at a choice point in a maze is a result of suggestion simply because they were reinforced for doing so. Consequently, neither must human subjects reinforced in analogous ways acquire their patterns through "suggestion." Erwin's example of a schizophrenic woman reinforced for carrying a broom in the Ayllon, Haughton & Hughes (1965) study does not seem to capture the notion of a pattern created through suggestion; it only illustrates the case of a patient for whom a chosen psychoanalytic interpretation is doubtful when it transpires psychologists have been reinforcing broom-carrying patterns. The behavior in question did not *necessarily* originate because broom-carrying was suggested by experimenters. I say "not necessarily" because suggestion is not altogether ruled out either; but neither is it guaranteed. Despite the possible irrelevance of operant strategies to the issue of suggestion, Freud nonetheless had little justification for making his exclusionary remarks, especially in the light of his limited access to this patient population.

Lastly, on what basis did Freud contend psychotics are impervious to suggestion in the context of his 1909 dismissal of "suggestibility" as a "catchword," not to mention its lack of clear definition? Impervious to what? Evidently, the conceptual laxity Freud is permitted by loyalists is off limits to critics like Grünbaum. Sachs (1989, p. 355) takes Grünbaum to task for the latter's fuzzy notion of "suggestion," while Erwin (1993) is forced to grapple with several senses of the term in order to cover all the possibilities of meaning spawned by its ambiguity. Ironically, Sachs seems more impatient with Grünbaum's failure to clarify the meaning of "suggestibility" when criticizing Freud, than he is with the latter for failing to do likewise in his critique of Berheim's theory of suggestibility in hypnotism (Freud, 1888; Ellenberger, 1970; Sulloway, 1992).

The theory/therapy marriage is indisputable in the seduction papers, whatever the looseness of the connection in post-1987 theorizing. Despite this, modern theorists who wish to disengage psychoanalytic theory from the support given to it by therapeutic effects must grapple with the larger issue of justifying the system. Loyalists cannot maintain there is something worthwhile about psychoanalytic theory unwed from those therapeutic effects and explanatory virtues serving to distinguish it over rival theoretical accounts. If a putative recovery of a repressed "memory" fails to ameliorate symptoms any better than alternative approaches, what is the evidential basis for contending the pathogen is a *memory*, whether of an actual or fantasized event? True, the theory may receive confirmation in other areas of inquiry, like experimental or epidemiological investigations. However, support for it from these quarters, while occasionally suggestive, is in the main equivocal or poor.

The point here should not be misconstrued. It is not that psychoanalytic theory is necessarily *vacuous* unless psychoanalysis can be shown to be therapeutically sound or superior; it is only that in the absence of differential treatment results, what is to recommend it, given the existence of equally effective—and less lengthy or expensive!—treatment alternatives? If this is crassly pragmatic, so be it.

4   Freud's "hysteria," as defined in his paper *Hysteria* cuts across several diagnostic categories listed in the DSM-IV, the current official manual of psychiatry nosology (American Psychiatric Association, 1994). The constellation of clinical disturbances observed by Breuer and Freud in 1895 may have represented time-bound Victorian syndromes (Sulloway, 1992, p. 59) or "culture-bound syndromes" (Simons & Hughes, 1985). Webster (1966) has indicated that "hysteria" functioned as a "diagnostic dustbin," embracing conditions that from a modern psychiatric perspective are quite distinct. For example, the patients in Freud and Breuer's *Studies in Hysteria*, manifest symptoms across a range of disabilities, including conversion disorder, dissociative disorder, post-traumatic stress disorder, generalized anxiety disorder, obsessive-compulsive disorder, amnestic syndrome, brief reactive psychoses, etc. Complicating the diagnosis of "hysteria" is the promotion of an illusory purview for *psychogenesis*, based as it may be on premature calculation. The conviction that a condition must be a purely "functional" or "non-organic" one—in the sense it lacks a physiological underpinning—may have fostered misdiagnoses. Symptoms of "hysteria" may spring from organic disorders that are unclassifiable due to the unavailability of relevant diagnostic procedures during a given era. If "hysterical" is medical shorthand for disturbances of function that cannot be readily attributed to known neuropathological processes, it does not follow that psychogenesis is the forced alternative. As Webster observes, the etiological bases for such cases still remains an open question.

In a more comprehensive sense, there is no category of pathology theoretically exempt from neurophysiological causation, since all behavior, normal or otherwise, is mediated by the central nervous system. If so, "organic" and "psychogenic" simply denote distinguishable realms of disorder that are ultimately physical: those that have (or may come to have) specifiable etiologies and those that do not (or will not). For what is the alternative? A purely "mental" etiology without causal physical underpinnings, as under Cartesian dualism? Even Freud, who surmised that all psychic processes would eventually be described in physical terms, implied that there is no such thing as a purely "psychic" disorder. Accordingly, the conjecture by Bowlby (2004) that "Breuer and Freud's initial insight that hysterical symptoms represent not a chemical imbalance but a mental conflict" may involve a category mistake (Ryle, 1949).

In line with the foregoing, the possible problems of a diagnosis of "hysteria" are at least four in number: (1) it may cover a protean variety of symptoms as to be virtually meaningless as a classificatory tool; (2) it may refer to symptoms springing from a *known* neurological disorder like torsion dystonia, yet get misdiagnosed by psychiatrists overlooking an organic basis all too familiar to neurologists; (3) it may cover symptomatic pictures of physical conditions unknown to *all* practitioners in a given era; and (4) it may *necessarily* and ultimately pertain to neurophysiological anomalies in accordance with assumptions central to a philosophical position on the mind-body relationship (i.e., identity theory).

[5]   In referring the putatively high level of childhood sexual abuse required by the ST, Freud emphasized that it did not correspond quantitatively to the incidence of the disorder, hysteria, attributed to it. The abuse had to be greater than the prevalence of hysteria, since the latter is the delayed consequence of the abuse. Consequently, more abuse was being perpetrated than its symptomatic manifestations indicated, since the latter were only the accumulated results over time.

[6]   Schimek (1987) was among the first to call into question whether Freud's patients actually disclosed early sexual abuse. However, he finesses his psychoanalytic stand by attempting to diminish the significance of Freud's switch from reality to fantasy of abuse. In this connection he writes: "…actual seduction in early childhood played only a limited, though indispensable role in the complex and lengthy process of symptom formation. This early trauma was significant only to the extent that its unconscious memory had a 'delayed' action at puberty…It is only when the unconscious memory

has acquired a new meaning in a different context at a later age that it becomes a psychic trauma. Internal psychological processes and transformations already play a central role in the seduction theory. Thus Freud's later shift of emphasis from reproductions of real events to fantasies (which contain fragments of actual past experience) did not represent such a radical break in the continuity of his thought" (Schimek, 1987, p.939). On the other hand, and despite Schimek's valiant effort to establish continuity of Freud's thought in the landmark reversal of 1897, what more important difference can you have than the one between reality and fantasy?

7   Sulloway (1992) may have exaggerated the originality of key figures of Freud's circle, like Wilhelm Fliess. In developing his thesis that the latter's influence on Freud has been generally underestimated, Sulloway faults the editors of the Fliess correspondence for failing to recognize that Fliess "was a pioneer in the field of infantile sexuality" (Sulloway, 1991, p. 250). However, just as Fliess's contributions to bisexuality and infant sexuality should not be obscured by attributing his views to Freud, so too should Fliess not be portrayed as scooping what had already been thematic in Victorian pediatric medicine. To correct the record, discussions of infantile sexuality were numerous, not sparse, before Freud and Fliess. They began after the middle of the nineteenth century, although they did not proliferate in the Continental literature until later on (Carter, 1983). The widespread pre-Fliessian belief that hysteria was sexual in nature inspired investigations of sexuality in hysterical children. Accordingly, clinical reports on infant sexuality—a majority of which focused on masturbation—were authored by Behrend in 1860, Jacobi in 1876, Fleischmann in 1878, Lindner in 1879, Smith in 1880, Scherpf in 1884, and Herz in 1885 (Carter, 1983). As for Freud's objection in *The Aetiology of Hysteria* to the argument that the infantile sexual episode cannot be the cause of hysteria because such episodes were more common than its later clinical picture, he was only responding to conjectures about the relationship between the two as discussed in the pediatric literature of his day (Carter, 1983, p. 194). In an

eye-opening monograph, Kern (1973) details the way in which many of the alleged Freudian discoveries, from infantile sexuality to psychosexual stages of fixation and their impact on later character traits, made a prior debut in the nineteenth century pediatric literature. Such studies were conducted shortly after the midpoint of the century. The conviction that it was Freud alone who originated this intellectual tradition is undoubtedly due to the promotional efforts of psychoanalysts to advertise the revolutionary nature of his discoveries. More often than not, this was at the expense of ignoring the more extensive literature that preceded him. As a case in point, we find Freud in his 1905 *Three Essays* declaring the uniqueness of his contribution to the understanding of sexuality in children: "So far as I know, not a single author has clearly recognized the regular existence of a sexual instinct in childhood" (Kern, 1973, p. 118). This pronouncement is astonishing in light of the depth of understanding about the subject detailed in the pre-Freudian work of Maudsley in 1867, Perez in 1886, Groos in 1899, Bell in 1902, Ellis in 1903, Sollier in 1891, Barnes in 1892, Dessoir in 1894, Dallemagne in 1894, and probably numerous others.

[8] It was Cioffi (1988) who first questioned whether all sexual games—like doctor and nurse games—initiated by children should be characterized as *abusive*. Were enemas, decades ago thought to be a home remedy for assorted gastrointestinal ailments, sexually abusive when administered to children on a more frequent basis than nowadays considered medically advisable? Lastly, is sexual abusiveness toward children definitionally linked to the legal notion of *mens rea* in the mind of the perpetrator? In other words, can adults sexually abuse children if the episode in question is accidental or non-purposeful? Under the looser Freudian definition of "trauma" in the originary period, accidental frottage during the sexually precocious phase might have met criteria for a pathogenic event, although perpetrator intentionality would have been lacking. Are enemas abusive if the parent mistakenly believes irrigation of the bowels on a regular basis is feasible as a health measure? Perhaps

it is necessary to distinguish between what is *traumatic* and what is *abusive.*

9   It was not only the foreboding aspect of the landscape at the foothills of the Carpathians, nor the sinister demeanor of Count Dracula that caught Jonathan Harker's attention in his travels to Eastern Europe. As if to set the stage for the terrifying drama that was to unfold, Harker's racially tinged remarks about the peasants and villagers he met along the way to Castle Dracula are also noteworthy. He finds them fearful, superstitious, strange-looking, and sickly despite their gay attire. Their food is good, although it makes him "thirsty." The women are pretty, except when you draw close to find "how clumsy they are about the waist." The Slovaks are the most "barbaric": while "picturesque," they are not "prepossessing," and on stage they would be mistaken for an "Oriental band of brigands." They are, he reassures himself, quite harmless and "rather wanting in self-assertion." Harker's reaction to Eastern Europeans is the initial nicety or expression of wonderment, followed by the patronizing remark. He is quintessentially the western European, oblivious to his sense of racial superiority. On the other hand, Count Dracula's litany of virtues about his own "race," harkening back to Attila the Hun, betrays his conviction that his lineage is moribund. Indeed, the literal and lineal notions of "blood" shift imperceptibly back and forth at the beginning of the novel—authored in the auspicious year of 1897!

References

American Psychiatric Association (1994). *Diagnostic and statistical manual of mental disorders, fourth edition.* Washington, D.C.: American Psychiatric Association.

Austin, J. L. (1960). *Sense and Sensibilia.* Oxford: Oxford University Press.

Ayllon, T., and Haughton, E. (1964). Modification of symptomatic verbal behavior of mental patients. *Behavior Research and Therapy,* 2, 87-97.

Ayllon, T., and Haughton, E. and Hughes, H. (1965). Interpretation of symptoms. Fact or fiction? *Behavior Research and Therapy,* 3, 1-7.

Balmary, M. (1979). *L'Homme Aux Statues: Freud et la Faute Cachee du Pere.* Paris.

Baroja, J. C. (1965). *The World of the Witches.* Chicago: University of Chicago Press.

Bowlby, R. (2004). Introduction to *Studies in Hysteria.* London: Penguin Books.

Breuer, J. and Freud, S. (1895). Studies in hysteria. *SE,* 2.

Carter, K. C. (1983). Infantile hysteria and infantile sexuality in late nineteenth-century German-language literature. *Medical History,* 27, 186-196.

Cioffi, F. (1972). Wolheim on Freud. *Inquiry.* 15, 171-186.

Cioffi, F. (1974). Was Freud a liar? *Listener,* 91, 172-174.

Cioffi, F. (1988). "Exegital myth-making" in Grünbaum's indictment of Popper and exoneration of Freud. In P. Clark and C. Wright (Eds.), *Mind, Psychoanalysis, and Science.* Oxford: Basil Blackwell, pp. 61-87.

Cohen, L., Berzoff, J. and Elin M. (1995). *Dissociative Identity Disorder.* Northdale, New Jersey: Jason Aronson, Inc.

Crews, F. (1986). *Skeptical Engagements.* New York: Oxford University Press.

Crews, F. (1995). *The Memory Wars: Freud's Legacy in Dispute.* New York: New York Review of Books.

Crews, F. (Ed.) (1998). *Unauthorized Freud: Doubters Confront a Legend.* New York: Viking.

Ebersole, P. and Ebersole, S. (1993). *The Abuse of Innocence: The McMartin Preschool Trial.* Buffalo, New York: Prometheus Press.

Ellenberger, H.F. (1970). *The Discovery of the Unconscious.* New York Basic Books.

Erdelyi, M. (1984). The recovery of unconscious (inaccessible) memories: Laboratory studies of hypermnesia. In G. Bower (Ed.), *The Psychology of Learning and Motivation: Advances in Research and Theory,* Vol. 18, New York: Academic Press, pp. 95-127.

Erwin, E. (1993). Philosophers on Freudianism. In J. Earman, et. Al., *Philosophical problems of the internal and external worlds. Essays on the philosophy of Adolph Grünbaum.* Pittsburgh and Konstanz: University of Pittsburgh Press and Univestätsverlag, pp. 409-460.

Esterson, A. (1993). *Seductive Mirage: An Exploration of the Work of Sigmund Freud.* Chicago, Illinois: Open Court.

Farrell, J. (1996). *Freud's paranoid quest: Psychoanalysis and modern suspicion.* New York: New York University Press.

Féré, C. S. (1884). La famille névropathique: Theorie teratologique de l'hérédité et la dégénerescence, *Archives de Neurologic, 7,* 1-43.

Fish, S. (1986). Withholding the missing portion. Power, meaning and persuasion in Freud's "The Wolf Man" *Times Literary Supplement.* August 29, 935-938.

Fishberg, M. (1911). *The Jews: A Study of Race and Environment.* New York: W. Scott.

Freud, S. *The Standard Edition of the Complete Psychological Works of Sigmund Freud.* 24 volumes. James Strachey (Ed.) London: Hogarth Press and the Institute of Psycho-Analysis (1953-1974). (Hereafter referred to as *SE*).

__________. (1988). Hysteria. *SE, 1,* 41-57.

__________. (1896a). Heredity and the aetiology of the neuroses. *SE, 3,* 143-146.

__________. (1896b). Further remarks on the neuro-psychoses of defence. *SE, 3,* 162-185.

__________. (1896c). The aetiology of hystera. *SE, 3,* 191-221.

__________. (1905). Three essays on the theory of sexuality. *SE, 7,* 123-243.

__________. (1912-1913). Totem and taboo. *SE, 13,* 1-161.

__________. (1918). From the history of an infantile neurosis. *SE, 17,* 7-123.

__________. (1925). An autobiographical study. *SE, 20*, 7-74.

__________. (1931). Female sexuality. *SE, 21*, 221-243.

__________. (1964). *The Letters of Sigmund Freud.* New York: McGraw-Hill.

__________. (1886a). Report on Freud's studies in Paris and Berlin. *SE, 1.*

__________. (1886b). Preface to the translation of Charcot's lectures on the diseases of the nervous system. *SE, 1.*

__________. (1893). Charcot, *SE, 3.*

Gay, P. (1988). *Freud: A Life For Our Time.* New York: Doubleday.

Gilman, S. (1993a). *Freud, Race, and Gender.* Princeton, New Jersey: Princeton University.

Gilman, S. (1993b). *The Case of Sigmund Freud: Medicine and Identity at the Fin de Siecle.* Baltimore, Maryland: The John Hopkins University Press.

Glicklhorn, J. and Glicklhorn, R. (1960). *Sigmund Freuds academische Laufbahn im Lichte der Dokumente.* Vienna and Innsbruck: Urban & Schwartzenberg.

Gould, S. J. (1981). *The Mismeasure of Man.* New York: W. W. Norton.

Grünbaum, A. (1979). Is Freudian psychoanalytic theory pseudo-scientific by Karl Popper's criterion of demarcation? *American Philosophical Quarterly, 16,* 131-141.

Grünbaum, A. (1984). *The Foundations of Psychoanalysis: A Philosophical Critique.*

Berkeley, California: University of California Press.

Grunbaum, A. (1991). Etiology and therapy in psychoanalytic theory. *Behavioral and Brain Sciences, 14,* No. 4., December, 729-732.

Hacking, I. (1995). *Rewriting the Soul: Multiple Personality and the Sciences of Memory.* Princeton, New Jersey: Princeton University Press.

Henningsen, G. (1969). The papers of Alonso de Salazar Frías: A Spanish witchcraft polemic 1610-14. *Temenos.* Studies in comparative religion presented by scholars in Denmark, Finland, Norway, and Sweden, 5, 85-106.

Henningsen, G. (1980). *The Witches' Advocate: Basque Witchcraft and the Spanish Inquisition.* Reno, Nevada: University of Nevada Press.

Israels, H. and Schatzman, M. (1993). The seduction theory. *History of Psychiatry.* 4, 23-59.

Kern, S. (1973). Freud and the discovery of child sexuality. *History of Childhood Quarterly, 1,* 117-141.

Krasner, L. (1958). A technique for investigating the relationship between the behavior cues of the examiner and the verbal behavior of the patient. *Journal of Consulting Psychology, 22,* 364-366.

Krull, M. (1986). *Freud and His Father.* New York: Norton.

Levin, K. (1944). *Freud's Early Psychology of the Neuroses: A Historical Perspective,* Pittsburgh, Pennsylvania: University of Pittsburgh Press.

Lynn, S. and Rhue, J. W. (1994). *Dissociation.* New York: Guilford Press.

Macmillan M. (1991). *Freud Evaluated: The Completed Arc,* New York: North-Holland.

Masson, J. M. (1984). *The Assault on Truth: Freud's Suppression of the Seduction Theory,* New York: Farrar, Straus, and Girox.

Masson, J. M. (1985). *The Complete Letters of Sigmund Freud to Wilhelm Fliess: 1887-1904,* Cambridge, Massachusetts: Harvard University Press.

McGrath, W. J. (1986). *Freud's Discovery of Psychoanalysis: The Politics of Hysteria.* Ithaca, New York: Cornell University Press.

Monter, E. W. (1969). *European Witchcraft,* New York: John Wiley.

Murray, C. and Herrnstein, R. J. (1994). *The Bell Curve.* New York: The Free Press.

Sachs, D. (1989). In fairness to Freud: A critical notice of *The foundations of psychoanalysis* by Adolph Grünbaum. *The Philosophical Review,* vol. XCVIII, No. 3, July, 349-378.

Salzinger, K. and Pisoni, S. (1958). Reinforcement of affect responses of schizophrenics during the clinical interview. *Journal of Abnormal and Social Psychology, 57,* 84-90.

Schatzman, M. (1992). Freud: Who seduced whom? *New Scientist, 21,* March, 35-37.

Schimek, J. G. (1987). Fact and fantasy in the seduction theory: A historical review. *Journal of the American Psychoanalytical Association, 35,* 937-965.

Sebald, H. (1995). *Witch-Children: From Salem Witch-Hunts to Modern Courtrooms.* Amherst, New York: Prometheus Books.

Smith, M. and Pazder, L. (1980). *Michelle Remembers.* New York: Congdon and Lattes.

Stewart, L. (1976). Freud before Oedipus: Race and heredity in the origins of psychoanalysis. *Journal of the History of Biology, 9,* 215-228.

Stratford, L. (1988). *Satan's Underground.* Eugene, Oregon: Harvest House.

Sulloway, F. (1991). Reassessing Freud's case histories: The social construction of psychoanalysis *Isis 82,* 245-275.

Sulloway, F. (1992). *Freud: Biologist of the Mind.* Cambridge, Massachusetts: Harvard University Press.

Szasz, T. S. (1961). *The Myth of Mental Illness: Foundations of a Theory of Personal Conduct,* New York: Harper & Row.

Thornton, E. M. (1983). *The Freudian Fallacy: An Alternative View of Freudian Theory.* Garden City, New Jersey.

Vetter, I. (1988). *Die Kontroverse um Sigmund Freuds sogennante Verfuhrungtheorie.* MA thesis Bayern: Catholic University Eichstatt.

Weber, E. (1986). *France, Fin de Siècle.* Cambridge, Massachusetts: Belknap Press of Harvard University Press.

Webster, R. (1996). *Why Freud Was Wrong: Sin, Science and Psychoanalysis.* New York: Harper Collins.

Wilcocks, R. (1994). *Maelzel's Chess Player: Sigmund Freud and the Rhetoric of Deceit.* Lanham, Maryland: Rowman & Littlefield.

Young-Bruehl, E. (1995). A history of Freud biographies. In Micale, M. S. and Porter R. (Eds.), *Discovering the History of Psychiatry,* (pp. 157-173). New York: Oxford University Pres

Kierkegaard's Cold Feet

Most scholarly interpretations of the astute, complex and categorically diverse aspects of Søren Kierkegaard's thinking are often sympathetic to seeing the fate of his relationship with Regine Olsen in his own terms. While critics feel they can unearth sundry explanations for it, they are for the most part variations on those Kierkegaard himself outlined (Roberts, 1959).

On the other hand, some experts have averred that there may be other explanations for why Kierkegaard turned away from marriage. Yet clinging to the idea that the rejection of Regine would parallel a similar scenario for any other woman with whom he might have become infatuated embraces a picture of his disengagement as driven by the reasons the philosopher himself put forth. This amounts to a view of the rejection as only a singular instance of what would prove to be marriage to anyone, despite the way other liasons might have been played out.

It was no secret that Kierkegaard could cast an appreciative eye on other women, including twenty-two year-old Bolette Rordams, the daughter of family friends in whose home he first met Regine. (The philosopher deleted from his journals any mention of dallying with Bolette lest prying eyes jack up its significance).

And he had a thing for the Berlin soprano Hedvig Schulze, whom he fantasized approaching with less than what he called "the purest intentions." The soprano reminded him of Regine, although his continuing ascetic mode in 1841 prevented him from becoming an avid suitor after the singer's performance as Elvira in Mozart's *Don Giovanni*. Another 1841 journal entry makes note of a "pretty girl" who caught his eye while reassuring himself that his fidelity to Regine all but precluded an interest in this young woman.

Most critics also assume that the rejection of Regine was one based exclusively upon Kierkegaard's internal reality, not on the external reality of Regine Olsen. In other words, a scholarly consensus has it that because Kierkegaard felt that the idea of marriage was unacceptable, his decision to repudiate one with Regine was not based on her individual characteristics, since for him she was a matchless woman in every respect. Whether the assumption is correct depends upon the truth of a counterfactual: that *any* relationship with a woman headed for marriage with Kierkegaard was doomed to failure. What if such an assumption were wrong, as implausible as this may strike us? After all, it was never put to a crucial reality test. And acknowledging this is hardly inconsistent with the view held by scholars like Fabro (1967) that a predominance of Kierkegaard's later output bore the stamp of the rejection of Regine that made such an "indelible mark" on him.

Most commentators on Kierkegaard's philosophy are likewise convinced his relationship with Regine not only dramatically affected him personally, but also drastically colored his subsequent thinking on virtually every other issue he chose to address. Yet in reviewing over three thousand titles about Kierkegaard authored by a wider community of scholars (Lapointe, 1980) it's odd that only eleven (two in English) chose to give that relationship sole focus in a published work or essay. It seems to have been a subject in many articles, but usually only in passing.

To recapitulate several of the events in the on-again-off-again affair between Søren Kierkegaard and Regine Olsen, the following may serve to set the stage for fuller exploration of their dissolution.

Regine's first contact with Kierkegaard was on a spring day in 1837, when she was fifteen and he was twenty four. Later, she recalled him making a strong impression upon her, a feeling that was reciprocated by the philosopher. He began pursuing her over a longer period of time, finally deciding to court her. His declaration of love for her took place after a chance encounter near her home on September 8, 1840. They both repaired to her parlor where she began playing her piano. In a flurry of seeming impatience with the musical interlude, Kierkegaard declared that it was she he wanted, not the music, announcing that he had wanted her for two years. Subsequently, he pleaded his case for marriage to Regina's father, Councilman Etatsraad Olsen, who granted his suit, and the two became engaged.

The day after the understanding was finalized and Regine agreed to the match, Kierkegaard harbored reservations about it and on August 11, 1841 broke off the engagement, sending Regine a farewell letter together with his engagement ring. Devastated by the rejection, she threatened to commit suicide if he did not retract his decision.

In order to drive home the reality of renouncing his marital intentions, Kierkegaard took it upon himself on October 11, 1841 to meet with Regine in person to reinforce his decision. Her father intervened to announce to Kierkegaard that his daughter was in a desperate, suicidal state of "total despair" and that because of this the philosopher should reconsider his decision. Regine's rather dramatic, if not histrionic, reaction to the rejection should perhaps be understood in the light of the social position of women in mid-nineteenth century Scandinavian Europe: a constricted one in which marriage and motherhood—interspersed in her case with painting miniatures and dutifully attending Sunday church meetings—were pretty much the narrow aspirational niches a young woman of her time might hope to occupy.

Kierkegaard, overwhelmed with remorse about the effect his retraction had on Regine, attempted to soften its damage by adopting a *faux* callousness, pretending that his feelings for her were those of a "vulgar imposter," rather than suffused with an ardor she mistakenly attributed to him. In this regard, and in response to a question Regine asked him about whether he would ever marry, he responded, "Yes, in ten years, when I have begun to simmer down and I need a lusty young miss to rejuvenate me." The pretense was belied by the torment his decision was to have on him. Both he and Regine spent nights weeping in their beds over his decision.

What was a forlorn philosopher to do, given the impact jilting his lover had on him? What any miscreant might undertake after such a dramatically charged *volte face*: get out of town. Kierkegaard undertook a trip away from Copenhagen that broke his Kantian pattern of confining himself exclusively to his home town. Two weeks after the break with Regine, the philosopher headed for Berlin, Germany, ostensibly to attend lectures on F. W. J. Schelling's philosophy.

Disappointed with Schelling's take on Hegel, Kierkegaard, in an apostrophe that would betoken a talent for humor that most serious-minded scholars would probably dub "irony," wailed that he was "too old to listen to lectures, just as Schelling is to old to give them" (Garff, 2005, p.210). Several years before in 1838 in a jibe at editors, he remarked: "Since I know that you will probably not read it, and if you did would not understand it, and if you understood it would take exception to it, may I direct your attention only to the externals: gilt-edges and Morocco binding." A study in irony perhaps, but fast-forwarded to our modern era: the closest thing to a stand-up comedian you're likely to see in the annals of philosophical commentary.

Kierkegaard returned to Copenhagen in early March of 1841, but brooding over his decision hounded him mercilessly. With a wounded consciousness, his public authorship of separate treatises went undercover in a flurry of a half dozen pseudonyms: Victor Eremira, Johannes Climacus, Virgilius Haufiniensis, Hilarius Bookbinder, Johannes De Silentio among others—as though hiding his face were driven by a personal subtext in addition to whatever scholarly reasons he had for remaining anonymous in the face of critical reaction to his radical religious commentary.

Kierkegaard's ruse of callousness with Regine is reminiscent of a similar theme in the philosopher's spin on the Abraham/Isaac biblical relationship, as expounded in *Fear and Trembling*. In it, the patriarch takes ownership of the intended sacrifice of his son rather than have the latter believe it was ordered by God. The ruse served to offset any less than suitable notions about the Almighty Isaac might harbor should the actual authorship of the intended sacrifice be revealed.

What may strike one as odd about Kierkegaard's retraction of marital intention is his sudden discovery that it could not go forward despite his earlier enthusiasm about marrying Regine. For the philosopher, his continuing melancholy, his *vita ante acta* (i. e., his wayward youthful ways), or his being a penitent were the reasons he gave for the retraction. In 1841, however, he added that "there was a divine protest" against the marriage to Regine, and after noting that "she fought like a tigress" Kierkegaard reiterated his conviction that "God had lodged a veto," and had it not been otherwise, the marriage would have taken place. Of course, in inquiring into reasons for the retraction, it was the philosopher's opinion on what he personally considered his religious mode to dictate that prevailed. It would be a stretch to imagine Kierkegaard felt that that God spoke to him directly, unless we are partial to believing he was experiencing something with an Old Testament trope, as in instances of actual voices embodying heavenly will from on high, not the crisis-oriented existential faith Kierkegaard originated.

Of course it was possible that in the flurry of enthusiasm about marrying Regine before his about face, he was acting impulsively with what he characterized in his journals as "the firm purpose of deciding the matter," heedless of the natural misgivings prevailing at the point of the retraction. Yet a paradox still persists, since by his own accounting he was contemplating a permanent relationship with Regine for fully two years prior to the fateful meeting with her on September 8, 1840. This was more than enough leeway in time to ponder the wisdom or drawbacks of marriage to her (or anyone else); certainly enough time to determine what heavenly opinion or personal inclination was or should be about the marriage.

Critics like Fabro (1967). In addressing the issue of Kierkegaard's retraction are among a group of commentators who tend to mystify it by adopting an overly reverential (if not to say sentimental) stance on this chapter in the life of the philosopher. In this connection, he declares that because Kierkegaard exhibited "such an exceptional power of renunciation'" his motives are "not accessible to psychological analysis" since they pertain "to the sphere of the spirit" (p. 391).

Going on, Fabro complains that the "most recent extravagances of psychoanalysis" are nothing but "a dull and crude objectification," hardly an "authentic approach." Such remarks amount to little more than obscurantism: psychological inquiry into the motives of anyone is possible, whether or not it proves to be promising or fruitful. Nor need it be drenched in what is fast becoming a museum relic these days: psychoanalysis (Grünbaum, 1984; Macmillan, 1991; Crews, 1986, 1995, 1998). Whatever its complexion, it would not in any case detract from Kierkegaard's importance as a thinker or somehow diminish his stature. His references to the "curse" that hung over him in not daring "to permit any being to be intimately attached to me" should not derail any number of different possible interpretations, including psychological ones.

Søren Kierkegaard was not alone when it comes to commentary about thinkers whose passions are analyzed in terms congenial to their way of seeing things. On the other hand, there's a pitfall in an all too narrow focus on a philosopher's system as the expression of his or her psychological make-up, regarding it as a direct or indirect reflection of personal hang-ups. This spin on things runs the risk of side-stepping what is conceptually authentic about the thinker in question. For example, earlier in his life Albert Camus was subject to fits of despondency. Later on, in *The Myth of Sisyphus*, he declared that the fundamental question of philosophy is deciding whether to commit suicide (Camus, 1975).

One can speculate that Camus' insistence that the idea of suicide as a *philosophical* problem sprang from a personal subtext. Yet whatever its motivational thread, leaving the matter mired in psychology might forfeit the opportunity to examine the relationship he posited between the Absurdity of life and suicide, even acknowledging the underbelly of his theorizing. One might even hazard the guess that it was precisely through a darker personal subtext that Camus was able to develop a metaphysical thesis that should be evaluated on its own terms. One can dispute his philosophical view without declaring that psychological analysis is the sole or principal intellectual task.

In a like vein, Freud was a confirmed atheist who conjectured that the belief in God was the projection of an unconscious need for a father figure. Even if true, the theory has little bearing on an ontological issue about God's existence. Accordingly, one can be an orthodox Freudian and remain a believer without a clash between convictions about unconscious wish-fulfillment and religious faith, even in the face of contrarian views on the part of atheistic or agnostic peers.

While one should distinguish between a philosophy and its motivational basis, the relationship between the two can take several forms. Perhaps the most extreme version of this was developed in the past by a philosopher who, taken with the promise of psychoanalytic theorizing, seemingly went for broke (Lazerowitz, 1959; 1968). He maintained that, for example, Spinoza's utterance, "Something cannot be made out of nothing," was not merely a symptom of the philosopher's concern with his being puzzled over the problem of birth, but actually amounted to *nothing more* than this psychological subtext. According to Lazerowitz, philosophical statements possess only "the delusive appearance" of words used to make them. Psychoanalysis, he conjectured, alone can discover what philosophical utterances really say, "as against what they delusively appear to say" (1959, p. 153).

Parlor psychoanalyses of such a runaway character risk being hoisted on their own petards. In deconstructing the propositional content of philosophical statements in favor of their unconscious sourcings, why are the latter exempt from the same denuding of discourse it proclaims is the lot of other systems of thought? In other words, how can one take seriously what this radical form of psychoanalysis preaches about underlying motives in philosophizing when it too is merely a product of the unconscious processes it commemorates? And faced with this kind of deconstructing effort, where does Truth itself gain a proper foothold?

Despite the foregoing, in circumventing a genetic fallacy, or confusing the assessment of a point of view with a thinker's motivation for having it, one can also forfeit the opportunity to contribute to an understanding of personal history that can be informative in its own right, without sacrificing the propositional integrity of a system, true or false.

Kierkegaard's spiritual problems ran neck in neck with his physical complaints, as anyone familiar with his individual and family history knows. Critics have poured over his self-described list of symptoms, as well as reports by persons who knew the philosopher or had protracted contacts with him, like Regine Olsen. The problem with much of this commentary is that diagnoses in the mid-nineteenth century lacked the sophistication of modern medicine, so that many of the older judgments about the philosopher's physical condition were in the nature of pure guesswork. All the same, in an 1854 Journal entry entitled *About myself*, Kierkegaard describes himself as "Slight, delicate, and weak, denied in almost every respect the physical requirements in order to pass for a complete man." The compensatory trait as described by him was a "pre-eminent intelligence." One might quibble with the former description, but not, in any reasonable universe of discourse, the latter.

Backhouse (2016) has reviewed past diagnoses of the philosopher that have been put forth without granting any of those hunches legitimacy. His litany includes orthopedic anomalies, seizure disorder, Potts paraplegia, myelitis, porphyria, and syphilis, inherited or contracted. Elsewhere, dizziness, hemorrhoids, constipation, insomnia and, improbably, leprosy and a curved penis, were cited as possibilities. As to syphillis, and as Garff (2005) has indicated, "how often and with what result" as a young adult the philosopher cavorted with ladies of the night in Peder Madsen's Alley is unknown (p. 104).

There is some dispute over the possibility that a young Søren visited bordellos; hence, the surmise over contracting syphilis. The truth about this remains elusive, while there are hints in the Journals that perhaps some kind of sexual activity occurred. For example, in a 1848 entry, Kierkegaard references a melancholic early life "which threw me for a time into sin and debauchery." It is perhaps oversacralizing his life to hold that "sin and debauchery" could not refer to sexual impropriety. In a Journal entry a year later in 1849, the philosopher references a woman, Frederica Bremer, who wanted to have sexual intercourse with him although he remained "virtuous." But virtue at age thirty six tells us nothing about earlier years of his self-described free-wheeling ways. At any rate, while scholarship hints at a range of possible medical fragilities, Kierkegaard himself attributed his physical problems to a childhood fall from a tree.

Backhouse's take on Kierkegaard's infirmities seems to founder when it comes to the philosopher's most celebrated complaint: his depression. Here, and despite his numerous references to the despondency he was subject to, Backhouse nonetheless maintains that depression is an "armchair diagnosis" that is simply "too pat" (p. 82). He reasons that because depression is a "debilitating illness" this diagnosis is inconsistent with producing "reams and reams of material, working and reworking their ideas long into the evening" and producing writing that is "not all miserable"..."Sadness, yes, but also joy, humour, worship, and puppy love can be found in the pages" (p. 82).

Backhouse's spin on the philosopher is that, contrary to being depressed, he was simply mercurial. But "mercurial" is not a psychiatric term, although what it variously denotes can perhaps be fitted nicely into formal psychiatric categories, depending upon the specific patterns of behaviors so designated.

What is more to the point is Backhouse's deficient understanding of the common cold of psychiatric conditions, depression. The diagnosis he has in mind and disputes is in all likelihood major depression, often associated with neurovegetative signs like appetite and sleep loss, ahedonia, amotivational states, psychomotor retardation, and suicidal mentation or attempts. Yet depression, unlike its severest form, can have any number of clinical presentations, from mild to severe, while the latest manual of standard psychiatric nomenclature lists over forty forms this affective state may take, including diagnoses like Cyclothymic Disorder or Bipolar Disorder in which periods of heightened creative activity can find a place, as they do in Dysthymic forms of the disorder. Again, this should not be taken to be authoritative commentary on Kierkegaard's proper diagnosis. Rather, it is only to acknowledge that complaints of what he called "my great melancholy" should be taken at face value as some form of ongoing depressive state, while fine-tuning its accurate diagnostic niche remains indeterminate.

Forms of depressive disorder have plagued other philosophers. Wittgenstein was a modern example. His assessment of the importance of Kierkegaard as a thinker was summed up in his view that the Dane "was by far the most profound thinker of the last century...a saint," presumably because he was "always making one aware of new categories" (Drury, 1984, p. 88).[1] Wittgenstein felt another kind of solidarity with the Danish philosopher in believing that "we are not here in order to have a good time" (Drury, 1984, p.88), a sentiment that is indisputably Kierkegaardian. In a journal entry of 1851, the philosopher declares that official Christianity has misrepresented religion as providing "nothing but consolation, happiness, etc." adding that, "I do not wish to be made happy by an illusion."

It might be added that while both philosophers were subject to depressive states of mind, Wittgenstein's may have been of a more serious cast. He battled thoughts of suicide throughout his adult life, with family history mirroring the despondency: he had three brothers, Hans, Rudolph, and Kurt, all of whom committed suicide. Kierkegaard, on the other hand, was given to a melancholic/obsessional style informing both his personal life and his philosophy.

As keen as Kierkegaard's self-insights were in the minds of scholars, might they on occasion have amounted to an overplayed hand? Earlier in his career on August 31, 1835, he modestly opined that he was "still far from having reached so complete an understanding of myself," a reservation that would seem to leave wiggle-room for misconstruing some of his motivations. His insights evidently did not serve him well before his retraction, while subsequent efforts to compensate for the latter, like regarding Regine as someone who had a claim on his devotion with a facsimile of marital commitment (not to mention the remains of his estate [2]) bear traces of a reparation that had a Johnny-come-lately hollow ring.

As was mentioned, Kierkegaard enumerated three reasons for his retraction. However, in envisioning other possibilities this may understate the number. It should nonetheless be kept in mind that any hunch about the philosopher's motivations for his retraction is speculative. In the event that fresh data would serve to shed light on other reasons for it, this might highlight the fact that when it came to matters of the heart, the philosopher on occasion may have fallen short of the Socratian ideal of knowing oneself, an eventful failing in 1841.

What strikes one about the Wittgensteinian family history is the strong suggestion of hereditarian taint. Research evidence for such a reality (especially studies on the high concordance rates for affective disorder in identical twin populations in contrast to fraternal twins and control groups) is by now a well established psychiatric finding (Lyons, Elsen, Goldberg, et. al., 1995; Shih, Belmonte & Zandi, 2004; Kendler, Pederson, Neale & Mathe, 1994).

In Wittgenstein's case, family history is suggestive evidence for a genetic transmission of depression. In Kierkegaard's case, by contrast, blight might be more akin to an underlying preoccupation, not any facet of family history establishing hereditarian influence. And here we might envisage the possibility of Kierkegaard's thoughts about nuclear family background being at least one component in his repudiation of Regine. If only to consider reasons for other kinds of factors in the retraction, we might pose a question about whether Kierkegaard's preoccupations were driven in part by an apprehension that in marrying Regine he might damage her or their future progeny because of his own physical vulnerability.

Kirkegaard's preoccupation with a family curse is more than idle speculation. However, and as was mentioned, this may not have encompassed taint in the strictly biological sense of the term. Indeed, scholars have speculated that Kierkegaard's father, Michael Pederson Kierkegaard, was considered by his youngest son to provide an "important common ground in a few strange ideas" (Updike, 2005). Another 1848 journal entry mentions "the dread with which my father filled my soul" and "his own frightful melancholy" and "other things in this connection" Kierkegaard failed to commit to paper.

Michael was a person who, as a young Jutland shepherd boy, cursed God and later fathered a child with a servant girl, Ane Sorensdatter, while his first wife Kirstine was still alive although sickly. After the latter died, Michael married Ane. Kierkegaard was Ane's seventh and last child, so that the philosopher might have considered himself one of the many living illustrations of Michael's sinful ways. Consequently, "being tainted" in Michael's mind was more like a fateful bane, a heavenly retribution that was visited upon his family. The curse he earlier had hurled at God in his mind could later revisit him as some form of divine comeuppance. The burden took on a singular complexion: his fear that his children would all die before the age of thirty-four, so as not to outlive Jesus Christ.

Divine retribution nonetheless proved to be an ambivalent affair: five of Michael's children, two brothers and three sisters, died before the age of thirty-four, whereas Søren lived to forty-two. His older brother Peter, depressed and hyperreligious to the end like his father, lived to the ripe age of eighty-two. In his journals, Kierkegaard referenced the "dark background of my life" from his earliest days and the "anxiety with which my father filled my soul," a presentiment he chose not to flesh out in writing. To assume all this had little impact on the later direction of Kierkegaard's life—including his relationship with Regine—may be short-sighted.

Accordingly, the specter of blight visited upon Regine if he were to marry her might have been one underlying motive in Kierkegaard's retraction, although not recorded by him. If this preoccupation were a hidden or unconscious motive, it was bound up with a concern about the effect a union with Regine would have on her, rather than on the philosopher's scholarly or religious obligations to himself. And Kierkegaard's preoccupations, whether declared or otherwise, might have switched between Me-oriented and Other-oriented concerns, while there is nothing to negate the possibility of both kinds of motives operating simultaneously.

There are other variations on Other-oriented possible motives. Lukacs (1978) mentions Kierkegaard's wariness about marriage as "wrecking Regine:" that "she would have been ruined…for I should constantly have had to strain myself trying to raise her up. I was too heavy for her" (p. 33). While such passages from the journals do not specify why Kierkegaard thought the strain existed, apprehension over it clearly takes the form of concerns about Regine, as well as himself. "She would have wrecked me too…I was too heavy for her, she too light for me, but either way there is most certainly a risk of overstrain" (p. 33). Lukács suggests that the philosopher felt it was his duty to "save Regine's life" (p. 32).

Another possible Me-oriented motive might have been Kierkegaard's doubts about his own ability to become an adequate husband, not because this would mean encroachment on his philosophical/authorship time alone, but also because he felt he lacked the personal skills to assume such a role, dedication to religious pursuits notwithstanding. In short, there might have been a nagging sense of inadequacy about stepping into a marital role, whatever the professional direction of his life. This might or might not be the case, but if it were, the religious mode of existence became all the more compelling, in part because the ethical mode (fealty to marriage and its social bonds and responsibilities) posed unworkable challenges for the philosopher! Accordingly, on this hypothesis, pursuing the religious mode in a curious way might have served as a default route undertaken in part because of the strain the ethical mode placed on his view of capability.

"Overstrain" as a burden on Kierkegaard would be another example of the sacrifice *he* would have to make in marrying Regine, and the Me-oriented aspects of his retraction seem to be predominant ones figuring in commentary about it. Thus, most of the latter takes the retraction to be based on the sacrifices he thought he would have to make to ongoing writing, philosophical pursuits, and dedication to God while married. Yet the same commentary rarely broaches the issue of just why Kierkegaard believed marriage would interfere with those goals. Consider: what if it turned out that Regine would have been the ideal spouse for maintaining a household that enhanced his religious/philosophical pursuits. After all, she could have tended to the daily chores and requirements of living, like meals, paying bills, cleaning, and supervising servants (or replacing them) that the philosopher would have to undertake himself as a bachelor. Far from marriage frustrating his philosophical role, maybe it would have furthered it by subtracting out the time it took to discharge other lower-level or menial responsibilities!

It was already mentioned that the tide of critical opinion has it that whatever reasons Kierkegaard had for abandoning Regine stemmed largely from his own internal wish for a life in the religious dimension of existence, out of devotion to God. This motive ostensibly circumvents doubts about Regine's ability to fulfill the marital role herself. Here, and despite extolling the virtues of his intended before and after the retraction, could it be that Kierkegaard, in his interactions with Regine especially around the time of their engagement, suddenly realized how needy she was, too much so to qualify for being the kind of wife he envisioned? Such a motive, while being Me-oriented with respect to meeting the intended marital goals of the philosopher, might have sprung from his sensing a drawback in Regine that did not in any event diminish his love for her. Perhaps this motive is a less plausible one, although it would go hand in hand with Kierkegaard's sudden realization that Regine was unable to sacrifice herself for his ongoing philosophical identity.

Another possibility is that Kierkegaard's 1841 case of cold feet was driven by the apprehension that a departure from his ordinary mode of living was not something he figured he could negotiate comfortably. In other words, and despite all the fanfare about philosophy and religion, the philosopher was not up to facing the idea of a major change in life circumstances, a theory that is no stranger to personalities apprehensive about departures from familiar ways.

Finally, there is the possibility of wariness over a growing dependency on Regine in adapting to a life with her. This motive, a scion of the need to separate from her in order preserve familiarity, in Kierkegaard's mind may have sprung from anticipating the myriad ways the love of his life might grow on him—to the tune of mindless devotion leading to deflection from higher appointed tasks. On this interpretation, far from either Søren or Regine falling short of being an enthralled partner, perhaps the former needed to back away from what he sensed was going to prove to be too much of a good thing.

Endnotes

[1] Despite Wittgenstein's high opinion of Kierkegaard, he complained he had no appetite for rereading the latter whom he thought was too "long-winded…saying the same thing over and over again. When I read him I always wanted to say, 'Oh all right, all right, I agree, I agree, but please get on with it'" (Drury, 1984, p. 88).

[2] Kierkegaard's once estimable fortune inherited from his father Michael had been virtually depleted by the time of the philosopher's death on November 11, 1855. Regine consequently could not avail herself of the inheritance in any case. The gesture should not be understood as a slap in the face, especially if we cannot ascertain just what Kierkegaard knew about the state of his finances while he lay dying in Frederick's Hospital. His terminal penury in a curious way fatefully mirrored Michael's caveat to his youngest son: "You will never become anything as long as you have money."

References

Backhouse, S. (2016). *Kierkegaard: A Single Life.* Grand Rapids, Michigan: Zondervan Publishers.

Camus, A. (1975) *The Myth of Sisyphus.* London: Penguin Books.

Crews, F. (1986). *Skeptical Engagements.* New York: Oxford University Press.

___________ (1995). *The Memory Wars: Freud's Legacy in Dispute.* New York: New York Review of Books.

___________ (Ed.) (1998). *Unauthorized Freud: Doubters Confront a Legend.* New York: Viking.

Drury, M. O'C. (1984). Some notes on conversations with Wittgenstein. In In R. Rhees (Ed.) *Recollections of Wittgenstein,* Oxford: Oxford University Press, pp. 76-96.

Fabro, C. (1967). Why did Kierkegaard break up with Regina? *Orbis Litterarium,* 387-392.

Garff, J. (2005). *Søren Kierkegaard: A Biography.* Princeton: Princeton University Press.

Grünbaum, A. (1984). *The Foundations of Psychoanalysis: A Philosophical Critique.* Berkeley, California: University of California Press.

Kendler, K. S., Pederson, N. L., Neale, M. C. & Mathe, A. A. (1994). The clinical characteristics of major depression as indices of the familial risk to illness. *British Journal of Psychiatry, 165* (2), 66-72.

Lapointe, F. H. (1980). *Søren Kierkegaard and His Critics: An International Bibliography of Criticism*. London, England: Greenwood Press.

Lazerowitz, M. (1959). The relevance of psychoanalysis to philosophy. In S. Hook (Ed.) *Psychoanalysis, Scientific Method, and Philosophy*. New York: New York University Press.

___________________(1968). *Philosophy and Illusion*. New York: Humanities Press.

Lukács, G. (1968). *Soul and Form*. Cambridge, Massachusetts: The MIT Press.

Lyons, M. J., Elsen, S. A., Goldberg, J., et. al. (1995). A registery-based twin study of depression in men. *Archives of General Psychiatry, 55 (5)*, 468-472.

Macmillan M. (1991). *Freud Evaluated: The Completed Arc,* New York: North-Holland.

Shih, R. Belmonte, P. L. & Zandi, P. P. (2004). A review of the evidence from family, twin and adoption studies for a genetic contribution to adult psychiatric disorders. *International Review of Psychiatry, 16* (4), 260-283.

Updike, J. (2005). Incommensurability. *The New Yorker*, 1-15.

Acting Theory and Psychology

We know too much psychology

—Iris Murdoch, *Existentialists and Mystics*

It should come as no surprise that there are few important areas of behavior left untouched by psychology. It addresses many human patterns, albeit fraught with friction among disciplinary factions when it comes to explaining them. Within the profession certain categories of mental phenomena have been an arena of spirited controversy for some time, although longer than might be expected given psychology's advanced methodologies of inquiry. Skirmishes over such topics as consciousness, memory and language acquisition (Skinner, 1957; Chomsky, 1959; MacCorquodale, 1970; Ross, 1991; Loftus & Ketcham, 1994) can be decidedly heated. Collegiality of discourse frequently masks clashes of outlook laced with ferocity of opinion. Actors have not been spared the discipline's attention, although psychological issues bedeviling the performer's art continue to persist despite a continuing focus on them.

There is quite a stretch between the creative life of performers and theories of acting they may happen to endorse. The latter involve principles about the practice of the craft formulated in different schools of training. But stage life, both inside and outside the studio, is more than just theory. It is a wider, more complex world that can no more be encapsulated in popularized acting systems than do the realities of political life boil down to principles enshrined in foundational law, like the Constitution. Sometimes psychology steps into theatrical discourse, hoping to clear away whatever cobwebs of confusion or misunderstanding have accumulated in the history of the art.

The relationship between acting principles and psychology, while a frequent subject of commentary, has its own share of problems. How close knit are psychological theories and acting principles before and after the curtain goes up? An accepted folklore has it that the two are inextricably wedded. But in what way? Here, we should distinguish between two separate issues: (1) the psychological analyses of scripts or acting principles and (2) theatrical depictions of historical events of psychological interest. The latter are exemplified in, for example, Cixous's (1976) *Portrait of Dora*, a feminist glossing of Freud's famous case, Mark St. Germain's (2011) *Freud's Last Session*, Terry Johnson's (1993) drama, *Hysteria: Or Fragments of an Analysis of an Obsessional Neurosis*, or Nicholas Wright's (2010) *Mrs. Klein*, a dramatic treatment of Melanie Klein's problems of her own parenting abilities.

Psychoanalysis. Proponents of different systems of actor training have been vocal about their favored approaches being those students should adopt. Similarly, many patients in psychotherapy attaching great significance to the treatment procedures they undergo, likewise champion their superiority. For example, psychoanalytic treatment has been touted by many as the chosen "depth" approach to self-understanding. Yet blind devotion to the practice may forestall the systematic attention this claim deserves. Can a treatment approach be fairly characterized as effective due to its "insight-oriented" capabilities before ascertaining whether the self-knowledge it produces is actually true? And how can any system of psychotherapy be "deeper" than its rivals in advance of determining its superior treatment efficacy? Less known is the finding that "insights" into why certain behavioral problems arise is not always necessary in order to achieve gains in psychotherapy (Bloom, 1994; Weisz, et. al., 1995).

Research on these issues in the behavioral sciences has been ongoing, yet inconsistent enough to be troubling. Systems of psychotherapy routinely gallop far ahead of their scientific validation, while proponents of this or that treatment approach strive to bring its concepts to bear on clinical results, dramatizing the deficiencies of competitors. Yet a patient's progress in psychotherapy, however gauged, does not ensure the validity of its constituent concepts. The value a patient attaches to psychoanalysis, effective or not, hardly guarantees the legitimacy of such notions as repression, forgotten sexual trauma, Oedipal strivings, free association, decoding presumed "symbolisms" in dream interpretation or rarefied discourse about transference and countertransference. One can acknowledge the personal growth attributed to psychological treatment the driving concepts of which nonetheless may fail to stand the test of time.

Similarly, actors may lead rewarding professional lives long after sundry systems of performer training lose their appeal. Enriched performance on stage may bear little or no relation to the validity of the training system thought to inspire it. When all is said and done, an actor's creative life cannot be summed up by a batch of theoretical principles supposedly driving it, any more than the exhilaration of driving an antique automobile springs from the quality of gasoline pumped into its fuel tank.

Comparisons between Method acting and psychoanalytic theory or treatment is an old story—and often a muddled one. The playwright David Mamet has characterized psychoanalysis as a "coeval harness-mate" to Stanislavsky's system, one that "can demand fealty and long-term devotion," but rarely "demonstrable results." In an ironic tone, he has declared that certain acting theories and psychoanalysis both absorb the time and attention of students "who would otherwise be hard put to fill an idle hour" (Mamet, 1997, p. 15).

Method actors and their instructors often wax eloquent about the training they undergo, as do patients—be they actors or otherwise—about the self-knowledge they acquire after lengthy exposure to psychodynamic therapy. Yet both types of enterprise are to a large extent supervised by gurus who engage overtly or covertly in a special pleading for their point of view. Both psychoanalysis and offshoots of Stanislavsky's system can be likened to grids brought to the experiences of patients and acting trainees. The capacity for both systems to embrace a wide range of patterns is broad enough for presumed "fits" between theory and practice to supposedly validate the former.

In his book, *Sanford Meisner On Acting* coauthored with Dennis Longwell (Meisner & Longwell, 1987), the revered acting teacher Sanford Meisner speaks of his own experience with psychoanalysis, and claims that it revealed how the death of his brother became "the dominant emotional influence" in his life (p. 5).

Meisner insisted on occasion that acting takes twenty years to learn. He felt that only within such a time frame can novices hope to become seasoned performers. As he indicated, the transformation is the result of laborious training. Cannot the same be said for the development of psychoanalytic insights? If Meisner, after years on the couch, came to realize the trauma resulting from a brother's death had effects on his personality he was able to pinpoint, why shouldn't this revelation likewise qualify as a product of sustained coaching? Did not Meisner's psychoanalytic therapy *train* him to perceive many aspects of his personality as the direct or indirect effects of his brother's death? Might his hang-ups have developed despite, and not because of, family history?

In psychotherapy, insights into the presumed causes of personality problems may be hampered by constraints on what is uncovered in hourly sessions contaminated by placebogenic effects, memory distortions, suggestibility and other non-specific factors (Sulloway, 1979; Macmillan, 1991; Sacks, 2013). They may also become complicated by mistaken causal hunches. For example, a patient, at the prodding of his analyst, may come to believe his obsessive-compulsive disorder is the effect of early severe bowel training, when this "insight" might turn out to be dead wrong, as in all likelihood it is (Bernstein, 1955; Beloff, 1957; Heatherington & Brackbill, 1963). A dream interpretation by a psychoanalyst may be open to doubt, especially when it conflicts with another put forth by one of his equally experienced colleagues. A patient may learn he has a stockpile of "repressions," while some investigators note the concept underwent a history of shifting meanings from the early to later stages of Freud's theorizing (Ross, 1991), while others claim there has been no rigorous evidence for any such process in sixty years of experimental research (Holmes, 1990). This in no way undermines a rich tradition of research into unconscious processes that goes back before Freud to nineteenth century researchers like Helmholtz (1821-1894) and Herbart (1776-1841). It continues on in a flowering tradition of contemporary neuroscience that makes a mockery of the concept of an unconscious when it is identified exclusively with psychoanalytic theorizing (Kihlstrom, 1987, 1992). What we don't know about ourselves consists in much more than our ignorance over the fancied sexual and aggressive nature of our alleged "instincts."

Perhaps Meisner no more knew precisely what effects his brother's death had on his personality than did his analyst. Yet together they collaborated on weaving a narrative magnifying the importance and influence of such life happenings. The result is a tale which, whatever its allegiance to inferential and possibly erroneous leaps, at least coheres. The accommodation of diverse life events to such coherent narratives is then taken as evidence that something has been explained.

In recent years, some psychoanalytic theorists, abandoning hope that causal connections of the type Meisner came to believe existed between his personality traits and certain life experiences can be rigorously established, have retreated to the position that constructing narratives of remarkable compass is pretty much all that remains of the house that Freud built. Nonetheless, it goes without saying that a tale with a comprehensive reach has its own manner of gripping the imagination. When it comes to what the psychoanalyst Spence (1982) calls "narrative truth," such tales are free for the asking, and ostensibly limitless in number.

There is virtually no experimental evidence to show the therapeutic superiority of believing one narrative over another, or that such narratives—as opposed to none at all—have implications for the treatment capabilities claimed for them. Spence (1985) maintains that analysand and analyst as unbiased purveyors of relevant processes derives from a model that contravenes all we have learned from an updated understanding of psychology.

Other psychoanalysts like Schafer (1992), facing the daunting task of replacing what he considered to be the "mechanistic language of Freud's metapsychology," speaks to a form of narrative interchange between analyst and analysand in which the baby is arguably thrown out with the bathwater. In this respect, his effort is not without a hint of the kind of relativism that thumbs its nose at striving for the certainty that is the goal of any scientific quest. Thus, he insists that the narrative can be construed as "versions of the true and the real," while "narratively unmediated," or unimpeachable access to truth either cannot be demonstrated, or remains an elusive ideal. In this respect, therefore, he denies any "absolute foundations for observers or thinkers"; each must select "his or her narrative or version" (pp. xiv-xv). Far from representing an advance on Freud's older orthodox formulation, one might view Schafer's version of the promised land to be an epistemological backwater, mired forever in he said/she said scenarios or "texts" of a postmodernist cast (Ellis, 1989; McGowan, 1991; Rosenau, 1992; Butler, 2002).

Earlier in his career, Freud flatly denied that any of his clinical results could be attributed to the effects of suggestion (Freud, 1988a). He maintained this stance despite his familiarity with the dispute between his mentor, the Parisian neurologist Jean-Marie Charcot, who felt hypnotic phenomena were the immediate and uncontested symptoms of "hysteria" conceived as neurological disorder, and Hippolyte Bernheim of Nancy, who was convinced they were largely a manufactured residue of suggestibility, just as did his predecessors Liébeault, Abbé Faria and James Braid. In the course of their debate, Bernheim's slant came to predominate in scientific circles. For him, hypnosis could not be regarded as symptomatic of "hysteria," since he held that aside from "hysterics"—currently a defunct psychiatric category of diagnosis—others not so diagnosed could likewise be hypnotized. And he turned out to be right.

There have been several works celebrating the connection between Method acting and psychoanalysis, among them Freed's *Freud and Stanislavsky: New Directions in the Performing Arts* (Freed, 1964). Its dust jacket declares it will prove to be of "inestimable value to young actors seriously concerned with their work." Yet there is little in the way of technique offered the aspiring student throughout the book. Rather, its slant is pretty much a form of literary criticism heavily laced with psychoanalytic concepts. Its chapters on such characters as Shakespeare's *Hamlet* fall short of providing the acting student with technical advice about how to approach the role on stage. Rather, the latter aim seems to have been hijacked by abstract discussions of character or script analysis from the psychoanalytic point of view. Even if students agreed with the tendentious analysis of *Hamlet* authored by Ernest Jones in *Hamlet and Oedipus: A Classic Study in the Psychoanalysis of Literature* (1949), specific acting approaches to the role do not ride piggy-back on such scholarly convictions. The student will still have to fashion a delineation of the role based upon clear acting strategies.

Drawing connections between Freud and Stanislavsky may be like comparing apples and oranges. Some such dissociation seems to have escaped the attention of many commentators and bedeviled comparisons between the two theorists. Sullivan (1967), despite a valiant attempt to draw significant parallels between the views of both men, was moved to confess that, "they differ in what they observed and formulated" (p. 98)

Stanislavsky was a theorist who attempted to develop a system of actor training that captured stage reality; Freud's psychoanalytic theory purports to supply an explanatory framework for all behavior, normal and abnormal. Needless to say, both systems are on quite different wave-lengths. There are no learned behavioral patterns falling outside of the assumed compass of psychoanalytic theory. Because of this, there are no unique "Freudian" roadmaps to theatrical portrayals; any interpretation of a role will, in virtue of the scope of the theory, lend itself to a psychoanalytic spin. Consequently, all dramatic approaches to *Hamlet* will accommodate to this kind of interpretation.

Freud originally posited the Oedipus complex as a *universal* unconscious scenario: everyone harbors it. He deemed it to be such an ingredient aspect of human development that the latter would be impossible without it. Accordingly, we would be hard pressed to come up with a specimen of ongoing behavior exempt from its imputed, albeit invisible effects. Presumably, and according to orthodox psychoanalytic theory, there are no personality styles, whether normal or abnormal, without the stamp of the complex. Whether resolved successfully or not, it underlies the development of all behavior, despite the enormous range of human patterns that exist. If so, it seems paradoxical to characterize a particular pattern like that of Hamlet as evidence of the complex when there are no counterexamples against which it can be meaningfully contrasted. In other words, any possible behavior patterns engaged in by the Prince of Denmark can be viewed as stamped by the complex—as it is for everyone else.

Freed describes the "miscarriage" between art and psychology, referencing a mistake he felt Sir Laurence Olivier and director Tyrone Guthrie committed in a 1937 staged version of *Hamlet* (Freed, 1964, pp. 24-25). The directorial error involved is more accessible to audiences in Olivier's 1948 film version of the tragedy. In the movie, one that Olivier admitted was inspired by Ernest Jones's treatise, the closet scene between Hamlet and his mother Gertrude (Act III, scene 4) involves berating the queen (Eileen Herlie) for her liaison with his uncle, Claudius (Basil Sydney), the then reigning king of Denmark. In an interview with the critic Kenneth Tynan in 1956, Olivier maintained that he thought the Jones analysis of the tragedy provided a "water-tight case" for the psychoanalytic point of view.

Olivier, in the role of the hero and enraptured by the Oedipal spin placed on the play by Freud and Jones (both he and Guthrie traveled to Hampstead, England to confer with Jones about Shakespeare's play), in one scene planted a deep kiss on Gertrude's mouth that was suggestively sexual. If taken to be a direction inspired by psychoanalysis, this cinematic conceit, as Freed noted, is misconceived. It in effect confuses a scene open to psychoanalytic interpretation of a text with a graphic depiction of an unconscious scenario that by definition is not overt (sexual possession of the maternal figure—according to theory, a repressed wish).

If any mother-son interaction is consistent with an Oedipus complex, why should Act III, scene 4 of the tragedy command any greater attention from what psychoanalytic theory dictates than other scenes between characters in the play? Any interpretive enactment of the bedroom scene in *Hamlet* (or any other Shakespearean scene, while we're at it) is subject to psychoanalytic explanation, since the theory covers all facets of human behavior. There is consequently no such thing as "psychoanalytically-inspired direction," if we take this to mean an enactment of a role more consistent with Freud's formulation than with some alternative personality theory—or, as the case may be, none at all.

Another way of framing the issue would be to compare Olivier's portrayal of Hamlet with the one that was previously a signature role for his contemporary, Sir John Gielgud. Although Olivier, during the interview with Tynan, said he was convinced that the Jones interpretation was "the absolute resolution of all the problems concerning Hamlet," would a spectator discern any difference between the portrayals of the two actors as this bears on a psychoanalytic interpretation of characterization? "Psychoanalytic interpretation" pertains to a literary or psychological analysis of character or script, not the way an individual performer chooses to enact a role on stage. That is, should partiality toward psychoanalytic interpretation be favored, Gielgud's portrayal likewise exemplifies the theory.

Similar observations were made by Wilson (1985). He also considered director Guthrie and Sir Laurence Olivier to have "missed the point" in having Hamlet "grope his mother lecherously," since in classic psychoanalytic theory, underlying motives are unconscious "even to the characters themselves." (1985, p. 53). However, the Olivier enactment smacks of redundancy, since any mother/son pattern of interaction is fully consistent with psychoanalytic theory. If so, why should a director strive to emphasize the theory's applicability by artful displays of what is misleadingly construed as its visible instantiations? Wilson notes that psychoanalysis enjoys more popularity among humanities scholars than it does among scientifically-minded psychologists. Many of the latter regard it as more metaphorical than scientific, the same criticism lodged by thinkers who were contemporaries of Freud, like Kraus (Szasz, 1976) and Wittgenstein (1966).

The third chapter of Hornby's critique of Method acting (Hornby, 1992) is entitled "Are Actors Neurotic?" It has the rare good sense to challenge the folderol that often passes for excursions into the psyches of performers, as though such parlor games were not foredoomed to redundancy. Hornby notes that both orthodox analysts and their latter-day brethren, the so-called ego or identity psychoanalysts, had little to say about "theatre, acting or actors at all" (p. 28). However, there are occasional mavericks like Weissman who, in his 1965 *Creativity in the Theater: A Psychoanalytic Study,* takes the fanciful plunge. He declares that actors are persons who fail to develop normally, suffering from depersonalization, exhibitionism, and related perversions." Hornby goes on to quote Weissman as believing actors also may "develop severe acting-out neuroses or even psychoses" (p. 29).

Hornby quite rightly will have none of these glib overgeneralizations. Except his arguments lapse into the same genre of error he criticizes. Neurotics, avers Hornby, "usually make bad actors" (p. 30); performers have a seeming "childishness" that derives actually from their "self-esteem" and a "firm sense of being fully adult" (p. 31). However, if it is transparently unfair to lodge blanket indictments of actors as "neurotic," it is no less extravagant to attribute to them maturity levels outshining non-performers. The mistakes here on both sides are the baseless speculations about the inferior or superior qualities of entire populations of persons, irrespective of whatever talents or limitations each of them may chance to illustrate. And both Hornby and Weissman would do well to acknowledge that the term "neurotic," while a common enough lay designation for abnormal psychological patterns, carries no currency in present day psychiatric diagnoses, having been expunged from the professional lexicon for many years (Wilson, 1993). Its banishment from professional discourse was resisted to the end by the constituency most forlorn over the disappearing snows of yesteryear: the psychoanalysts. Despite this, even Freud was careful to differentiate among varieties of "neurosis." Toward the late part of the nineteenth century, he distinguished among neurasthenia, the anxiety neuroses and the psychoneuroses. It was the last of these that was the springboard for his theories about repression, the Oedipus Complex and infantile seduction.

Routine paeans to psychoanalysis have been an expectable stance in the theater arts community, as is the case in a now diminishing form of literary criticism in the academy. Lee Strasberg was reported to have advised his acting trainees to seek analysis, and encouraged them to appeal to the unconscious while in training (Walsh, 2013, p. 35). But the times they are a-changin,' as Dylan observed. Clinical practitioners who laud the importance of discoveries that smack of a bygone vintage—while reminding us that psychoanalysis has moved on to appropriate more modern ways of thinking—may be in for a rude awakening.

Psychoanalysts nowadays contend that their "science" has advanced well beyond the earliest days of Freudian innovation, currently incorporating more up to date practice. What is left out of this modernization is an acknowledgement that the extent to which the evolution in question departs from older forms, to that extent does it approximate therapeutic transactions of alternative theoretical orientations and procedures. On the other hand, to the extent psychoanalytic practice retains methods like dream interpretation or free association, it remains weighed down with the scientifically questionable detritus of yesteryear.

Outcome studies in behavioral science over the past several decades have generally supported the view that psychoanalysis fares no better than many other forms of psychotherapy when it comes to behavior change or symptom removal. (On balance, it probably does worse, since the patients it treats are usually gleaned from more clinically intact patient populations.) In the absence of scientific validation, high-sounding pronouncements about "transference," "symptoms," "dreams," "repressions," "symbolic representations," and other paraphernalia of the practice, should be assessed for what they are: empirically groundless.

In the opinion of the present author, psychoanalytic analyses of Shakespeare's plays likewise represent misdirections in a proper assessment of the canon. Interpretations of the motives of, say, Hamlet or Iago, fail to do what they purport: plausibly explain the behavior of central characters in plays. In psychoanalytic commentary, we are treated to such interpretations of Hamlet's "procrastination" in avenging his father's death as being due to his unconscious Oedipal fantasies surfacing uncomfortably close to consciousness were he to murder his uncle outright. On the other hand, we are told Iago's hatefulness supposedly camouflages his homosexual desire for Othello or Cassio or both.

The Othello theme is not a unique one in the psychoanalytic grab bag. A favorite spin in the commentary of this professional community is latent or unconscious homosexuality. It seems currently to have exhausted its rueful grip on American letters awash in the same kind of thinking. From all indications, it is an older, but now wearied preoccupation of academics who congregated principally in humanities departments. Many of its scholars in the past fastened onto the theme as a protean explanatory rubric. Perhaps one reason for its diminished role in commentary is the more recent drift toward abandoning outdated ideas about persons of diverse psychosexual identities. Accordingly, repressed homosexuality in literature and the theater seems to have run its tortuous course up to that point in time at which everyone stopped being a nervous Nellie about the possibility that the condition was lurking cryptically behind his or her daily patterns.

American plays in which homosexuality is an ingredient theme, like Tennessee Williams' *Cat On A Hot Tin Roof,* are often those in which the motive is not *repressed* in the psychoanalytic sense, but *suppressed.* Big Daddy Pollitt, in the powerful second act of Williams' play, forces his son Brick to face the erotic, and not especially unconscious, desire for his dead sports pal. Brick returns the lesson in truth-telling by informing Big Daddy he is dying of colon cancer. The father, furious that his condition has been kept from him, exits shouting that everyone—except his conflicted son—is a liar. The "odor of mendacity" on Big Daddy's plantation is relieved only by revelations that for father and son have been too hidden to face prior to their searing confrontation.

Psychoanalysis, which Thomson (2015, p. 97) sees as having become a cottage industry in Los Angeles in the 1940s, is currently being questioned in widening segments of the professional community as a viable avenue of explanation and treatment. Patients sometimes improve in this kind of psychotherapy, but they also improve in alternative forms of therapy. As was indicated, suggestibility, placebogenic effects and biogenic factors are always relevant considerations, although behavior change in treatment is most of the time attributed to applications of the explanatory system involved, as if the logical fallacy of *post hoc ergo propter hoc* were too much of a temptation for the enchanted to avoid committing.

The business of evaluating the effectiveness of psychotherapy is a tremendously complicated task for researchers. Effectiveness has to be the statistically significant advantage of any treatment approach over the advantage of receiving no treatment at all or comparisons with suitably designated control groups. Despite Sontag's noting approvingly that some see psychoanalysis as "a new and higher level of consciousness" (1967, p. 258), the convictions psychoanalysts have for decades proclaimed about their "discoveries"—predicated as they are on the flimsy crucible of consulting room experience and speculation—only underscore the system as perhaps the preeminent pseudoscience of an age. (Cioffi, 1974; Swales, 1982; Grünbaum, 1984; Medawar, 1985; Crews, 1986, 1995; Macmillan, 1991; Esterson, 1993; Scharnberg, 1993; Dawes, 1994; Webster, 1995; Erwin, 1996; Bucci, 1997; Dufresne, 2000, 2007).

Behaviorism. In like-minded speculation over applying psychoanalytic theory to matters theatrical, confusion may saddle notable attempts to bring behaviorism to the same subject matter. Stanislavsky purported to follow Pavlov, less so Sechenov, whose writings were recommended to Stanislavsky by Kommissarzhevsky (Carnicke, 1998, p.162). Nonetheless, his contact with both their systems was limited. Vladimir Prokofyev of the Moscow Art Theatre, in a visit to the United States in 1964, indicated there was an exchange of letters between Pavlov and Stanislavsky, revealing that the physiologist once requested a copy of *An Actor Prepares* while the latter was writing it (Munk, 1967, p. 68). Recent attempts to keep pace with a scientific tradition on acting have been made (Schulman, 1973; Stern & Lewis, 1968; Konijn, 2000; McConachie, 2008). Lee Strasberg, during actor training sessions, made glancing references to emotional responses being "conditioned" (Hethmon, 1965, p. 113).

Both Stanislavsky as well as his latter-day interpreters like Strasberg failed to note a possible down side of the Pavlovian model by ignoring the role of extinction in any process based upon classical conditioning. Extinction refers to the weakening of conditioned responses when they are no longer paired with the unconditioned stimulus. In the original paradigm, a dog was trained to salivate (conditioned response) at the sound of a bell (conditioned stimulus) after the latter was paired enough times with food powder (unconditioned stimulus). However, the conditioned response to the sound of a bell would tend to disappear over time unless pairing bell and food was reinforced (i.e., repeated).

Whatever acting theorists imagine the conditioning process to be in the theatrical context, it has dire implications for the length of time an actor may depend upon Pavlovian, or classical, conditioning. In the case of a lengthy run of a play, a conditioned response should weaken over time without reinforcement. At any rate, it should be less durable than it would be in a short run. By implication, should reliance on a technique like affective memory derive from a "conditioning process" as Stanislavsky and Strasberg both assumed, its effect would be naturally time-limited. This, despite the fact that the way classical conditioning is construed by acting theorists to be a functioning process in their techniques is not without a degree of fuzziness from the outset. In affective memory, what precisely corresponds to conditioned and unconditioned stimuli? Have Method actors noted that the use of affective memory diminishes in power over time in the same role, as it should when the inner stimulus corresponding to the unconditioned factor is no longer paired with the one corresponding to the conditioned stimulus? Alternatively, perhaps reliance on affective memory involves a process resistant to weakening because its application does not represent Pavlovian conditioning in the required technical sense. Indeed, what, after all, corresponds to reinforcement in the Stanislavskian reliance on this form of "conditioning"?

Schulman (1973) sees Method acting and behavioral psychology as sharing a common goal of controlling behavior. He distinguishes them as the difference between observing others and having oneself as the subject. As in many such ventures devoted to drawing close comparisons, it is sometimes difficult to distinguish separate emphases implied by the undertaking. On the one hand, "applying behaviorism" may involve equipping the actor with a set of self-management tools to resolve persistent problems of the craft. On occasion, the technology can be a useful way to eradicate bothersome sources of interference to the performer's task. A second emphasis involves a redefinition of the actor's task in behavioristic theoretical terms. This is analogous to psychoanalytic interpretation becoming merely theory-saturated discourse of a particular script.

As an example of the first kind of behavioristic emphasis, Schulman recommends techniques like Joseph Wolpe's systematic desensitization for anxious performers (Wolpe, 1956). This procedure combines deep muscle relaxation with imagining anxiety-evoking situations. Eventually, the actor learns to relax in the presence of the feared situation, enabling him to substitute a more appropriate response (Schulman, 1973, p. 54). Such applications of behavior-theory have obvious implications for reducing performance hang-ups like phobias, stage fright, and other anxiety-sourced problems. They might have assisted such artists like Sir Laurence Olivier, the tenor Franco Corelli, pop singer Carly Simon and actor Phillip Bosco, performers who were stricken with severe anxiety or panic attacks before or during performance.

On the other hand, a second behavioristic emphasis may have little or no import for performance problems or strategies, since it consists merely in the appropriation of a theoretical terminology into which performance ideas or problems are recast. For example, such notions as "positive reinforcement," are concepts at home in Skinner's operant psychology (Skinner, 1953). All the same, it remains to be seen whether behavioral analyses of actors' training procedures are merely a new-fangled way of describing slices of experience, adding little to what trainees already know. To the extent behaviorism represents for the students a novel way of speaking merely, it purchases applicability at the price of triviality. Lexical revision in which ordinary language terms such as "praise," "feedback" or "encouragement" are recast as "positive reinforcement" in a fancied behavioristic approach would seem to represent little more than altering a vocabulary of discourse. Needless to say, such revisionism has little import for how an actor should delineate a particular role or rid himself or herself of troublesome problems or distractions.

Another problem area in the crossover from psychology to performance consists in mischaracterizing an effort, even within the behavioristic scheme appropriated. Schulman (1973) sketches how certain procedures used in the Actors Studio to train performers may be based on such behavioristic tools as "successive approximations," involving shaping processes by which acting goals can be attained through step-by-step reinforcement of stages inching toward the final product.

Schulman contends that students in Lee Strasberg's classes at the Actors Studio became "increasingly spontaneous" and creative when it came to training exercises such as rhythmic movements. The technique involved apparently resembles one placing the emphasis on a practical technology of self-management. When instruction at Actors Studio is thus characterized by Schulman as relying on a technique of successive approximations, the model or template for the procedure is a representative arrangement of conditions in the animal laboratory. Here, a pigeon can be taught to peck at a disc twenty consecutive times before it is reinforced with a food pellet. But creating a twenty-peck response pattern right off the bat is unlikely or impossible. Understandably, the animal could never be brought to a response criterion of twenty consecutive pecks had the experimenter waited for this completed cycle before delivering reinforcement. Accordingly, initial training cannot be predicated upon impossible goals. The pigeon must be brought to criterion in stages by first being placed on more modest schedules, like one or two responses before reinforcement. After this is established, the response criterion can be slowly increased until the pigeon is maintained on a schedule of twenty responses per reinforcement. The schedule of reinforcement is said to be in strength when, based upon the pigeon's reinforcement history, it continues indefinitely to emit twenty responses before reinforcement. A fixed ratio schedule (FR 20) is designated as such because it is governed by the number of responses and the reinforcement contingent upon this.

When Schulman describes Method instructional methods at the Actors Studio as incorporating techniques like successive approximations, he refers to an experimentally uncontrolled environment. True, his description would be accurate were teachers like Lee Strasberg to have behaved like ideal reinforcement machines. This would have been extremely difficult to verify unless the pedagogy involved were monitored at all times. Suffice it to say, the grapevine suggests a different story, and it is hard to know where the truth lies. Since Studio training is conducted in less than a tightly controlled environment like a Skinner box, it is only speculation that an actor's growth can be plausibly attributed to techniques of the kind Schulman discusses.

The appropriation of behavioristic terminology for Studio training as this encompasses schedules of reinforcement comparable to those in animal laboratories may be a case of wishful thinking. Any such retranslations have as their goal the attempt to prettify training—in the sense of downplaying the painfulness of the learning process for the actor (in Skinnerian terms, its aversive aspect). As a case in point, one initially enthusiastic member of the Studio, James Dean, widely regarded as one of its stellar alumni, was so traumatized by Strasberg's criticism of scenes the actor presented in class, he was loath to repeat the experience in front of assembled colleagues. Cheryl Crawford documents this in her autobiography (Crawford, 1977, pp. 221-222). In it, she indicates the actor "turned bitter and left" after two later scenes that were not well received.

Despite his discouragement, Dean's membership in Actors Studio continued, as it did later for all permanent members. Dean's acting ability, to the extent aspects of it could be reasonably attributed to Studio training, would hardly seem to have derived from steady doses of positive reinforcement. The Studio appears to have functioned in part in his case as a suppression of ongoing behavior, or punishment in the Skinnerian sense of this term. Accordingly, when performers emerge from the Studio as accomplished artists, their achievements, far from being a triumph of the method of successive approximations, may for all we know have developed independently of the training the program afforded. After the fact there is no way to tell, although hype about the maturation of talent under Studio auspices is a widely advertised tale. Actually, there is as much evidence for assuming the opposite.

Studio membership from the outset comprised and still comprises a glamorous assembly of actors whose talents were the reason they were originally inducted into its ranks. Many publications about the Method invariably list the number of famous movie stars who count themselves as members. Accordingly, an impression is left that the Studio has created (or enhanced) an astonishing array of talent. This may not be true. The talent may have developed, for all we know, independently of Studio instruction or was obvious prior to membership in it. While it may be the case that the Studio had in some ways a creative impact on many film or stage careers, it is difficult to determine in just what way this is so.

Ironically, James Dean may not be the exception to the rule. As a forum for training, Actors Studio has a membership that in the past was inconsistently involved in scene presentation. Shortly after its creation, members who were deemed non-participating or lacking the requisite talent were asked to leave, a policy subsequently reversed because of its demoralizing effect on the membership. The fruits of non-contingent reinforcement, however, are not without response-cost. What the Studio membership gained by way of tenure, it may have lost in the way of incentives to participate in scene study. Unless observational learning (Bandura, 1971) i.e., attending classes without scene participation had instructional payoffs for members, inclusion in the program by non-participating professionals may mean little more than reaping the advantages of networking (a not unimportant perk for the frequently unemployed actor), or having an eye-catcher on a resumé signifying membership in a theater aristocracy.

Robert Lewis, a founding member of Actors Studio who, like Strasberg, was given to lengthy speeches about the art of acting during classes supposedly devoted to developing it (Lewis, 1958), experienced a similar problem of non-participating attendees. One might hazard the guess that recalcitrance on the part of student members may have been due in part to an environment not always brimming with the satisfactions of a utopian community like *Walden II* (Skinner, 1948). Nor is the Studio forever entitled to such cheerful designations as "positively reinforcing." Perhaps this is as reality must dictate. For many performers, the heartache of launching careers, whatever the training milieu, may abound in more turmoil and angst than most optimists are wont to admit. Hethmon, in his introduction to tape-recorded sessions of Lee Strasberg at the Actors Studio, has provided a compelling view of the more anguished side of performers' lives (Hethmon, 1965, pp. 1-23).

It should be kept in mind that the notion of reinforcement has distinguishable meanings in the Pavlovian and Skinnerian paradigms.

For Pavlov "reinforcement" is the number of times the conditioned stimulus (bell) is paired with the unconditioned stimulus (food powder); for Skinner "reinforcement" is the event which increases the probability of a response-class when delivered following its emission. For Pavlov, the responses in question are called *respondents*; for Skinner, they are called *operants*. The former, like reflexes, are essentially under the control of the autonomic nervous system, the latter are for the most part instrumental behaviors, or basically the wider range of voluntary behaviors.

The diminishing appeal of the Method, whatever its implication for the future of actor training, is a more recent trend. There are in all likelihood broader sociological reasons for this, including demands on performers for wider capabilities on stage. Being a "triple threat" talent (acting, singing, dance) now represents more of a requirement for work on the Broadway stage (especially musicals) than it did when the Actors Studio was founded. Yet such demands doubtlessly contribute to what many aspiring performers are forced to regard as a fuller plate of challenges. When a young Burgess Meredith approached Harold Clurman with a request to receive Method training, the latter dissuaded him, explaining that Meredith had too many interests already (Hethmon, 1965, p. xi). But "too many interests" fairly characterizes the mandatory professional lot of many of today's young performers. This reality may be partially a consequence of the type of theatrical vehicle favored by contemporary audiences, together with narrowed opportunities for performers in a competitive market place. Yet discursive dogfights over the Method can reach a feverish pitch, as if they were being aired in a scholarly vacuum insulated from the ever-changing face of theater history.

In his chapter, "I Hate Strasberg: Method Bashing in the Academy," Krasner (2000) dutifully provides a response to critics like Counsell (1966), Brustein (1958), Hornby (1992) and Mamet (1997) who, among a tide of other commentators soured on the Method regard it as "psychobabble," its avid enthusiast as "[playing] himself, not somebody else," or acting out of motives that are "basically a form of emotional release" (p. 17). But Krasner's venture in counter-reformation strikes a peculiar note. According to him, Method actors should be seen as exemplars of, *mirabile dictu*, free will. Here we are no longer in the realm of psychology, but cozying up to metaphysics to boot! Krasner insists that the Method actor views the world "as a logical construct of human sense-experience" in opposition to determinism which he maintains sees free will as an illusion (pp.19-20).

Rather a mouthful, to be sure. It would be hard to suppose that any struggling Method actor is likely to see this as a proper depiction of a world-view—should he or she even harbor one. Moreover, Krasner confuses philosophical theories like idealism and realism with free will and determinism, not to mention mischaracterizing the latter. Only the form of determinism known as incompatibilism (Edwards, 1961; Van Inwagen, 1975; Strawson, 1994; Harris, 2012) denies free will. Another form of the persuasion, termed compatibilism (Nowell-Smith, 1954; Dennett, 1984; Nahmias, 2005) grants it with what can only be discerned in the philosophical literature as academic gusto. A more modest intermediate position is the "agnostic autonomism" of Mele (2014). Determinism, in short, is a house divided against itself on free will. As in all attempts to apply paradigms from a broader range of social science and philosophical systems to acting theories, the cautionary note can be summarized in one word: carefully.

In summary, when it comes to acting theory, not to mention a slew of much larger issues, both psychoanalytic and behavioristic practitioners and theorists sometimes may be biting off more than they can chew.

References

Bandura, A. (1971) *Psychological Modeling.*New York: Lieber-Antherton.

Beloff, H. (1957) The Structure and Origin of the Anal Character, *Genetic Psychology Monographs, 55,* 141-172.

Bernstein, A. (1955) Some Relations Between Techniques of Feeding and Training During Infancy and Certain Behavior in Childhood. *Genetic Psychology Monographs, 51,* 3-44.

Bloom, P. B. (1994) Is insight needed for successful treatment? *American Journal of Clinical Hypnosis, 36,* 172-174.

Bucci, W. (1997) *Psychoanalysis and Cognitive Science: A Multiple Code Theory.* New York: Guilford Press.

Butler, C. (2002) *Postmodernism.* New York: Sterling Publishing Company.

Brustein, R. (1958) America's new cultural hero: Feelings without words, *Commentary, 25,* 123-129.

Carnicke, S. M. (2009) *Stanislavsky in Focus: An Acting Master for the Twenty-first Century.* London: Routledge.

Chomsky, N. (1959) A Review of B. F. Skinner's *Verbal Behavior* in *Language, 35,* No.1, *26-58*

Cioffi, F. (1974) Was Freud a liar? *Listener,* 91, 172-174.

Cixous, H. (1976) *Portrait of Dora. The Selected Plays of Hélène Cixous,* In E. Prenowitz (Ed.) London: Routledge.

Crawford, C. (1977) *One Naked Individual: My Fifty Years in the Theatre*. New York: The Bobbs-Merrill Company.

Counsell. C. (1996) *Signs of Performance: An Introduction to Twentieth-Century Theatre*. London: Routledge.

—————— (1986) *Skeptical Engagements*. New York: Oxford University Press.

—————— (1995) *The Memory Wars*. New York: New York Review of Books.

Dawes, R. (1994). *House of Cards: Psychology and Psychotherapy Built on Myth*. New York: The Free Press.

Dennett, D. C. (1984) *Elbow Room: The Varieties of Free Will Worth Wanting*. Boston: MIT Press.

Dufresne, T. (2000) *Tales From the Crypt: The Death Drive in Text and Context*. Stanford: Stanford University Press.

——————— (2007) *Against Freud: Critics Talk Back*. Stanford: Stanford University Press.

Edwards, P. (1961) Hard and soft determinism. In S. Hook (Ed.) *Determinism and Freedom in the Age of Modern Science*. New York: Collier Books. Pp. 117-125.

Ellis, J. M. (1989) *Against Deconstruction*. Princeton, New Jersey: Princeton University Press.

Erwin, E. (1996) *A Final Accounting: Philosophical and Empirical Issues in Freudian Psychology*. Cambridge, Massachusetts: The MIT Press.

Esterson, A. (1993). *Seductive Mirage: An Exploration of the Work of Sigmund Freud*. Chicago: Open Court.

Freed, D. (1964) *Freud and Stanislavsky: New Directions in the Performing Arts.* New York: Vantage Press.

Freud, S. (1988a) *The Standard Edition of the Complete Works of Sigmund Freud, 24 Volumes.* James Strachey (Ed.) London: Hogarth Press and the Institute of Psycho-Analysis (1953-1974), *1*, 41-57.

__________ (1988b) *The Standard Edition of the Complete Works of Sigmund Freud, 24 Volumes.* James Strachey (Ed.) London: Hogarth Press and the Institute of Psycho-Analysis (1953-1974), *16*, 452.

Grünbaum, A. (1984) *The Foundations of Psychoanalysis: A Philosophical Critique.* Oakland, CA: University of California Press.

Heatherington, E. M. and Brackbill, Y. (1963). Etiology and Covariation of Obstinacy, Orderliness and Parsimony in Young Children, *Child Development, 34*, 919-943.

Hethmon, R. H. (1965) (Ed.) *Strasberg at the Actors Studio: Tape-Recorded Sessions.* New York: Theatre Communications Group, Inc.

Harris, S. (2012). *Free Will.* New York: Free Press.

Holmes, D. S. (1990) The evidence for repression: An examination of sixty years of research. In J. L. Singer, *Repression and Dissociation: Implications for Personality Theory, Psychopathology, and Health.* Chicago: The Chicago University Press. Pp. 85-102.

Hornby, R. (1992) *The End of Acting: A Radical View.* New York: Applause Theater Books.

Johnson, T (1993). *Hysteria: Or Fragments of an Analysis of an Obsessional Neurosis.* London: Methuen.

Jones, E. (1949) *Hamlet and Oedipus: A Classic Study in the Psychoanalysis of Literature.* Garden City, New York: Doubleday & Company.

Kihlstrom, J. (1987) The cognitive unconscious. *Science, 237*, 1445-1452.

______________ (1992) The psychological unconscious: Found, lost, and regained. *American Psychologist, 47*, 788-791.

Konijn, E. A. (2000) *Acting Emotions.* Amsterdam: Amsterdam Univeristy Press.

Lewis, R. (1958) *Method—or Madness?* New York: Samuel French.

Loftus, E. and Ketcham, K. (1994) *The Myth of Repressed Memory: False Memories and Allegations of Sexual Abuse.* New York: St. Martin's Press.

MacCorquodale, K. (1970) On Chomsky's review of Skinner's *Verbal Behavior. Journal of the Experimental Analysis of Behavior, 13*(1): 83–99.

Macmillan, M. (1991) *Freud Evaluated: The Completed Arc.* New York: North-Holland.

Mamet, D. (1997) *True and False: Heresy and Common Sense for the Actor.* New York: Pantheon Books.

McConachie, B. (2008) *Engaging Audiences: A Cognitive Approach to Spectating in the Theatre.* New York: Palgrave Macmillan.

McGowan, J. (1991) *Postmodernism and Its Critics.* Ithaca: Cornell University Press.

Medawar, P. B. (!985) *The Limits of Science.* Oxford: Oxford University Press.

Meisner, S. and Longwell, D. (1987) *Sanford Meisner on Acting.* New York: Vintage

Books.

Mele, A. R. (2014) *Free: Why Science Hasn't Disproved Free Will.* New York: Oxford University Press.

Munk, E. (1965) (Ed.) Stanislavski preserved: An MAT discussion. In *Stanislavski and America: "The Method and Its Influence on the American Theatre.* New York: Fawcett World Library, pp. 66-73.

Nahmias, E. (2005) Agency, authorship, and illusion. *Consciousness and Cognition, 25,* 27-41.

Nowell-Smith, P. H. (1954) *Ethics.* London: Penguin Books.

Rosenau, P. M. (1992) *Post-Modernism and the Social Sciences: Insights, Inroads, and Intrusions.* Princeton, New Jersey: Princeton University Press.

Ross, B. M. (1991) *Remembering the Personal Past: Descriptions of Autobiographical Memory.* New York: Oxford University Press.

Sacks, O. (2013) Speak, memory. *New York Review of Books.* February 21, Vol. LX, No. 3, pp. 19-21.

Schafer, R. (1992) *Retelling a Life: Narration and Dialogue in Psychoanalysis.* New York: Basic Books.

Scharnberg, M. (1993). *The Non-Authentic Nature of Freud's Observations* (2 Volumes). Stockholm, Sweden: Almqvist & Wiskell International.

Schulman, M. (1973) Backstage behaviorism. *Psychology Today,* June, 51-88.

Skinner, B. F, (1945) The operational analysis of psychological terms. *Psychological Review, 52,* 270-294.

————— (1948) *Walden II.* New York: The Macmillan Company.

————— (1953) *Science and Human Behavior.* New York: The Free Press.

——————— (1957) *Verbal Behavior.* New York: Appleton-Century-Crofts.

Sontag, S. (1967). *Against Interpretation.* New York: Farrar, Straus & Giroux.

Spence, D. P. (1982). *Narrative Truth and Historical Truth.* New York: Norton.

Stern, R. M. and Lewis, N. L. (1968) Ability of actors to control their GSR's and express emotions. *Psychophysiology, 4,* 294-299.

Strawson, G. (1986). *Freedom and Belief.* Oxford: Oxford University Press.

St. Germain, M.(2011). *Freud's Last session.* New York: Dramatists Play Service, Inc.

Sullivan, J. (1967). Stanislavski and Freud. In E. Munk (ed.) *Stanislavski and America: "The Method" and Its Influence on the American Theatre.* New York: Fawcett Library, pp. 88-109.

Sulloway, F. (1979). *Freud, Biologist of the Mind.* New York: Basic Books.

Swales, P. (1982). Freud, Minna Bernays and the Conquest of Rome: New Light On the Origins of Psychoanalysis. *New American Review, I,* 1-23.

Szasz, T. (1976). *Anti-Freud: Karl Kraus's Criticism of Psychoanalysis and Psychiatry.* Syracuse: Syracuse University Press.

Thomson, D. (2015). *Why Acting Matters.* New Haven: Yale University Press.

Van Inwagen, P. (1975). The incompatibility of free will and determinism. *Philosophical Studies, 27,* 185-199.

Walsh, F. (2013) *Theatre & Therapy*. London: Palgrave Macmillan.

Webster, R. (1995). *Why Freud Was Wrong: Sin, Science and Psychoanalysis*. New York: Basic Books.

Weissman, P. (1965) *Creativity in the Theater: A Psychoanalytic Study*. New York: Basic Books.

Weisz, J. R., Donenberg, G. R., Han, S. S., & Weiss, B. (1995) Bridging the gap between laboratoty and clinic in child and adolescent psychotherapy. *Journal of Consulting and Clinical Psychology, 63*, 542-549.

Wilson, G. (1985) *The Psychology of the Performing Arts*. London & Sydney: Croom Helm.

Wilson, M. (1993) "DSM-III and the Transformation of American Psychiatry: A History". *The American Journal of Psychiatry, 150*, pp. 399–410.

Wittgenstein, L. (1966) *Lectures and Conversations on Aesthetics, Psychology and Religious Belief.* Oxford: Basil Blackwell.

Wolpe, J. (1958) *Psychotherapy By Reciprocal Inhibition*. Stanford: Stanford University Press.

Wright, N. (2010) *Mrs. Klein*. London: Nick Hern.

Unpublished Letters to the Editors
of *New York Review of Books*

Professor Thomas Nagel's engaging review [*New York Review of Books,* May 12, 1994] of yet two more works on Freud, this time by Richard Williams and Paul Robinson, exhibits all the sentiments of loyalist screeds. Coming as it does on the heels of the Frederick Crews bashing, one wonders whether some found in Nagel's piece the recompense they felt timely in what was doubtlessly a deluge of indignant letters from psychoanalytic devotees.

Nagel indicates that Freud's influence is powerful. However, Freud's having altered the intellectual landscape is hardly a reality his detractors would care to question. Consequently, it is quite beside the point when considering the scientific merit of his theories that Nagel would aver it is unlikely they will be "expunged" or fail to have sociological effects that go "much deeper than can be captured by a set of particular hypotheses." As Nagel points out, the same can be said for the influence of Hobbes or Descartes on contemporary thought, although few of us would argue that political theory or philosophy of mind must remain forever wedded to their view of humanity. I hasten to add that historical influence is also a feature of astrology, theosophy, phrenology, pyramidology, and—to bring the point closer to home—biorhythms, female inferiority and nasal determinism. Unlike psychoanalytic theory, such curiosities have not enjoyed the luxury of avoiding critical scrutiny by beating a hasty retreat into "hermeneutics": the escape hatch through which concepts central to scientifically false, limited or vacuous formulations can be recycled by humanities scholars into crowning metaphors of existence.

Freud's influence is not quite the consensus Nagel takes it to be. Psychoanalysis elsewhere enjoys nowhere the popularity it does in the United States. This fact awaits explanation by a definitive sociology of the psychoanalytic movement (as opposed to the compromised hagiographies of sectaries up and down Park Avenue, within literary circles, among Hollywood celebrities and throughout British philosophy circles.) Also, Freud was always less the rage for students of experimental medicine and psychology than he was for scholars whose views are more readily disseminated through the media. Professor Nagel cannot have it both ways. He cannot persuade us that psychoanalytic theory is "scientific," and, like its staunch advocates, go ballistic whenever incisive critiques like Adolph Grünbaum's appear.

The lengths apologists go to defend the sacred terrain are remarkable. Psychological explanation is an amazingly protean rubric for experimental psychologists. Yet it is virtually equated by Nagel, Wollheim and Robinson with Freud's motivational psychology exclusively, as if criticizing it were somehow an assault on any explanation lying wholly outside the physiological domain. Is it impossible to understand human behavior as parsed through any but psychoanalytic categories of discourse?

Professor Nagel's flirtation with *petition principii* is everywhere apparent in his review. For example, he regards Frederick Crews as "fatally benighted" because the latter refuses to see psychoanalysis as "an extension of familiar forms of insight." However, the issue of whether such extensions are valid or deserve to be considered "insights" is precisely the theoretical bone of contention. Whether Freud, as Nagel insists, actually "extended the range of [psychological] explanation to unheard-of lengths" is the conclusion of the scientific argument, not an indisputable premise of understanding on which it rides piggy-back.

In my opinion, Nagel does a disservice to the complexity of scientific issues rife in psychoanalytic theorizing. His commentary downplays experimental issues, a tendency manifested by his dismissal of both the importance and possibility of controlled experimentation in adjudicating the claims of psychoanalysis. For example, something he terms "statistical confirmation"—as though statistical inferences were a necessary feature of all controlled experiments (what about single-case experimental designs?)—is for him "completely impossible" in chosen interpretations. As a result, he informs us we are forced to fall back on whatever psychodynamic hypothesis is most "plausible." But what are the criteria of plausibility for these interpretations? That they sound good, like the view of depression as "sadism toward the introjected love-object?" Why is that explanation so plausible, other than the reasons provided by the insular community? When we come to such a seminal concept as repression, the need for controlled experimentation to validate it as the overriding concept Freud took it to be is more imperative than ever. Nagel's conjecture that it is an "explanatory concept" evidence for which "comes from a variety of sources" is hardly reassuring, especially in the light of such controversies swirling around it as the early childhood sex abuse, false memory and ritual abuse themes.

Nagel's dismissal of an experimental approach to psychoanalytic theory is nowhere more apparent than his falling for those beguiling anecdotes of psychoanalysts designed, as one can well imagine, to dispel vestiges of skepticism through the vehicle of sudden, prophetic insight. Nagel is taken with one interpretation of the case of a patient who challenged his specialist to explain why he fell asleep at the point stock market reports were being broadcast. Is it too late in the game to remind Nagel that such prophetic "hits" when they occur are standard fare in mediumship and sundry parlor games? The proof of any system of prediction is an analysis including the number of times an interpretation is found incorrect. Before I credit a chimpanzee with being a Shakespearean scholar, I should want to know just how long he had been hammering away at a typewriter prior to writing the first line of *Twelfth Night*!

The conviction grows in reading Nagel's review that he believes the house that Freud built is, in some unexamined way, unassailable. Unassailability, following Wittgenstein, is a property of "world pictures," not sciences. Freudians have a tendency to behave as though they were in the grip of the former, while proclaiming how truly dedicated they are to the latter. Michael Brearly and peter Hobson have already raised the question as to whether psychoanalysis is a "form of life." If so, criticisms of it are greeted as though they were like colonial depredations against an insular culture, self-justified on its own terms.

Finally, Nagel, like so many philosophers before him, devotes principal energies to arguing for the *coherence* of Freud's system. We are already beyond that. Our primary epistemological aim at present is to determine whether it is *true*. I submit this cannot be done through such tainted procedures as "clinical observation" or "analytic insights." In the last analysis, it is only the experimental approach to the complex issues of psychology that will permit us to determine whether Freud was wise, or merely ingenious.

In his otherwise commendable overview of Daniel Kahneman's contributions to psychology, Freeman Dyson winds up in the latter part of his review close to a conceptual tailspin. Bemoaning Kahneman's failure to reference Sigmund Freud in his book or its thirty-two pages of endnotes, Dyson launches into a broadsides about the omission that bear further scrutiny.

Dyson duly notes the scientific *diminuendo* of enthusiasm for Freud's psychoanalysis, both as an explanatory enterprise and treatment approach, and references commentary by Sir Peter Medawar and Frederick Crews. The contemporary disenchantment, however, is far more widespread than many suppose, and includes critical commentary by such notables as Thomas Szasz, Ernest Nagel, Sidney Hook, Karl Popper, Karl Krauss, Vladimir Nabokov, Adolph Grünbaum, Malcolm Macmillan, H. J. Eysenck, Ludwig Wittgenstein, not to mention a long tradition of academic psychology over a century old. Yet Dyson, opting to ignore the fact that this dissenting tradition includes spokespersons who have harbored abiding doubts about the scientific and empirical basis for Freud's system, clings to the belief that Hahneman's work somehow lacks appreciation of the "insights" of the founder of psychoanalysis. The stance is all the more paradoxical, since Dyson elects to characterize the difference between Freud and Hahneman as between "literary" and "scientific" contributions. (As early as 1895, we find Freud admitting that "It still strikes me as strange that the case histories I write should read like short stories and that, as one might say, they lack the serious stamp of science.") But if the value of an explanatory system is its appeal to a "literary" rather than a "scientific" sensibility, why is it a *scientific* shortcoming to ignore it in a fresh approach to psychological theorizing? And just why are Freud's alleged insights "complementary," rather than "contradictory" to Hahneman's, as Dyson avers? In just what sense does literary value "complement" scientific value in a purely *scientific* formulation?

Dyson makes several other curious observations. As against Hahneman's experimental approach, he contrasts William James along with Freud as a thinker more given to literary, rather than scientific contributions, calling the two "artists" rather than "scientists." James is an unfortunate example to illustrate his point, since in 1890 he published his seminal *Principles of Psychology*, a ground-breaking work that along with the laboratory studies of Wundt, Fechner and Helmholtz in Germany in the same century set the stage for what was to later become a rich tradition of experimental psychology. And contrary to Dyson, it was not Hahneman who "was to make psychology an experimental science, but a tradition begun a century or so before he was born! Nor did he "revolutionize" psychology; he only made an important contemporary contribution to it.

Other of Dyson's comments would appear to suggest that his familiarity with psychology may be somewhat on the deficient side. According to him, "strong emotions and obsessions cannot be experimentally controlled," a proposition that seems to be confusing ethical constraints on certain types of research with methodologies that are quite equal to the explanatory challenge. At any rate, investigators like Stanley Milgram, Harry Harlow, Joseph Wolpe and Philip Zimbardo might take exception to any opinion that they were not dealing in their studies with strong emotions. And a long tradition in physiological psychology investigating arousal states from anxiety to penile tumescence is rich in precisely the kind of knowledge Dyson seems to be maintaining is off limits to its methods.

PITFALLS OF MEMORY

To the Editors:

In Oliver Sacks's otherwise beneficial essay on the ways our memory of the past may mislead us [*NYR*, February 21], he maintains that such phenomena as "source confusions," "autoplagiarisms" and "cryptomnesias" document its frailties. What we sometimes consider to be veridical memories of events may be no such thing and may, in fact, be false. He references the disastrous legacy of the so-called "recovered memory" movement in psychology, aimed at uncovering repressed memories of early sexual abuse. Unfortunately, it is still with us. Assuring us that we possess no cortical mechanisms for determining the truth or accuracy of our recollections, Sacks goes on to underscore the often elusive character of "historical" as opposed to "narrative" truth: what we deem to be past realities may be constructions of our imagination. But then he avers that such aberrations are "relatively rare" and that our memories are for the most part "solid and reliable."

You cannot have it both ways. If we lack inborn mechanisms to determine the truth or falsity of our memories, on what basis can we be sure that most of them are, as Sacks insists, reliable? He takes pains to illustrate the vagaries of memory by referring to Freud's contribution to the subject, indicating that the father of psychoanalysis uncovered "grosser distortions" of memory when he realized that patient accounts of early sexual abuse were "fantasies." Commentary on the subject in recent years has raised doubts over whether Freud really obtained "reports" or was actually confusing patient memories with interpretations he forced upon them. If the latter, then memory distortion can even assail investigators pioneering the study of the subject. Accordingly, if false memories can infiltrate hallowed corridors of received wisdom, maybe sometimes it's *not* better to let sleeping dogmatists lie.

Psychotherapy as Moral Enterprise

The practice of psychotherapy is on occasion seen as charged with the value-systems of those who practice it. As a consequence, its interventions may be viewed as often harboring the moral persuasions of its practitioners. By "moral persuasion" is meant that fabric of professional activity having to do with values, ethical norms and moral-judgmental moves of a game.

Characterizing psychotherapy as embodying a "game" is not to derogate it, only to deem it something for which sets of governing rules can be uncovered, however problematic the challenge proves to be. Accordingly, being rule-governed amounts to playing different kinds of "games," without implying that anything as auspicious as the care of souls is no more consequential than checkers or bingo.

When the practice of psychotherapy as administered by psychiatrists, psychologists, social workers and other types of counselors is viewed inescapably as possessing moral or evaluational ingredients, this does not also imply that clinicians are thereby doing something unacceptable in practicing their profession, although serious ethical lapses when they occur understandably trigger moral concerns.

It is quite another thing to maintain that these professions are so bound up inherently with issues of value that they amount to practicing moralities. To understand the full import of this is not to merely imply the importance of therapists striving to understand their own value assumptions, lest their practices get mistakenly construed as value-free. Moral structure is not an ingredient of psychotherapeutic transaction that can in principle be shaved off or separated from ostensibly empirically grounded operations ostensibly at the heart of a professional calling. The matter is more complex than this.

It is hardly surprising that treatment of the human condition bears the unmistakable stamp of values unique to a given historical era. Needless to say, psychotherapy—not to mention its corollary activities like diagnosis—inevitably plunges practitioners into a furnace of value-imbued decision-making and normative assumptions. Some future anthropologist might explore contemporary forms of psychotherapy incorporating time-bound moralities with not so much as a dissenting note by colleagues reviewing the history of the profession. But it is a far cry from declaring a minimal or additional infusion of values to the thesis that the very terms and concepts of clinical theory are so value-imbued, it would be doing violence to them to categorize them as other than evaluative in substance, however much they masquerade as value-free.

Terms like "symptoms," "diagnoses" or "behavioral problems," are cases in point. Whatever the upshot of opinion about their meaning, they connote patterns that are undesirable given a system of values. To grant this is not likewise to assume that clinical practice is reprehensible in some austerely moral or religious sense. Accordingly, it would hardly be a challenge to the view that clinical concepts are normative that they are not the foci of high moral controversy. A clinician may thus frame an essentially value issue as, aseptically, an "objective," "factual" or "scientific" one without so much as an inkling that his or her enterprise is a cryptically moral one. For example, just because diagnosing a personality disorder does not catapult opposing clinical factions into hotly contested moral colloquies hardly shows that diagnostic classification must be other than an evaluative act, even when designated as purely "descriptive," "factual" or some other bloodless synonym. The very notion of "abnormality" pertains to an evaluation, as much as it does a description of behavior, as do the retinue of myriad contenders for purely descriptor status: "aggressive," "inappropriate," "hostile," "narcissistic," "grandiose," "antisocial," "withdrawn," etc.

When psychotherapy is construed as an applied science, this can be taken to mean two very different things: (1) it incorporates procedures or techniques that can be investigated by methodologies aimed at empirically determining such parameters as effectiveness; (2) it *has* incorporated techniques authenticated by sound research in the field. Historians of the subject might appreciate that while (1) holds true of most schools of psychotherapy, (2) is not particularly true of any but a minority of practices within the larger enterprise. The evolution of psychotherapeutic theory and practice is not for the most part driven by data gleaned from rigorous outcome studies. It pretty much has a life of its own. The runaway character of the field is consequently not a historical phenomenon resting upon a carefully vetted body of knowledge accumulated as a result of rigorous research. Its course is largely determined by more capricious factors in addition to whatever value-presuppositions of the day embedded in human traditions are its stock and trade.

Despite the lack of scientific support for most psychotherapy as currently practiced, many treatment specialists prefer to view their efforts as being derived from "science:" in above sense (2) not merely in sense (1). On rare occasions, the attribution is fitting, although as was mentioned, less frequently than clinicians care to admit. Actually, as a professional class, psychotherapists have habits of self-description that are not without a touch of irony. The more they reference their activities as "our science," the more they believe the designation holds true. In the past, when psychoanalysis was struggling for disciplinary recognition, embarrassments in the form of professional scandals, schisms, the emotional instability of many of its pioneers, turf warfare or later on, disappointing results of outcome studies, were events regarded by devotees as "setbacks for *our science*." Such terminology, continuing to this day, obscured the political, if not self-serving, atmosphere of the psychoanalytic establishment. Its historical chapter holds more sociological interest than it does the unmistakable stamp of an applied experimental psychology.

What is the nature of the value-laden or moral enmeshment of psychotherapy? While psychotherapists from time to time grant that their professional activities are suffused with values, they are generally unwilling to admit how far this goes. If I am not mistaken, the picture of the field in the minds of most of its practitioners is a laminated one. That is, they feel there is a layer of value-laden strains infiltrating their practices that can be sharply distinguished from a "scientific" layer, however difficult such an separation may prove to be. Thus, the received picture of the profession in the minds of its practitioners is that the field runs merely an occupational risk of a moral-judgmental intrusive element when practitioners are not alert to its incorporation. Supposedly, the challenge is then spun as the task of differentiating that element from an ethically neutral core of practice with an eye toward suspending or controlling the element.

The possibility of purifying psychotherapy of moral texture is a fantasy not simply because the task is difficult or impractical. Psychotherapists are not occasional moralists, as when they presumably lapse from playing the scientific game or its applications. They are inveterate moralists, whether or not they own up to this. To be a psychotherapist is consequently to apply a system of values to a subject matter, albeit one fostered in a unique instructional mode. The morality in question is an invisible one, imparted for the most part as though it were a set of moves in a quite different kind of game. Specialist and patient are thus both of them beguiled by respective pictures of the practice. If there is talk of victimization (a chosen metaphor of our age), then everyone, practitioners and patients alike, are victims of a misleading picture.

When I say that psychotherapy is suffused with values or moral doctrine, I am not referring to anything as tangible or identifiable as an "ideology," as we have come to understand the term. I speak of doctrines that are more subtle, embedded and invisible than this. And they cut across all types of psychotherapeutic interventions.

Construing psychotherapy as an applied value-system or morality is not likewise to assume there are as many different value systems as there are practitioners. The moral moves in question are shared by communities of therapists, one reason why it is easy to confuse them as aseptic scientific ventures. Were every psychotherapist to preach unique and different moral tenets, the nature of a practice would be all too obvious. It is the encompassing reality of a moral consensus on a great many issues that masks the nature of the calling. In order to flesh out the foregoing remarks, we shall take up illustrative examples, one from the past and one from a more recent professional example.

A word of warning. The reader should not suppose that our remarks are an attack on psychotherapy. Construing it as essential value doctrine is not tantamount to indicting or dismissing it. It is not like discovering one's doting mother is really like Joan Crawford, one's hives is really leprosy, or one's obstetrician Victor Frankenstein. On the contrary, I think moral doctrine, even when dispensed in as cloaked a form as psychotherapy, can be as important and valuable a thing as any other form of beneficial moral suasion.

Pascal's Other Wager

One of the most enjoyable features of Blaise Pascal's *Provincial Letters* is the way he feigns pie-eyed innocence in his debates with Jesuits who have condemned a Jansenist for heresy. Pascal was convinced of the piety of the accused, a certain M. Arnauld, who reportedly challenged a papal interpretation of the writings of the founder of Jansenism. Pascal's attempted refutation of the Jesuit scholars took the form of a disarming dialogue with several of them that belied its mathematical precision and dialectical ingenuity. The Jesuits took him on as a seemingly ingenuous theological novitiate, little realizing how much this impressive intellectual talent was out for the kill.

In his first letter, Pascal sets out to consider a question of presumed "fact:" was M. Arnauld presumptuous in asserting—against a bevy of bishops, to boot—that higher ecclesiastic authority was wrong in imputing heretical opinion to the founder of Jansenism. That Pascal himself was not prepared to conclude that M. Arnauld was anything but unpresumptuous in his approach shall not concern us. What does is another question: just what kind of alleged "fact" was it that he was or wasn't presumptuous? Had Pascal been a contemporary clinician, he might have posed the question in a slightly different form: was M. Arnauld's behavior appropriate or inappropriate? If it is either one or the other, it is tempting to regard the disjunction as patently a factual option.

Whether M. Arnauld actually authored the document in which church authorities found evidence of presumption could be considered a factual affair (providing there were no paradoxes in his claim to authorship). But the accusation in question itself is not a *description* of

M. Arnauld's behavior, but an *evaluation* of it in the light of certain moral principles. And to judge his act this way is not akin to providing a summary depiction of its empirical features, but locating it within a system of values. What is more, to pass moral judgment, much like decisions from the bench in courtroom procedures, means handing down a verdict. In the courtroom, two jurists can review the same set of "facts," yet come to completely different conclusions about them. Here, the disagreement is routinely not over an issue which can be adjudicated solely by an appeal to the empirical features of a case. Disagreements among jurists or agents of moral judgment obviously take place in the context of scrutinizing certain facts over which disputes arise, but clashes of moral or legal viewpoints are more than purely factual affairs.

In Pascal's case, it was impossible to judge M. Arnauld as "presumptuous" without first ascertaining other matters. We must determine whether or not it is allowable in church law to challenge a papal opinion that is not an *ex cathedra* pronouncement or ecclesiastical verity. It is, of course, conceivable that within the clerical rules of the game at his time, M. Arnauld, although possibly correct on a theological issue, was nonetheless "presumptuous" for expressing an opinion when it ran counter to those enunciated by pope and bishops. Since he might still be judged "presumptuous" irrespective of the correctness of his opinion, theological stance and personal attitude or behavior were separate considerations under scrutiny by an ecclesiastical tribunal.

On the other hand, perhaps while being wrong during Pascal's time would make expressing the opinion in question audacious in the extreme, maybe the only out for diminishing a charge of presumptuousness was being right. Had a tribunal discovered that M. Arnault was theologically correct, then the imputation of presumption might have conceivably been withdrawn. In all of this, it is intriguing to note that a charge of presumption—putatively a behavioral description—might well rest on determining other intricate theological issues. And what, after all, does M. Arnauld's being right theologically amount to? Is his being right or wrong a fact—not a simple one like being widowed, a Frenchman, a father or six feet tall—but a fact, nonetheless?

If M. Arnauld's being right amounted to a judgment about whether his theological views could be accommodated in an orthodox tradition, it would appear that the answer requires a type of jurisprudential assessment. Accordingly, the answer can only be established by implicit moral argument. "Presumptuousness" within the context of religious discourse at that time is therefore the upshot of a moral argument, not a "fact" in the flatfooted empirical sense. If so, what about its modern counterparts "appropriate" and "inappropriate" patterns of behavior?

The problem with modernist counterparts of seventeenth century Catholic theological concepts is not that seeing them as morally tinged as opposed to exclusively empirical results in complicating the task of determining when a pattern is "appropriate" or otherwise. In most cases, the task is easy because of moral consensus on so many normative issues arising during the course of treatment. The problem is that we have been led to think that most of the stock terms of clinical usage have a purely descriptive function without moral or normative underpinnings. Morality in clinical theorizing or diagnostic appraisal has in effect gone to a masked ball: *Un Ballo en Maschera*, as Giuseppe Verdi would have had it.

Some time ago I was asked to review a paper submitted for publication to a leading psychiatric journal. Its author undertook to address issues in the uneasy interface between psychology and religion, psychotherapy and spirituality. The author maintained that patients should never be pressured or coerced into accepting the viewpoint of the therapist, whatever the belief system of the patient and specialist happen to be. "This is only ethical," the author declared.

My first hunch was that the author's statement was excessively pious. After all, therapists not only do pressure clients into accepting their point of view, I wasn't so sure this was in many cases a bad thing to do. In other cases I was convinced it was an ethical mandate, especially when the belief system of the patient is a damaging one to him or others. Indeed, was not "pressuring" a client to adopt a newer adaptive pattern what the therapeutic enterprise amounted to in many cases? We may thus call the thrust of certain efforts "cognitive behavior change," as in the CBT approach. But doesn't producing such change often constitute a form of suasion bordering on or constituting pressurized or coercive strategies? What, after all, is the intended goal of treatment with an individual diagnosed with Antisocial Personality Disorder?

The proof of my position—or so I thought at the time—was shown in two cases I provided as illustrations of the ethical use of pressure. The first instance was that of a therapist who attempts to convince a paranoid patient no one was actually out to "get" him. The second case was that of a patient diagnosed with Dissociative Identity Disorder who "remembered" being a Satanic cult breeder despite unimpeachable evidence she had never been pregnant. In these two cases, I assumed that efforts to wean patients away from mistaken beliefs at strategic points in treatment, was not any the less "pressured" or "coercive" even when ethically justified.[1]

The irony is that while the author and I appeared to be in disagreement over general ethical principles of treatment, we may have been of one mind about the approach taken in the two cases cited. Yet how is this possible, when we differed over the admissibility of the use of pressure or coercion?

What I had failed to realize was that the disagreement was more complex than I had supposed. Was the author correct in assuming that patients should never be pressured into accepting a practitioner's viewpoint except in circumstances in which interventions could be deemed ethically sound because the notions of "pressure" or "coercion" were made to have attenuated application? In short, both concepts, depending on the circumstances, can undergo moral transformations.[2]

In other words, ethical consensus among practitioners who seem to be in moral disagreement might be achieved by finessing the application of terms in broadly defined ethical standards, rather than regarding them as saturated empirically with straightforward reference to descriptive features of practitioner behavior.

So the difference between the author's position and mine might not, in one way of looking at the matter, represent a disagreement over what practices were unethical. It may have amounted to honoring the exceptionless character of moral codes at the expense of finagling their application in particular cases. That is to say, for him ethical principles are exceptionless and universally true, although how they apply in particular cases is up for grabs, awaiting the outcome of moral assessment. Consequently, to honor exceptionless principles isn't necessarily to be clear over what procedures instantiate them in every case. If "pressure" or "coercion" is open-textured (Waismann, 1963) as are all empirical concepts, the possibility exists that theorists who appear to be in disagreement over abstract ethical codes may be on the same plate when it comes to appraising individual cases or circumstances. When one insists on the universality or binding force of ethical or moral principles, one is not boxed in, as it were, by moral rigidity or austerity. Upholding principles may only mean that "pressure" or "coercion" are weasel words, deployed for the most part only after the moral dice have been cast. Accordingly, terms are made to fit—much in the manner of a suit of clothes. They are not deployed as descriptive labels in some uniform or flatfooted empirical sense, but as linguistic residues of preconceived ethical judgments.

We have, in short, two substantially different tacks on "pressure" and "coercion." One of these is the view that deployment of these terms is wedded to ethical perceptions of therapeutic practice already in place. They are thus not deployed as purely descriptive labels but as the aftermath of preconceived ethical judgment. The alternative view is that the terms are descriptors with unambiguous meanings. On this view, their use involves the practice of looking to see whether as a matter of cold, empirical fact pressure and coercion turn out to be characteristic of given patient-therapist interactions.

A Contemporary Example

In a more recent controversy of note, the Nomenclature Committee of the American Psychiatric Association in 1973 removed homosexuality from the DSM-III, replacing it with the diagnosis "ego-dystonic homosexuality." The decision was a paradoxical one right off the bat for commentators who declare that abnormality, or those conditions which are "disorders" or "treatable" can from time to time undergo transformations into patterns no longer classifiable as such, being reworked as variants of normalcy.

"Ego-dystonic homosexuality," however, was in the seventies a remnant of an ethical game that was reluctant to let homosexuality completely off the hook of "abnormality." In contrast to more recent thinking about psychosexual identity, this diagnosis established a unique criterion for a disorder: personal distress. That is, the profession declared that in the gay population, only those whose sexual orientation caused personal distress qualify as having a "disorder." The importance to the APA of the element of distress is intriguing inasmuch we do not accord distress similar significance in a great many other instances in which behavioral patterns are accompanied by it. Thus, and at the instigation of family, friends, church or social reference groups, a youngster may be brought to grief over having sex before marriage, marrying outside the faith or ethnic group, wearing long hair, getting a tattoo, smoking weed, or having a taste for rock music. It is conceivable that the discomfort might prompt a youngster to seek professional help, although the discomfort in question might come to be viewed by a therapist as nothing more than a residue of generation gap tensions. It is also possible that therapists in such cases might seek to increase intra-familial understanding, rather than regard the upset in question as a sign of a "disorder." Yet the architects of the older DSM-III elected to designate "distress" over one's homosexuality as more consequential than merely the aftermath of societal pressure. Personal distress evidently made the difference between a sex orientation that was abnormal and untold numbers of other patterns that are not, although distress may be a consistent theme in all of them.

Cutting to the chase, we may acknowledge the existence of many patterns causing personal distress, although we are not moved to alter them despite the unhappiness they produce. The noteworthy example that readily springs to mind is, of course, heterosexuality. Its exclusion from pathology is engineered by what might be characterized as a conceptual sleight of hand, belying psychiatric double-standards.

When heterosexuality causes distress, this is somehow parsed as the problem of "impotence," "aggression," "infidelity," "marital discord," "insensitivity," or some such thing. Accordingly, when a straight person is distressed, it is "sexual dysfunction," that is the disorder; when a gay person is distressed, it is his or her "homosexuality" that is the problem!

Perhaps the Nomenclature Committee of the APA felt obliged to formulate a diagnosis of ego-dystonic homosexuality if only for the reason that some gays presented clinically as distressed over their sexual orientation, while straights usually do not. Here, we might examine the implications of another possibility. Hypothetically, suppose some straight persons present as distressed over their sexual orientation, what then? Would this prompt the inclusion of a DSM category of ego-dystonic heterosexuality? Why not, if consistency were the rule?

Heterosexuality is not established as a "normal" mode of psychosexual identification as a result of any decision grounded in data, research, or empirical considerations. The "normalcy" of heterosexuality is a social fiat, a moral decision to accept it as a standard of acceptable sexual orientation, deviations from which are judged otherwise—hence "treatable." Heterosexuality can no more be discovered to be a disorder than can the standard meter rod in the Parisian Bureau of Standards be discovered to be less or more than a meter long. The Parisian rod *defines* how long a meter is. Questions about whether heterosexuality is disordered are senseless, not empirical. And investigations into the pathological basis of homosexuality—which were rife decades ago [3] are now virtually non-existent. We have come a long way from the seventies, which progress dramatizes a lesson to be drawn: how is the drastic change in the psychiatric classification of homosexuality possible if diagnosis is a putatively empirical affair? How is a pattern of behavior a "pathology" at one point in time and a variant of "normalcy" at another if empirical truth is the arbiter of any new outlook on a "condition"?

I am in agreement with Meehl's thesis that psychotherapists function as "crypto-missionaries" (Meehl, 1959), except the strain colors all of their transactions, not merely those touching on religious or spiritual themes. For example, diagnosing "narcissistic personality disorder" is not simply an exercize of attaching a formulaic label to an unambiguously defined set of verbal and non-verbal behaviors; it is *judging* whether the label is the proper assessment of a pattern in a quasi-jurisprudential decision. Disagreements over diagnosis are usually not disagreements over the empirical features of a behavioral pattern, but over how these might be classified through a ruling that has much in common with decision-making in the ethical and judicial spheres.

With respect to what Hart (1963) has called the "defeasible" character of judgment, among criteria for the diagnosis "Antisocial Personality Disorder" (F60.2 in DSM-V) include "Failure to conform to social norms with respect to lawful behaviors, " and "Consistent irresponsibility, as indicated by repeated failure to sustain consistent work behavior or honor financial obligations." Far from regarding such criteria as purely descriptive, they can be likened to rulings in law that are the outcome of judgments blending fact and law. "Irresponsibility" is thus a feature of behavior that is *ascribed*, rather than being purely descriptive of it. As such, clinicians, just like lawyers, may disagree over whether the criterion has been met in a particular case without any disagreement over the empirical features of that case. When it comes to homosexuality, revising older thinking about it celebrated in DSM-III is not the result of amassing new empirical information about the pattern, but doing nothing less than expanding a common understanding of how "normalcy" should be defined. The move is value impregnated, so that viewing it as the outcome of a purely factual discovery is barking up the wrong tree from the outset. And who can argue with expansion, especially when it goes in the sensible direction, courtesy of a revised moral outlook?

An expected objection to the reclassification of homosexuality as devoid of empirical substance is that the same reasoning might be extended to patterns that are indisputably disorders, like schizophrenia or epilepsy. If one hitherto acknowledged "disorder" can be denuded of scientific foundation, what's to prevent a similar move in these two cases? How can one countenance the view that schizophrenia is a treatable "condition" only in virtue of a set of values in contrast to a palpable scientific truth than it is an illness independently of any value-system brought to bear on its status? Isn't it hard or impossible to view the pattern as anything other than pathology, irrespective of socio-cultural context? The answer to this is that it is difficult to see how schizophrenia can come to be a positively valued pattern in whatever socio-cultural setting it is considered. The closest we have come to such an implausible reformulation was a strain in the writings of R. D. Laing (Laing, 1960; 1961) in which the condition was viewed as an insightful window into the reality of a society that savaged patients so designated. Nor should we forget that epilepsy was once viewed as a divine condition created by visitations from the gods, and not a completely negative phenomenon.

Both schizophrenia and homosexuality were both once devalued as a consequence of moral-judgmental moves, except the former would never be declassified from being a pathological condition since, unlike homosexuality, there is an unchanging moral consensus concerning its undesirability to this day.

On a final note, certain religious zealots with a presumed pipeline to the Almighty have declared that AIDS is his punishment for a sexual orientation that is *contra naturum*. Unfortunately, the argument inevitably backfires since it is the heterosexual population that has the monopoly on the three most frequent venereal scourges: syphilis, gonorrhea and chlamydia. The group with the lowest rate of venereal disease is gay women. (In yet another finding, they are judged to be the most competent in the parental role.) I take this to mean that if zealots listen closely enough to what God might be saying about sexual orientation, they may not like what they hear.

Endnotes

1   As an aspect of the point of view we are defending, the virtual
identification of "coercion" or "pressure" may be fatefully linked to
the moral perception of an intervention. Accordingly, when efforts
to dissuade an antisocial personality from engaging in destructive
patterns, the therapy is parsed as "suasion" or "influence," not
the harsher-sounding "coercion" or "pressure." The latter,
presumably descriptive of ethical missteps, are more readily applied
to interventions in which, for example, a therapist attempts to
challenge the religious beliefs or spiritual mind-sets of patients.
So we are said to "coerce" the innocent, but only "influence" the
miscreant through (wouldn't you know?) precisely the same kind
of psychotherapeutic interventions.

2   For present purposes, we are equating the "moral" and "ethical,"
although in other contexts and usages the former is viewed as a
sub-category of the latter.

3   Research purporting to show the pathological basis of homosexuality
document little more than disparities between experimental
populations. In a similar mind-set, several investigations by
Hooker (1957; 1961a, 1961b, 1963, 1965a, 1965b, 1968, 1969,
1971) purported to reveal the "normalcy" of homosexuality when
she found no difference between homosexual and heterosexual
experimental populations on certain measures. Ironically, the data
were presented by Gay Liberation representatives to the APA as
evidence for the view that homosexuality should be deleted as a
disorder from DSM-III. It would appear that both the activist
group and the Nomenclature Committee were of one mind in
believing that inclusion of sex orientation in diagnostic manuals
was an empirical issue to be adjudicated by the relevant research!
If such were actually the case, what would the conclusion be if

Hooker's results went in an unexpected direction? In other words, suppose studies were replicated and homosexuals fared better than matched heterosexual controls on any measure regarded as decisive? What should the conclusion be? A moment's reflection will show that "faring better" on experimental measures is likewise an elusive notion, precisely because of its value-tinged meaning. Assume the relevant measure was the level of some hormone, say testosterone. The results of one hypothetical study show that homosexuals have less average levels than heterosexuals, leading researchers to assume they have produced preliminary findings consistent with suspecting a pathological basis of homosexuality. But in another study, heterosexuals are shown to have a less average level of the hormone in the blood than homosexuals. Curiously, the conclusion would be the same for both studies, because we have defined pathology as any result that represents a significant departure from an ethically instituted standard of acceptable behavior.

References

Hart, H. L. A. (1963). The ascription of responsibilities and rights, In A. G. N. Flew, *Logic and Language*, Fifth Impression), Oxford: Basil Blackwell, pp. 145-166.

Hooker, E. (1957). The adjustment of the male overt homosexual, *Journal of Projective Techniques*, XXI, pp. 18–31.

————— (1961a). The homosexual community. *Proceedings of the XIV International Congress of Applied Psychology*, Munksgaard, Copenhagen.

————— (1961b). Homosexuality: Summary of studies. In Evelyn Duvall and Sylvanus Duvall (curr.), *Sex Ways In Fact and Faith*, Association Press: New York.

————— (1963). Male homosexuality. In: N. L. Farberow (cur.), *Taboo Topics*, Atherton: New York, pp. 44–55.

————— (1965). An empirical study of some relations between sexual patterns and gender identity in male homosexuals. In J. Money (cur.), *Sex Research: New Development*, Holt, Rinehart & Winston: New York, pp. 24–52.

————— (1965). Male homosexuals and their worlds. In: Judd Marmor (cur.), *Sexual Inversion: The Multiple Roots of Homosexuality*, Basic Books: New York, pp. 83–107.

————— (1968). Homosexuality. The *International Encyclopedia of the Social Sciences*, New York: Free Press.

————— (1969). Parental relations and male homosexuality in patient and non-patient samples, Journal of Consulting and Clinical Psychology, XXXIII, pp. 140–142.

————— (1971). In C. J. Williams and M. S. Weinberg (Eds.) *Homosexuals and the Military: A Study of Less Than Honorable Discharge*, New York: Harper & Row, pp. vii–ix.

Laing, R.D. (1960) *The Divided Self: An Existential Study in Sanity and Madness*. Harmondsworth: Penguin Books.

————— (1961) (1961) *The Self and Others*. London: Tavistock Publications.

Meehl, P. (1959). Some technical and axiological problems in

the therapeutic handling of religious and valuational material. *Journal of Counseling Psychology*, 6, 255-259.

Waismann, F. (1963). Verifiability. In A. G. N. Flew, *Logic and Language*, Fifth Impression), Oxford: Basil Blackwell, pp. 117-144.

The Mental Illness Myth and Troubled Taxonomies

In the early sixties, the psychiatrist Thomas Szasz was in the forefront of a libertarian thrust to thinking about the relationship between psychiatry and the law. The emphasis achieved its most visible realization in the abandonment of a "hands off" policy of the courts (Martin, 1975). This amounted to changing the law's posture of seeming judicial neglect when it came to protecting the civil rights of hospitalized mental patients (Begelman, 1975; 1982). An older legal tradition tended to defer to medical authority on patient rights issues, as though courts were wary of abridging professional prerogatives through judicial oversight. Even such jurisprudential mainstays as the insanity defense had formerly been interpreted as a set of rulings in which psychiatric opinion was nearly identified with what "insanity" was construed to mean (Goldstein & Katz, 1963; Gendin, 1973). The alternative judicial posture was that since "insanity" was essentially a legal notion, psychiatric testimony could *inform*, rather than *define* it.

Szasz's clarion-call for the reform of traditional thinking about mental illness was broadcast in his widely circulated book, *The Myth of Mental Illness* (Szasz, 1961a). Its central theme was that there was no such thing as "mental illness." The counterintuitive flavor of this pronouncement lessens once we realize that Szasz did not wish to dispute the existence of those psychological realities the term usually covers; he only intended to dispute the way they were conceptually disfigured by calling them "illnesses" (Szasz, 1963, p. 17).

A historical footnote to the controversy inspired by Szasz's point of view is that it served to highlight an older uneasy relationship among professional constituencies. Psychiatrists, with some exceptions, disparaged Szasz's thinking (Begelman & Tolor, 1966) while psychologists and other non-medical professionals were more sympathetic to it. They felt it addressed issues unresolved in their older chafing under what they took to be preemptive psychiatric power in the treatment of patients. Adding to these complaints were disciplinary disagreements over accepting the "medical model" as an adequate understanding of abnormal behavior. In giving more systematic attention to Szasz's viewpoint, it is important to separate the purely conceptual aspects of his thinking from institutional advances in rights issues for which he was a leading and courageous spokesperson. These have been taking place over the last half century.

The Mental Illness Myth

Szasz's assault on the mental illness concept embodied two distinguishable claims: (1) a conceptual flaw in the very notion of "mental illness," and (2) a social critique of the violation of individual rights of patients by a profession wielding such diagnostic labels. With respect to (1), he maintained that calling someone "mentally ill" is a "logically highly dubious proposition," the truth or falsity of which is virtually impossible to determine. Among other criticisms of the expression, he indicated its suspect nature was due to the "wide range of meaning that may be assigned to the term" (Szasz, 1961 b, p. 59). He went on to explain that clarification of its meaning was the only way to relieve the expression of its "logical opacity." Yet "infectious disease," "gastrointestinal disease" or "familial illness," similarly embrace a wide range of meanings, although saddling them with logical dubiety would appear to be a heavy penalty for merely possessing categorical sprawl.

In his book *Ideology and Insanity* Szasz characterized the medical model he criticized as the view that some physical defect is the basis of "all the disorders of thinking and behaviour," a theory he maintained precludes that people's troubles—epitomized as problems in living—can be seen as causative (Szasz, 1970, p. 13). Such remarks are problematic. First, there is a trivial sense in which any pattern considered to be a mental disorder is indisputably grounded in neurology only because all behavior, normal or abnormal, is so based. If so, it follows that patterns conventionally described as psychiatric disorders likewise come under a broader neurological compass. The only exception to this might be mental phenomena as construed by the philosophical theory known as *libertarianism*: the idea that mental states are not caused by material processes within the brain, and that human decision-making and other intentional states are unfettered by physical determinism. However, libertarianism itself is a scion of the dualism Szasz himself elsewhere took pains to criticize elsewhere maintaining that the dualism between mental and physical symptoms is a "habit of speech," and not scientifically grounded (Szasz, 1970, p. 13). He seems to have agreed that in the trivial sense discussed, all behavior including "mental illness," preferably recast as "problems in living," has an organic grounding, since mental events do not take place in a "neurological vacuum" (Szasz, 1961, p.91).

Second, positing that neurological defect preempts explanation based upon conflicting personal needs, opinions, social aspirations or values may be an example of what Szasz inveighed against in other contexts: a category blunder (Ryle, 1949). Psychological theories are no more necessarily inconsistent with those framed in neurological terms than are explanations in cosmology or physics on a predictable collision course with those cast in terms of chemistry or biology. Far from being opposed, these differing formulations can sometimes be viewed as independent, contrasting or corollary explanatory slants on the same subject matter.

The confusion here seems to have plagued the commentary of other psychiatric historians. Webster (1995) believes that Freud's psychoanalytic theory originated in the mistake of substituting psychological explanations of hysteria for its putatively neurological foundation—as though one type of explanation necessarily precluded the other in every case. In addition, positing an exclusively physical etiology for 19th century forms of "hysteria" regrettably forfeits the opportunity to have settled the issue through modern technologies like like microscopic staining and brain imaging. Accordingly, any such pronouncements about etiology more than a century after the fact while *suggestive*, are speculative—as are their purely psychological explanatory alternatives.

Szasz's distinction between physical illness and problems in living raises another question: what human capabilities according to him are thereby sacrificed in acknowledging a psychiatric condition to be traceable to the former, rather than the latter? By inclusion in a class of physical diseases, one imagined implication is that anyone so diagnosed is *afflicted* by a condition, rather than *voluntarily* acting in ways instantiating responsibility or rationality. For example, in one slant on the physical disease model, bipolar disorder is a condition in which a patient, because of the organic hardwiring of the problem, is subject to mood swings outside his or her control; the schizophrenic person is likewise disadvantaged by hallucinations experienced involuntarily. In both instances individuals do not have a free hand in creating the physical condition experienced, and the notion of responsibility for resultant patterns seems excluded (or markedly diminished). On the theory that both persons are having problems in living solely, responsibility would seem to be reinstituted; patients are, as it were, in the driver's seat. Yet why should the two explanatory schema necessarily exclude each other? In other words, why should my responsibility for my actions be ruled out on the chance discovery that they are foundationally tinctured by some physical anomaly?

Szasz allowed for the possibility that certain conditions like schizophrenia may eventually be shown to be effects of central nervous system diseases, although this has not transpired to date. He was less clear about what corresponding social changes would or should take place in the wake of such discoveries. Questions still remain coming on the heels of demonstrating schizophrenia to be a biological condition. For consider: viewing schizophrenia as brain pathology does not imply that loose associations, delusions, hallucinations, or social withdrawal are "diseases." It is little more than a truism that patterns of behavior or thought, abnormal or otherwise, are not themselves "diseases," and this would be trivially true, even in the event of discovering the biogenetic basis of such patterns. Szasz himself agreed that a factual claim should be clearly distinguished from truths that are definitionally true. Acknowledging this, in one published work he opines that behaviour cannot by definition "be a disease" (Szsaz, 2008, p. 11).

Going on, complications plague the stance that there are unambiguous expectations attached to positing biogenesis. Individuals with the same neurophysiological underpinning may behave in distinguishable ways, depending upon the culture involved. For example, Malaysian, Alaskan, or Oceanic psychoses rarely, if ever, incorporate "voices" from Jesus Christ or delusional beliefs about him, unless the patient in question had converted to Christianity. Yet an organic etiology in such instances may conceivably turn out to be similar to cases of American schizophrenics whose psychoses register Christianized themes.

Third, it is unclear what expectations are introduced in event of new causal discoveries. From the purely social standpoint, it is schizophrenic *behavior* that is the focus of concern, not any fancied neurophysiological underpinning, however informative this might be from an etiological standpoint. Moreover, the character of biogenesis is itself dependent upon a moral/social assessment of the behavioral pattern to which it gives rise. The brains of geniuses like Mozart, Euler or Gauss are conceivably different from those of average individuals. Yet we do not consider that the three cases of genius are due to a neuroanatomical *defect*, because the accomplishments of these men are socially valued. The most we can claim is that their abilities may be traceable to a biogenic *factor* or *component*, not *defect*. Consequently, it is a mistake to imagine that any given neurophysiological finding stamps the moral character of a substrate independently of the social patterns attributable to it. Furthermore, no question arises over what treatment regimen individuals with the genius "factor" should be consigned; it is their plight to be *esteemed*, not *treated*, on any acceptable social response to them.

The coupling or uncoupling of terminology from historical practices associated with it has dubious import for what we should expect given the upshot of future empirical discoveries. On the assumption that the etiology of schizophrenia (as a spectrum disorder or otherwise) is in future shown to be due to an organic anomaly, Szasz insisted that the condition would then be rightfully classified as a physical disorder, specifically, a disease of the brain. Yet this tells us little about the dispensation of cases of schizophrenia. At this point, and according to

Szsaz, would psychiatry or medicine still have a rightful claim to the treatment of schizophrenia-*cum*-brain disease providing its practices were modified to accommodate demands arising in connection with the newly understood disease entity? And from a purely social standpoint, what demands are these?

As examples of the logically distinct character of professional language from practice, it is noteworthy that many psychiatric reforms introduced by both the courts and newer philosophies of treatment have become a reality. One aspect of this historical shift has been the disestablishment of large mental institutions across the nation. These were sites in which egregious professional practices like lobotomies, insulin shock therapy, enforced hydrotherapy, deprivation of civil liberties, indefinite confinement and coerced medication regimens, were very much at home. Yet there has been no corresponding change in modifying terms like "mental illness" tied to older ways to which patient populations have been subject. I take this to show that drastic changes in medical practice can be independent of a language, argot or idiom descriptive of individuals to which they apply.

Reshuffling Taxonomies

In the first chapter of *The Myth of Mental Illness*, Szasz examined what he took to be a crucial chapter in the history of psychiatry, contending that it contained a misstep that came to haunt the discipline for many years thereafter. The historical context in question occurred in the late 19th century, and involved what in his opinion represented a strategic mistake in the history of his profession. At that time, such authorities as Charcot and Freud came to regard hysteria as a form of illness, rather than "malingering." According to Szasz, both engineered this taxonomic move by emphasizing the similarities between hysteria and real illness, rather than the similarities between hysteria and forms of pseudo-illness or medical fakery. Szasz felt they promoted the "successful medicalization of malingering" and the idea of mental illness as a medical specialty (Szasz, 2008, p. x). The move, he insisted, was undertaken in part because of an underlying social motivation to improve the plight of "patients" so diagnosed. Lest readers misinterpret the thrust of Szasz's critique, his occasional remarks in subsequent publications make his meaning crystal clear when he opined that one can fault Charcot for rejecting evidenc that "hysterical symptoms were the *willed, voluntary actions* of the so-called patients" (Szasz, 2008, p. 36).

Cases of 19th century hysteria present complexities. Professional wisdom about them in hindsight seems divided between regarding them as either a historically evaporating set of patterns, or a poorly defined batch of behaviours and complaints that were age-specific. In any case, explaining fuzzily understood symptoms that disappeared from the historical scene seems tantamount to exorcizing ghosts nobody has taken the trouble to define in ways that make discourse about them a sensible enterprise.

Cryptic social expectations or ulterior motives for new psychiatric labels or diagnoses is virtually thematic in Szaszian commentary. It is as though past and present professional establishments were operating as undercover agents for hidden agendas—whether or not they were aware of the subtexts involved. They were seen as secret connivers whose decisions, albeit often inspired by humanitarian motives, were contrary to "scientific" mandates. For Szasz, only demonstrable organic lesions qualify a pattern as an authentic medical subject matter lending itself to "treatment." In the absence of such a foundation, the motivation for newer classifications for him was questionable, and needed exposure as social subtexts behind new-fangled diagnoses.

An alternative view is possible: regarding hysteria as "illness" rather than "malingering" was driven by a genuine perplexity arising from the need to classify patterns that shared features of disparate phenomena. If a population of individuals who behaved as though they were neurologically impaired were shown to have no neurological lesions (or assumed not to have them), what classificatory system best fits the anomaly? A wrinkle in the Szaszian critique is the justification for leaving well enough alone, i.e., regarding hysterics as "malingerers" without further ado. But what justifies this older classification? In the absence of physical lesions, for Szasz the only alternative to a proper diagnostic fix on hysteria is "malingering," or deception. Is it?

Szasz felt that all the trouble started when Charcot and Freud undertook a taxonomy representing a sea-change from an older classification, as though there were little mystery in regarding hysterics as a special class of malingerers. The term "special" here is the weasel word, because many 19th century "hysterics" seemed not to be ordinary malingerers; they came packaged with stigmata of ostensible neurological impairment. Yet Szasz kept reverting to a motive of social engineering, as though "malingering" were not as troubling for a legitimate classification as was "illness." The conspiratorial subtext of Charcot's "promoting" malingerers to hysterics, he insisted, was driven by the conviction that "the sick role is socially more acceptable than the role of the social outcast" (Szasz, 1961, p. 28).

For Szasz, legitimate classification should be determined as a "scientific task," which leads us to an overwhelming question: what is the proper scientific classification of the hysterical pattern in question? Why is "malingerers" more beyond scientific reproach than "illness?" Another option would be maintaining that *all* instances of classifying hybrid phenomena are driven by underlying social subtexts, in which case we can dispense with questioning the wisdom of any psychiatric classification in favor of exposing the social implications of adopting it![1]

Considering the 19th century classification of hysterics as "sick" as a *scientific* mistake begs a critical question. In *Psychiatry: The Science of Lies* (2008), Szasz insisted that Charcot and Freud abandoned the empirical basis for distinguishing between "real" medical conditions and "fake" diseases of the mind, resulting in a "gigantic edifice" built on "poisoned ruins" of the error (p. 2). Accordingly, for Szasz hysteria is a "fake disease," since no physical disorder of the body can be discovered to justify the diagnosis. One effect of Szasz's exclusionary emphasis is a derisive attitude toward what he saw as deceptions rife in Charcot's caseloads. It was as though no other viewpoint except dishonesty should prevail, given the absence of neuropathic findings. The implication here is clear: in the absence of physical findings, hysterics or their diagnosticians must have been falsifying clinical data and playing dishonest games, much in the manner of liars who dissimulate in order to get sleep medication unavailable without a physician's prescription. Szasz has described Joseph Babinski as yet another famous physician intent upon writing about a nondisease "as if it were a disease" (Szasz, 2008, p. 44).

A word of warning here is in order. Szasz's critique of the Charcotian switch from "malingering" to "sickness" may have capitalized on singular cases of 19th century patients at the Salpêtrière who could be characterized deservedly as feigning symptomatology in the context of institutional pressures to behave in certain ways in order to satisfy the implicit demands of an illustrious and formidable neurologist. What may have amounted to the voluntary gamesmanship of this underclass of "patient" is a picture of reality endorsed by other experts (cf. Crews, 2017). One of the notable voices testifying to this behavioral gamesmanship was Jane Avril, a subject of Toulouse-Lautrec's poster art, hospitalized for a stint at Charcot's institution. Yet the voluntary and deceptive simulation of neurological-like or epileptiform patterns would not seem to apply to individuals—including many males—who evidenced patterns like "railway spine" or paralysis even before coming to the attention of medical guardians at the Salpêtrière.

The possibility of at least four distinguishable patterns of patient behavior complicates our understanding of life under Charcot at the Salpêtrière: (1) cases of authentic neurological impairment misidentified as functional disorder due to the lack of advanced diagnostic tools; (2) cases of non-neurological patterns developing naturally or independently of treatment-derived ministrations; (3) non-neurological conditions established iatrogenically as a result of suggestion or reinforcement by a treatment team, but lacking patient intentionality; (4) the conscious and simulated appropriation of a patient role based upon the perceived advantage of adopting it, as the kind referenced by Jane Avril. Moreover, combinatory forms of the four types are not beyond the realm of possibility.

Babinski himself was intent on drawing attention to what he felt were inherent paradoxes in his clinical cases. In observing vast numbers of them, he became convinced, as had most other neurologists, that many of his subjects were sincere and could not be considered "malingerers." Accordingly, he disputed pronouncing hysterics to be fakers or deceivers. This was precisely the conundrum of clinicians of the time who deliberated in a like-minded way over a subject matter posing difficulties for proper classification. Yet Szasz challenged Babinski's decision to reclassify hysteria, for the reason that "...Doctors have no way of knowing which of their patients is sincere" (Szasz, 2008, p. 44). Needless to say, the sword is double-edged; neither did Szasz know which of those patients was insincere.

Relying on a criterion of illness as cellular pathology formulated by Rudolph Virchow (1821-1902), Szasz pronounced any condition not meeting this standard as something other than "disease" or "illness" (Szasz, 2008). But he seemed to pass too swiftly from the finding that 19th century hysterics do not meet such criteria to the conclusion that fakery, deception or "malingering" must be afoot in such cases. His argument overlooks the possibility that there is yet another alternative. This is captured in the case of subjects who do not meet Virchowian criteria, yet neither are they instances of "malingering," however defined. They may illustrate a wider class designated as *psychosomatic*: cases in which no evidence of cellular pathology exists, nor are patients deliberately faking their symptomatology. O'Sullivan (2015) indicates that nearly one third of patients seen in contemporary neurology clinics manifest symptoms that cannot be explained, even when advanced diagnostic tools are relied on. Furthermore, she contends that when the brain activity of asymptomatic controls, patients with forms of conversion disorder and subjects instructed to feign paralysis are compared, quite different patterns of brain activity are observed. She concludes that psychosomatic illness does not involve pretending.

When Szasz insists that such cases should be designated as forms of malingering, his conclusion begs the question, since it assumes gratuitously something about the intentions of the person so diagnosed. Virchow's criterion of "illness" accordingly represents what Stevenson (1938) has called a "persuasive definition" of disease. That is, in mapping a definitional course for the application of terms like "disease" or "illness," Virchow's standard does not coincide with the way in which these expressions have been deployed by diagnosticians before and after him.

The conceptual waters are further muddied. Is Szasz's refusal to classify hysteria as "illness" due to its being "malingering" or does it likewise cover cases of disability in which the assumed absence of neuropathic lesions is not associated with dissembling? Obviously, in cases of fakery "illness" would be an inappropriate term to describe a condition. It is less clear why the term should not be extended to instances of the putative absence of neuropathy in which deception cannot be demonstrated or is not operating.

Going on, Szasz's theorizing runs the risk of being anachronistic when it comes to his view of troublesome 19th century formulations, as when he faults Charcot and Freud for not identifying the notion of "illness" with departures from physical integrity or a "visible deformity, disease or lesion' or "an abnormal change in the structure of a person's body" (Szasz, 1983, p. 62).

Charcot and Freud on hysteria mirrored the same kind of thinking we can identify as far back as Hippocrates (460 BCE to 370 BCE). His classification of mental illnesses was based upon presumed abnormalities in the levels and balance among the four humors or cambia included mania, melancholia, phrenitis, insanity, disobedience, paranoia, phobias, panic, epilepsy, Scythian disease (transvestism) and, *mirabile dictu*, hysteria! Hippocrates viewed psychological and mental illness as natural effects of nature on people and were treated just like other diseases. He was convinced that the brain was the seat of mental illness, which should be treated in a manner similar to physical illness. The same observations have already been made by Kendell (2005).

Both Asclepius and Hippocrates (the founder of ancient Greek medicine) developed treatment practices based upon a naturalistic approach to the treatment of illness. It included physical activity as an essential aspect of *both* physical and mental health, whereas there was no perceived incongruity between therapeutic approaches to both classes of phenomena. Obviously, neuropathic lesions were nowhere in sight in the Greek scheme of medicine, unless their analogues were the hypothesized (but hardly demonstrable) humoral imbalances. In faulting the ancient

Greek assimilation of mania and paranoia to the same category of such "illnesses" as plague or leprosy, a Szaszian who went back in a time machine might have informed Hippocrates of the error he was making.

Not so fast. Suppose we undertook the fanciful trip, only to find that Hippocrates' taxonomy was an unfolding affair that proceeded by stages. Imagine that mania and paranoia, as it turned out, were the initial foci of therapeutic concern, whereas plague and leprosy came later [2] If mania and paranoia first got their feet in the taxonomic door as "treatable illnesses" under Hippocrates and before plague and leprosy, would the foundation have been laid for calling mania and paranoia true diseases, but plague and leprosy only "metaphorical illnesses" due to their fundamental dissimilarity to paradigmatic cases of diseases? The example may be a wacky one, although it perhaps dramatizes the point that something more is required in establishing the metaphoric status of any condition than its bearing different empirical properties from original cases of the class in which it is assigned membership. Is the duck-billed, egg-laying platypus a metaphoric mammal or a real one with novel characteristics for a mammalian species?

Going on, if the principle driving the Szaszian separation between physical diseases and "problems in living" is their fundamental dissimilarity as categories, what is the conceptual thrust of "fundamental?" For consider: suppose Hippocrates treated malaria long after he discovered leprosy. How "fundamental" is the difference between the two conditions that warrants or prevents inclusion in the same category of physical illness within Greek medicine? For Szasz the inclusion would have been a no-brainer, since they are both physical conditions. By the same token, Hippocrates might have defended his inclusion of paranoia and leprosy as "illnesses" by insisting they are treatable conditions of suffering citizens.

Behavior: The Elephant In the Room?

As was mentioned, in efforts to pin down definitional parameters of true "illnesses," Szasz makes no bones about the purely *physical* nature of the subject matter he takes the expression to cover. He insisted that classifying thoughts, feelings, and behaviors as diseases is a logical and semantic error, like classifying the whale as a fish" (Szasz, *Summary Statement and Manifesto*).

Evidently, Szasz was not merely reiterating his view that "behavior" cannot be regarded as an "illness" in the purely trivial or definitional sense already discussed. He was maintaining that behavior (as thoughts, feelings and actions) cannot be regarded as a logically appropriate category of phenomena qualifying patients for "treatment" by a psychiatric establishment. Unfortunately, his criteria would not pass muster on even the most restrictive medical playing field. On any definitional compass honored by non-psychiatric medicine, "behavior" is a significant symptom (sign, marker) of pathology. For example, consider the field of movement disorders including Hypokinetic disorders (e.g., Parkinson's Disease, Hallevorden-Spatz Disease, Striatonigral degeneration, etc.) and Hyperkinetic disorders (Dystonias, Blepharospasm, Spasmodic Torticollis, Essential Tremors, Huntington's Chorea, Tardive Dysinesia, etc.). To the possible Szaszian objection that movement disorders can be nonetheless traced to neurological pathology, there are two responses: (1) like schizophrenia, not all movement disorders have been so traced to date, and (2) neurological tracing was not available to physicians for over two millennia. Yet these phenomena were classified as "illnesses" long before their neurophysiological foundation was suspected or revealed.

With respect to the dementias, their classification as "illnesses" was likewise established prior to the advent of available technologies of detection of cellular or vascular anomalies. Furthermore, such diagnostic signs as disorientation—whether in all three spheres or otherwise— were stigmata established ordinarily on the basis of "thoughts" (verbal behavior indicative of short-term memory dysfunction), not somatic symptoms.

The lesson to be extracted from the foregoing examples is that shifting dimensions of the omnibus notion of "behavior" have always been conceived as indicative of illness, and long before the arrival of Charcot or Freud on the clinical scene. Furthermore, the notion of illness was extended to cases for which physical lesions were never established up to the present day. In many such cases, behavioral patterns led to classificatory decisions remarkably similar to the 19th century cases of hysteria under discussion. And Charcot's earlier view of hysteria, while developed in the absence of neuropathological findings, incorporated the notion of hereditary transmission of illness (Charcot, 1887).

Mental Illness as Metaphor

When it comes to Szasz's often repeated claim that the expression "mental illness" is metaphorical, there are other lessons to be learned. In a colorful way, Szasz likened the "sickness" of mental illness to the sickness of spring fever, and other recognizably metaphoric locutions. Examples surfaced in the 1980 trial of Darlin June Cromer when in response to prosecutor Albert Cromer's questions, Szasz provided other examples of metaphors, like "You are a son of a bitch" or "The apple of my eye" (Szasz, 2004). He went on to declare that "sick minds" is a locution comparable to "sick jokes" or "sick economies" (Szasz, 2016).

In several other publications, Szasz insisted that the metaphoric status of the expression "mental illness" is revealed by the fact that it refers to patterns of behavior, not physical diseases. Since only the latter for him was a proper medical subject matter, behavior (whether conventionally regarded as normal or abnormal) is not the kind of thing that can be construed to be "disease."

A contrary viewpoint, and one favored by the present author, is that the term "mental illness" is not metaphorical, has as much conceptual legitimacy as the expression "physical illness," and that its deployment has been justified in a variety of historical approaches to problems of patients and non-patients alike. It should be noted that some treatment approaches would curry favor in Szasz's scheme of acceptable interventions. Among these would be his version of "autonomous psychotherapy," a form of consensual treatment involving voluntary interactions between client and practitioner (Szasz, 1965). Under no circumstances would it brook interventions limiting the personal freedom of the patient or bring him or her under any form of institutional control.

The idea that the term "mental illness" is metaphorical was emphasized throughout Szasz's extensive body of publications, as well as taken up by several other commentators in agreement with him (Danziger, 1990; Leary, 1990; Sarbin, 1967; 1990). Despite the repetitive aspect of this theme in their writings, one wonders how often their commentary begs the question. Sarbin in particular has been vocal about the role of metaphor in approaches to the problems of what he characterizes as the propensities of violaters of social rules (Sarbin, 1990, p. 300). He considered Teresa of Avila (1515-1581) to be an influential voice in shifting jurisdiction over "norm violaters" from ecclesiastical authorities to Renaissance physicians, thus rescuing hallucinating nuns from the purview of the Inquisition (Sarbin, 1990, p. 301).

Unfortunately, Sarbin's discussion of the role of Teresa of Avila as an innovator in medicalizing the approach to abnormal behavior is marred by faulty historical assumptions. [3] First, Teresa's admonitions about her cloistered nuns, like many theologians before and after her, were inspired by the view that the psychological state to which she and they were subject was melancholia. Even in the context of this blight of the Galenic system of medicine, Teresa distinguished among several ways it could be manifested, from total madness (for which the sufferer in question was for her excused from all responsibility) to shades of guilt laced with the ability to reason, for which the cure was levels of severe punishment or restriction within her order. Second, Teresa hardly pioneered a transformation in thinking about mental illness. Rather, her contribution lay in articulating remedies for the effects of a psychological vulnerability that was the imagined lot of women, in contrast to men. The same thinking about female frailty as an inborn handicap risking susceptibility to the wiles of the devil was traditional for clerics antedating Teresa by centuries. It was celebrated in the fifteenth century manual *Malleus Maleficarum*, and harkened back to numerous tracts on female inferiority, many of which were lost in the mists of antiquity. The medieval *Canon Episcopi*, the strictures of which were meant to counteract beliefs in certain aspects of witch's tales, circulated the view that witch transvections to covens aboard brooms or animals were delusional in nature. Consequently, it is a mistake to assume that the idea of a delusional belief had a scientific, psychiatric or medical provenance (least of all one initiated by Teresa of Avila), when it had an older theological one, commemorated centuries before the Renaissance or the Age of Reason.

As for Szasz's and Sarbin's view of "mental illness" as metaphorical, a metaphor is a figure of speech in which a term or phrase characterizes something to which it is not strictly applicable. Martin Luther's hymn "A mighty fortress is our God" celebrates the notion of how the deity serves to strengthen resistance to evil, not the idea that God is literally an armed castle. "His attitude is bestial" implies something ugly and primitive about another's attitude, not that someone is literally a jackel. Should the other in question actually be a jackel, the statement about him is true, and unmetaphorical.

Szasz's contention is that "mental illness" must be metaphorical because the patterns to which it applies are by their very nature those that do not literally qualify for being "illnesses." Whether mental illnesses do or do not qualify as "illness" is the *conclusion* of an argument, not an indisputable truth relied on to establish its own veracity! In this connection, what are the grounds for assuming that mental illness cannot qualify as illness, therefore establishing the metaphorical status of the expression? In buttressing Szasz's theory, one might argue the Virchowian point that only cellular pathology qualifies as "illness" although, as has been argued, this criterion does not jibe historically with the way the expression "mental illness" (or its linguistic equivalents) has been deployed as far back as Hippocrates. In short, if the actual historical deployment of terminology—antedating Charcot and Freud by millennia—defeats the claim about metaphorical status, Szasz's argument begs a critical question. It should be noted that the foregoing makes purely conceptual points about the use of certain expressions like "mental illness." This is quite independent of any empirical statements about etiology or the moral or legal propriety of past or present institutional practice.

Endnotes

1   Szasz's critique of contemporary psychiatric practice on occasion smacked of having a runaway character. In the second chapter of *The Myth of Mental Illness*, he maintained that the sixty or seventy years prior to its publication a "vast number of occurrences were reclassified as 'illnesses,'" among which he included "phobias, delinquencies, divorce, homicide, addiction, and so on almost without limit as psychiatric illnesses" (p. 43). Since when were all these considered illnesses by psychiatrists—or by anyone else for that matter? The confusion here may be identifying any diagnostic listing in the five DSM manuals as an "illness." There are many entries in those manuals that defy any such characterization by a modern psychiatric establishment. I am not considered "sick" by any psychiatrist because I have an expected adjustment reaction to the loss of a loved one, job or spouse, nor am I "mentally ill" because I receive a lower grade in some class due to my dragging my feet on homework assignments. Yet these conditions, depending on the character of individual cases, can be represented in diagnostic manuals. Going on, although such conditions may be listed as "treatable" in strikingly divergent ways by psychiatrists, they are far removed from being conditions the institutional approach to which inspires vigilance or commentary on the part of civil libertarians. No one gets railroaded into a mental institution because of a minor adjustment reaction to personal loss.

2   Perhaps for good reasons. Leprosy or Hansen's disease, a lesser contagion among infectious diseases, indeed could have been a late arrival for Hippocrates in comparison with mania and paranoia. Paranoia might have been a sometime casualty in the lives of Greek citizens reeling from the effects of incursions like those documented by Herodotus and Thucydides over clashes between Persia and Greece or Athens and Sparta.

[3] The sections of Teresa's commentary that Sarbin cites, Chapter VII of the *Book of the Foundations* in the third volume of *The Complete Works of Saint Teresa of Jesus*, make no mention of the Inquisition, nor its possibly punitive reaction to the disordered imaginations of her cloistered nuns. The Inquisition is referenced only three times in Volume III of the *Complete Works*, in no case in relation to the danger cloistered nuns ran due to patterns that risked coming under inquisitorial scrutiny. Teresa's wariness concerning inquisitorial intervention surfaces in her *El Castillo interior*, and the fact that she was a relative of a *converso* (i.e., Jewish convert to Catholicism). The Inquisition itself was founded on the need to detect "Judaizers," or Jews practicing their religion on the sly. At any rate, it was Teresa herself, not her nuns, who ran the risk of practicing what inquisitors might have construed as indulgence in private mystical rites of a heretical cast. In its investigation of Teresa, inquisitors had to distinguish between Judaizing or Protestant leanings and condemning what was, after all, an established Catholic tradition of mysticism going back to suggestive strands in the desert fathers of the 4th century C. E., Athanasius, Palladius and Cassian, the Eastern monks of the Hesychastic tradition, such female mystics antedating Teresa as Hildegaard of Bingen, Bridget of Sweden, Catherine of Sienna and Mechtilde of Magedeburg, not to mention the Spanish Francisco de Osuna. Accordingly, it was in all likelihood the possibility of challenging the Catholicity of an already acknowledged mystical tradition of the faith that led inquisitors to absolve Teresa of any trace of heretical taint.

References

Begelman, D. A. and Tolor, A. (1966). A taste of honey: Dr. Guttmacher on Dr. Szasz. *Psychological Reports, 18,* 531-534.

_______________ (1971). Misnaming, Metaphors, the medical model and some muddles. *Psychiatry, 34,* 38-58.

_______________ (1975). Ethical and legal issues of behavior modification. In M. Hersen, R. M. Eisler and P. M. Miller (Eds.) *Progress in Behavior Modification*, Vol. 1, pp. 159-189.

_______________(1982). Ethical issues of behavior modification. In D. Teicher-Zallen & C. D. Clements (Eds.) *Science and Morality: New Directions in Bioethics.* Lexington, Massachusetts: Lexington Books, pp. 163-173.

Charcot, J. M. (1887). *Clinical Lectures on the Diseases of the Nervous System.* London: The New Sydenham Society.

Danziger, K. (1990) Generative metaphor and the histry of psychological discourse. In D. E. Leary (Ed.) *Metaphors in the History of Psychology.* Cambridge: Cambridge University Press, pp. 331-356.

Gendin, S. (1973). Insanity and criminal responsibility, *American philosophical Quarterly, 10,* 99-110.

Goldstein, J. and Katz, J. (1963). Abolish the "insanity defense"-why not? *The Yale Law Journal, 72,* no. 5, 853-876.

Groopman, J. (2017). Sick but not sick. *New York Review of Books,* February 9, *64,* No. 2, 30-31.

Kendell, R. E. (2005). The myth of mental illness. In J. A. Schaier, *Szasz Under Fire: The Psychiatric Abolitionist Faces His Critics.* Chicago and La Salle, Illinois: Open Court.

Leary, D. E. (1990). *Metaphors in the History of Psychology.* Cambridge: Cambridge University Press

Martin, R. (1975). *Legal Challenges to Behavior Modification.* Champaign, Illinois: Research Press.

O'Sullivan, S. (2015). *Is It All in Your Head? True Stories of Imaginary Illness.* New York: Other Press.

Peers, E. A. (1946). *The Complete Works of Saint Teresa of Jesus.* Volume III, London: Sheed & Ward.

Ryle, G. (1949). *The Concept of Mind.* London: Macmillan.

Sarbin, Theodore R. On the futility of the proposition that some people be labelled "mentally ill." *Journal of Consulting Psychology* (1967), *31,* 447-453.

____________(1990). Metaphors of unwanted conduct: a historical sketch. In D. E. Leary (Ed.) *Metaphors in the History of Psychology.* Cambridge: Cambridge University Press, pp. 300-330.

Stevenson, C. (1938). Persuasive definitions. *Mind, 47,* 331-350.

Szasz, T. S. (1961a). *The Myth of Mental Illness.* New York: Harper & Row.

____________ (1961b) The uses of naming and the origin of the myth of mental illness. *American Psychologist, 16,* 59-65.

____________ (1963). *Law, Liberty, and Psychiatry: An Inquiry into the Social Uses of Mental Health Practices.* New York: Macmillan.

__________(1965). *The Ethics of Psychoanalysis: The Theory and Method of Autonomous Psychotherapy.* New York: Basic Books.

__________(1970). *Ideology and Insanity: Essays on the Psychiatric Dehumanization of Man.* Garden City, New York: Anchor Books.

__________(1973). *The Myth of Psychotherapy: Mental Healing as Religion, Rhetoric, and Repression.* Garden City, New York: Anchor Books.

__________(1983). Mental illness is a myth. In R. E. Vat and L. S. Weinberg (Eds.) *Thomas Szasz: Primary Values and Major Contentions.* Buffalo, New York: Prometheus Press. Pp. 61-97.

__________(2004). Reply to Simon. In J. A. Schaier (Ed.) *Szasz Under Fire: The Psychiatric Abolitionist Faces His Critics.* Chicago and La Salle, Illinois: Open Court. Pp. 202-223.

__________(2008). *Psychiatry the Science of Lies.* Syracuse, New York: Syracuse University Press.

__________(2016). *Thomas Szasz on Freedom and Psychotherapy.* Interview with Randall C. Wyatt. Psychotherapy.net. pp. 1-20.

Webster, R. (1995). *Why Freud Was Wrong.* New York: Basic Books.

McHugh's Psychiatric Misadventures

In the Fall 1992 issue of the *American Scholar,* Paul R. McHugh developed his idea of the ailments of contemporary psychiatry (McHugh, 1992). His phrase is "psychiatric misadventures," for the unfortunate paths the profession has elected to take in recent years. "Misadventures" include: (1) the premature discharge of hospitalized mental patients, especially those with schizophrenia; (2) the theories of the "antipsychiatrists" like Szasz, Laing, Goffinan, and Foucault, whom McHugh blames for inspiring the discharge policies; (3) sex reassignment surgery for transsexuals; (4) witchcraft; and (5) the belief there is such a thing as Multiple Personality Disorder. According to McHugh, these follies are traceable to the common "medical mistakes" of oversimplification, misplaced emphasis, and pure invention (McHugh, 1992, p. 498). He considers them the pitfalls of a profession addicted to "intermingling with contemporary culture" (McHugh, 1992, p. 497), and the path tread by those for whom "trendy thought," "salvationist aspirations," ·and "prescribing for the millennium" are carrots dangling from the stick of modernity. McHugh traces the persistent attraction of psychiatry to such "fads" to the rudimentary nature of the field. For him, the antidote is to return to the hard-core sciences of psychiatry, such as epidemiology, genetics, and neuropharmacology. McHugh's five misdirections of psychiatry are thus articulated against the backdrop of his own definition of the field. He would like it to be purified of cultural fancy, and not in the grip of "thralldom to the gusty winds of fashion" (McHugh, 1992, p. 501).

McHugh is correct in supposing that avoiding the trendy is beneficial when pursuing a fad corrupts an enterprise. Yet the admonition, because it is framed in the abstract, is not particularly instructive in relation to future trends. Moreover, to be fashionable in many cases is not necessarily to be wrong. Nor can dicta about the importance of avoiding the trendy substitute for arguments showing why a particular policy should be scrapped. The term "fad" connotes impermanence, frivolity.

Definitional truisms, however, only leave us scratching our heads over what policies qualify for the mantle. We are in the question begging mode should we insist our judgments about fads are validated by the mere expression of sentiment.

Alternative views on the five presumed "misadventures" may be elaborated. McHugh's critique of "antipsychiatry" is a curious blend of misunderstandings that are difficult to sort out. Faulting theorists such as Szasz, Laing, Goffman, and Foucault, he takes them to task for their scathing critique of mental institutions, and for promoting attitudes responsible for the premature discharge of chronic mental patients.

McHugh's assault on antipsychiatry runs together attacks on institutional care and theories of schizophrenia in ways that are neither fair nor searching. Be that as it may, he insinuates the havoc is somehow traceable to a mistaken theory of etiology, or "oversimplified opinions about schizophrenia" (McHugh, 1992, p. 498). With the possible exception of Laing, the so-called "antipsychiatrists" are notoriously short on theories of etiology. Their contributions are principally in the areas of law or ethics (Szasz, 1961), labeling-theory (Goffman, 1961; Becker, 1963), and postmodernist criticism (McGowan, 1991; Ryan, 1993). For them, the moral careers of institutionalized mental patients enter into a dimensional analysis largely independent of what caused their behavioral patterns in the first place.

A weightier basis for the discharge policies than the somewhat obscure views of antipsychiatrists was the introduction of the neuroleptics. These agents, in tandem with therapeutic maintenance programs, permitted effective reentry of the hospitalized patient into the social mainstream. In addition, legal precedents signaling abandonment of the "hands-off" policy of the courts in relation to the hospitalized mental patient was likewise important (Martin, 1975). They encouraged voluntary admissions and discharges, and sought to redress conditions in overcrowded facilities on a collision course with a libertarian direction in American law. Here, reform was sparked by the actual conditions prevailing in institutions, rather than by theories. It was nurtured by embracing legal and constitutional principles outside the purview of strictly scientific considerations. Many treatment practitioners—McHugh may be among them—still fail to appreciate that dignitary rights to self-determination are not accorded mental patients simply because such policies are *clinically* judicious. Unless mental disorganization is so pronounced another legal status can be conferred, a patient has the right to be discharged or to refuse medication, not because the decision is psychiatrically wise, but because the decision is *his/hers* (Begelman, 1971).

It is noteworthy that legal reforms curtailing dehumanizing practices and now widely accepted as routine institutional procedure were once thought to represent the savaging of professional prerogative by "troublemakers" like Szasz (Guttmacher, 1964; Begelman & Tolor, 1966; Vatz & Weinberg, 1983). McHugh's observation that viewing mental institutions as oppressive was a "fad" propounded by the antipsychiatrists is inattentive to how far we have come in the area of legal reform, whatever the cause of mental disorder.

For McHugh, the mismating of psychiatry and what he terms "cultural antinomianism" combine to produce their grimmest manifestation, sex reassignment surgery. McHugh declares he initially arrived at his position of Director of Psychiatry at the Johns Hopkins School of Medicine with a determination to end the practice. One gets the strong impression that his distaste for the surgery derives from an unspoken sensibility, as if it were for him an affront to an invisible system of natural law—in the theological sense. Some such sensibility seems to inform McHugh's description of the effects of sex transformation surgery: "the ghastliness of the mutilated anatomy" (McHugh, 1992, p. 503). The ethical status of sex-reassignment surgery involves the outcome of complex and extended bioethical analyses. Designating reassignment "mutilation" in the manner of McHugh only begs the critical issue. Indeed, were a criterion of surgically tampering with natural endowment to be appealed to in condemning reassignment, why not condemn colostomy, cardiac bypass, replacement surgery, and cosmetic surgery in general, not to mention circumcision? The use of terms like "mutilation" already prejudges the outcome of complex bioethical analyses. Whether the fault is, as he puts it, "in the mind or member" is simply not an issue resolved by facile reliance on canonical verities about bodily integrity. We don't endorse liposuction for anorexics upon request and do arrange for kidney and liver transplants and cosmetic surgeries. The notion of the organ as offending body part in the latter cases is a moral presupposition of practice. Accordingly, the charge of "mutilation" for time-honored surgical procedures can have meaning only in relation to alternative sets of moral standards, like those of, say, Luddites or Christian Scientists.

When it comes to alternative proposals, McHugh recommends dealing with transsexuals by understanding the "inner dynamics" of this "mental disorder," or by helping parents guide their children properly so as to avoid the development of such conditions. The belief that gender identity phenomena spring from dysfunctional family dynamics is, while popular, an unsubstantiated theory (Acosta, 1975; Leader, 1975). Ironically, while McHugh believes transsexuality is a sex identity "confusion" tied to homosexuality, he is silent about the presumed non-pathological status of the latter pattern. Should consistency on his part dictate that colluding with the fashionable was likewise responsible for the newer psychiatric stance on homosexuality? Or is McHugh's principal difficulty with fads one lasting only so long as they smack of the incontrovertibly newfangled? (i.e., up to that point in time at which their survival becomes so obvious, they are wearily accorded membership in that oldest of clubhouses: tradition).

In psychiatric history, entities that are a result of "pure invention" reveal the darker side of the discipline, according to McHugh. Taking witchcraft as an illustration of the trend, he faults the accepted proof of it in Salem Village, Massachusetts in 1692 as "bizarre," and condemns the Puritan reliance on spectral evidence (i.e., visitation by spirits which do the bidding of Satan, resulting in bewitchment). The proper diagnosis for the possessed of Salem was, insists McHugh, hysteria, not bewitchment, just as it is for what he deems to be alarmingly frequent cases of Multiple Personality Disorder. In 1692, several teenagers and children who had been secretly practicing occult rituals began to exhibit dissociative symptoms the Salem Village community pronounced to be possessed states. Why McHugh classifies the Puritan allegation of witchcraft as a *psychiatric* misadventure remains a mystery. A possible linkage here is to the theory that witches were psychiatrically ill, the formulation a variation of which was popularized by Johann Weyer in the sixteenth century (Mora, 1992).[2] It has been a bandwagon ever since (Zilboorg, 1935, Zilboorg & Henry, 1941). The theory has been largely repudiated by historians, since it tends to obscure the complex social bases for allegations of witchcraft, their escalation from the later fifteenth century to the end of the seventeenth century, reasons for the ensuing panics, and the contributory role of theologians, jurists, pamphleteers, and ecclesiastical and lay tribunals, in America as well as in central Europe and its periphery (Ankerloo & Henningsen, 1993). Moreover, McHugh's diagnosis of hysteria refers to the bewitched (i.e., "possessed"), not to the imagined perpetrators of their condition, witches.

For McHugh, the Salem exercises ought to have been discredited when, after the executions "there was no change in the distraught behavior of the young women" (McHugh, 1992, p. 505). However, it seems audacious to rule on what Salem villagers in 1692 should have concluded, given their mind-set. Should they have concluded bewitchment was a reality had the possessions ceased after the executions? The advantage of historical hindsight held no comparable consolation for Salem citizens, whose witch-panic was, according to recent studies, overdetermined (Boyer & Nissenbaum, 1974; Demos, 1982; Karlsen, 1987; Godbeer, 1992). It is also an exaggeration to imply, as does McHugh, that spectral evidence went unquestioned in seventeenth century thinking about witches, inasmuch as it was a subject of heated controversy, even in 1692. Cotton Mather, the theologian whose speculations fanned the Salem witch-panic, was himself skeptical about this form of evidence, and devoted considerable energy to undermining judicial confidence in it in his principal treatise on demonology (Mather, 1692). The entire unfortunate chapter in American history, like its counterparts in European history, seemed to have been characterized by judiciary sessions presided over by a citizenry grappling with what for it were complex and frightening phenomena. The Salem saga, as Kittredge has noted (Kittredge, 1929), was distinguished by the swiftness of its rehabilitation from the craze (it lasted only a year) and the fundamental integrity of the jurors. In

1696, the latter recanted their previous errors, expressing contrition and personal responsibility for it in one of the most poignant documents of American history (Kors & Peters, 1972).

McHugh's diagnosis of the Salem possessions as cases of hysteria, not bewitchment, has its ironic aspect. A third interpretation, lying or malingering, is less frequently conceived as playing a role in the 1692 patterns. Yet the possibility is strong that the Salem teenagers were on occasion dissembling possession as a vehicle of social control over elders who caught them red-handed in occult practices. In fact, reviewing primary source material does not altogether negate such a suspicion. Possessions as purely factitious phenomena have a documented lineage in the European literature on the subject (Robbins, 1959). The relevance of a factitious pattern becomes clearer when we consider that McHugh's critique of bewitchment and MPD can also be deployed against the condition he takes them to be, namely, hysteria.

If McHugh defines hysteria as "behavioral displays in which physical or mental disorders are imitated" (McHugh, 1992, p. 505), how is hysteria itself rescued from the limbo of psychiatric fancy, fad, or pure invention relative to a less exotic picture of the problem, dissembling? Moreover, what prevents us from generalizing McHugh's critique to other psychiatric concepts already accepted by him as traditionally woven into its fabric? The objection that hysteria cannot be analyzed as a factitious pattern because it demarcates cases for which no evidence of "lying" exists will not do. Historically, the creation of "hysteria" was conceptually wedded to quasi-legal decisions undertaken with respect to the concept of dissembling. The latter, being open-textured (Waismann, 1963) afforded diagnosticians the opportunity to reshuffle ways of applying it, depending upon the temper of an age. For example, should we have said that hysteria exists because the Salem teenagers were not shown to be obviously lying? Or, imbued with the strictures against "psychiatric inventions" promulgated by McHugh, should we have decided that being a liar isn't always the uncomplicated affair we hitherto deemed it to be? On this hypothesis, some "liars," like the Salem youngsters, might prompt us to expand the concept of malingering. Maybe they are more adept at malingering than most—so adept, in fact, they even fool themselves! And if inquiries, however exacting, into possible malingering fail to uncover its customary stigmata, should we nonetheless have clung to its reality in the Salem case, in preference to having gone "trendy" by manufacturing "hysteria"? Conceivably, we might have blocked the inclusion of hysteria into our inventory of psychiatric concepts by widening the compass of the factitious pattern. As we know, psychiatry—and McHugh along with it—chose the alternative strategy. Its history is quite properly construed as involving such conceptual shifts, as much as it is empirical discovery. Ironically, hysteria as psychiatric fiction is a formulation of a theorist McHugh has accused of oversimplifying the problem of schizophrenia, Thomas Szasz (Szasz, 1961). Szasz's viewpoint is that theorists like Freud somehow engineered an illicit shift in parlaying cases of "conversion" patterns from "malingering" to "hysteria."[3] McHugh accuses Szasz of arguing for the mythic status of schizophrenia, although he makes no connection between Szasz's campaign to expose its reification and his own designs on MPD. On one side of the fence when it comes to schizophrenia, McHugh is quite on the other in relation to MPD.

For McHugh, the connection between the Salem possessions and multiple personality disorder is that they are both disguised instances of the same diagnosis, transmuted to fit the dictates of "cultural fashion." In his opinion, the actual psychiatric subtext in both cases is hysteria. Despite the seeming opposition between the "antipsychiatrist" Thomas Szasz and McHugh, there is a certain similarity of viewpoint which, like the mythical frog, grins residually up at us from the bottom of the beer mug (Austin, 1961). One claims there is no such thing as mental illness; the other that there is no such thing as Multiple Personality Disorder.

The foregoing remarks should not be construed as attempting to prove a case for the reality of Multiple Personality Disorder as a clinical entity. They are only meant to show that the logic deployed against it by certain critics can also be turned against a wider range of psychiatric concepts already accepted by them. For example, Merskey's (1992) skepticism over Multiple Personality Disorder, like McHugh's, seems to be sparked by the unprecedented number of cases of it diagnosed in recent years. Yet his speculations about the treatment-originated provenance of the disorder are not extended to suspecting iatrogenesis in connection with recent "epidemics" of Panic Disorder, Obsessive-Compulsive Disorder (Ross,1989), Somatization Disorder (Othmer,1988; Vaillant, 1984; Swartz, et. al., 1991; North, et.al., 1994) and sundry other diagnoses. Such conditions have also proliferated over the past decade, relative to an older picture of their incidence/prevalence. Nor does the geographically selective distribution of, for example, Anorexia Nervosa and Bulimia (Yates, 1989; Barton, 1993), Somatization Disorder, or patterns bearing striking similarities to MPD, Trance/Possession States (Begelman, 1993), occasion skepticism concerning the reality of culture-bound syndromes (Simon & Hughes, 1985). TP states have an anthropologically documented wide, albeit selective, distribution around the world. Because of this, ought we to insist that shamans "create" possession states, or possession states create shamans? In former years, the partiality in American psychiatry for diagnosing "schizophrenia" for patterns diagnosed as "manic-depressive illness" in British psychiatry was apparent. Does this prove that American schizophrenia was iatrogenically produced?

Merskey's critique, predicated as it is on an assumption of an "overdiagnosis" of MPD, appears to represent little more than an exercise in second-guessing the true nature of the clinical patterns referenced by the nosological label, with a predilection for Bipolar Disorder. That the preponderance of cases examined by Merskey are gleaned from older historical records further compounds problems associated with his *post hoc* reconstructions. For all they are worth, like-minded exercises can be conducted on most clinical entities. For example, were we disposed to consider reports of delusions and hallucinations untrustworthy (and why not, if the only evidence for them is a patient's verbal report he/she experiences them?), we could similarly deconstruct "schizophrenia" to a factitious disorder, the creation of mental health professionals taken in by the gamesmanship of a social underclass opting for therapeutic, not penal ministrations. Some such "sweeping iconoclasm" in connection with a broader range of psychiatric concepts is touched upon by Aldridge-Marris (1991), whose critique is subtitled "An Exercise in Deception". The selectivity of this author is noteworthy, especially in the light of his willingness to open Pandora's Box on such mainstays of the psychiatric canon as hysteria and schizophrenia—conditions whose reality he, unlike McHugh, indicates may be up for grabs.

As if to illustrate the illegitimacy of the very idea of multiple personality disorder, Aldridge-Morris devotes an entire chapter of his book to the diagnostic confusion surrounding the trial of the serial killer, Kenneth Bianchi. But the author's attempt to undermine the concept of MPD here is a study in irrelevance. The primary issue in the Bianchi case was whether the defendant was malingering. In other words, the issue hinged on whether a diagnosis was applicable, not whether it was, as a clinical entity, legitimate. Had Bianchi presented as psychotic (in contrast to dissociative), his insanity defense would still have been plagued by comparable problems of determining malingering. On the other hand, during the trial of the serial killer, Jeffrey Dahmer, conflicting opinion among expert witnesses pertinent to a legal plea of insanity absorbed deliberation, although the issue of malingering never arose.

Doubts about the reality of MPD have an older lineage, one predating controversies that from time to time swirl about it. Indeed, the iatrogenesis, Satanic ritual abuse, and False Memory Syndrome issues seemed to have followed on each others heels in swift succession. One wonders whether an older type atheism plays into tumultuous chapters of current debate. McHugh himself is clearly a spokesman for a vintage skepticism. Judging by his remarks in another paper entitled "Psychotherapy Awry," (McHugh, 1994), McHugh apparently feels that the spate of .MPD diagnoses springs from a current of "romanticism" in current treatment practices. The retrograde trend, he avers, should be counteracted by hewing to the scientific tradition of "empiricism", an allegiance known for its antipathy to theories gone amok.

In order to salvage a modicum of legitimacy for a field agonizing over its bad press, McHugh's method involves bifurcating psychiatry into right-thinkers ("empiricists") and wrong-thinkers ("romanticists"). The dichotomy is ostensibly directed toward cleaning up the neighborhood in order to forestall further drops in property values. The typology is simplistic, and is itself the product of eleventh-hour efforts at damage control for a discipline that has always been the source of its own problems. As Lunbeck notes (1994), psychiatry's transformation from a custodial role in the treatment of the insane to magisterial purveyor of normal psychology was fateful, and traceable to several factors. McHugh attributes the current disrepute of the field not to the consequences of its historical obsession with being marginalized, but to a misdirected constituency within it which has wandered away from precincts of correctness. But is there any such thing as a foreordained path to empiricist wisdom that only the perverse ignore willfully? One might even say that McHugh wishes to psychiatricize the changing fortunes of psychiatry. He would like us to believe its problems are the handiwork of unmanageable waywards who refuse to tow the line, rather than a disciplinary compass that is the fancied birthright of the field.

As a maneuver, scapegoating the errant few for psychiatry's misfortunes is a ploy drenched in transparency, for culprits are always singled out after the fact. In the past, few psychiatrists seemed overly concerned about the mischief-making propensities of notions like repression before it wormed its way into controversies over "female inferiority," "recovered memories," "Multiple Personality Disorder" (or as the rebaptizers would have it, "Dissociative Identity Disorder,"[4] "false memory syndrome," "repressed sexual abuse," "cult programming," and other scutcheons of troubled theory. "Empiricism," panacea or not, may turn out to be the *deus ex machina* of a psychiatric establishment trying to put its house in order while the dynamite in the basement is going off.

"Romanticism," asserts McHugh, is readily discernible as the culprit in the Paul Lazano/ Bean-Magog tragedy of recent memory. In it, the eventual suicide of a patient, Paul Lazano, is attributed by McHugh to the "romanticism" of his psychiatrist, Dr. Margaret Bean-Bayog. The latter conducted what in McHugh's opinion was an inappropriately "evocative" therapy with the patient, one deteriorating to the point of neglecting standard psychiatric practice. In addition, Dr. Bean-Bayog was, according to McHugh, "...overcome by erotic feelings for the patient." (McHugh, 1994, p. 19).

Does the Lazano-Bean-Bayog affair illustrate the folly of what McHugh calls an unbridled "romanticism"? And is the latter the battery charge for sexual overinvolvement with patients? Or is the entire fiasco a sordid melodrama in which the failure to adhere to the barest semblance of ethical standards produced the tragedy? "Romanticism"—whatever tradition McHugh precisely means by the term—may be no more the real culprit in the affair than are the lobotomized and enslaved victims of older psychiatric practices the handiwork of "empiricism." Can we really attribute the centuries of brutality and rights violations—which, were it not for the restraining influence of the courts, might still be with us—to any such ideology? The indictment is based upon accepting such simple-minded typologies as "romanticism" and "empiricism" in accounting for specific historical trends. That they will not serve for the complex task of analysis is amply illustrated by considering a slightly different twist to the tragedy.

Regarded differently, cannot the Lazano-Bean-Bayog affair be attributed to the well known tendency for a union membership to shield itself in cases of obvious ethical infraction? True, a psychiatric board investigated the practices of the treatment specialist handling Paul Lazano's case. But it did so four or five years after the patient had been seen in ongoing therapy with the specialist in question, and at the point ethical infractions were too egregious to palliate by customary guild efforts at damage control. McHugh allows us an inside look by referring to warnings by the staff at Harvard's McLean Hospital that Dr. Bean-Bayog was overly involved with her patient. A psychiatrist at McLean warned her on June 23, 1987 that there was a question about how much her treatment was stirring up conflict-laden feelings in her patient (McHugh, 1994, p. 19).

The fact that physicians would go out on a limb to fault a colleague's practices on record should alert us to the way the panic button was being pressed—without any corresponding call to effective action. No official apparatus to halt the outrageous treatment was activated—for understandable reasons. The reticence within the medical profession for taking action against its own is well known. For example, the unwillingness to testify against guild members in malpractice cases, rather than being seen as betokening a clubhouse mentality, is viewed within the medical community as springing from the "ethics" of the profession. Curiously, it is also perceived as consistent with the Hippocratic Oath, despite its sometime conflict with consumer interests. In this, the profession views itself as far less than a mutual protection society on the order of Knights Templar.

Despite the failure of a putatively "empiricist" collegial network to take appropriate in-house action to forestall the impending tragedy, McHugh is nonetheless quite ready to attribute the Lazano-Bean-Bayog matter to "romanticism". Why not attribute it to a surrounding conspiracy of silence and inaction on the part of "empiricist" heroes of the day too professionalized to step on a guild member's toes?

After Paul Lozano took his own life on April 2, 1991, McHugh's *post mortem* became a study in irony. He goes on to reference the sexually explicit nature of the relationship between therapist and patient detailed in Lozano's photographs, letters and audiotapes subsequently turned over to the Massachusetts Board of Registration in Medicine (McHugh, 1994, p. 20).

McHugh would have us believe that alerting the Massachusetts board was occasioned by the evidence contained in the written material perused in 1991, although that something was rotten in Denmark was evidenced by complaints about the treatment recorded as early as 1987. Could the delay be due to the fact that ignoring written material was more legally incriminating in the event of a publicized *cause celebre?* Furthermore, McHugh persists in attributing the affair to romanticist proclivities, although Paul Lozano's suicide took place after he was placed on a "vigorous" empiricist regimen of antidepressants, lithium, and electroconvulsive therapy by his new therapeutic team! The failure of the heroic regimen, McHugh implies, is due to the prior taint of romanticism, not to the empiricism so ceremoniously recruited for last minute salvation.

McHugh is also not above commentary on such lively topics as memory. Does not the experience of the children of Chowchilla, California, buried in sand for hours tell us that traumatic events are invariably recalled, not repressed, he asks? The children remembered every detail of their harrowing ordeal, claims McHugh. The example is a curious one to illustrate the lack of support for repression theory. Since the current controversy over publicized childhood memories of trauma was sparked by issues pertaining to their *reporting,* not forgetting, allegedly traumatic events, McHugh may have succeeded in critiquing a straw man. Recent controversies over "memory" involve distinguishable themes for children and adults. The controversy over children's testimony (as is illustrated, for example, in day-care nursery and "ritual abuse" cases) is whether disclosures of remembered events can be regarded as sufficiently free of coaching taint to prove judicially reliable. The controversy over adult memories of early "abusive" experiences is whether putatively forgotten memories recovered despite seemingly amnestic barriers are reliable. McHugh has these two types of cases mixed up. He imagines there is a group of "trendy" treatment practitioners who insist children don't remember recent harrowing ordeals. On the contrary, a relevant test of the view McHugh believes plays mayhem with clinical realities would be the fate of childrens' memories twenty or thirty years after the ordeal, would it not?

Parties to current debates over recovered memory may sometimes fail to distinguish between (1) claiming one *remembered* an event and (2) sustaining a belief a particular event occurred. Did the patient actually recover something that deserves to be called a "memory", or are memory fragments already accessible reinterpreted as yielding a new scenario? In the former case, we recover something justifiably classified as "memory", whereas in the latter case we reinterpret something already available. To complicate matters, there is also a difference between a patient whose cognitive mistake consists in *misnaming* a mental event (e.g., in mislabeling as a "memory" what boils down merely to a fresh interpretation of past events) and *misidentifying* an interpretation as a true memory (e.g., coming to believe that one's interpretation of memory fragments was actually a freshly recovered memory). Despite these complications, once having distinguished memory and belief and their combinatory forms, one is still obligated to establish the evidential basis for applying a concept to a particular case. Making such distinctions themselves does not clinch the case that what therapists do primarily is to manipulate beliefs in contrast to facilitating memory retrieval. In fact, we are not entitled to maintain any univocal position on the matter before looking at individual cases. Current waves of opinion given to sloganeering over such concepts as repression--especially in advance of the outcome of laboratory research and forensic studies--do a disservice to fair-minded attempts to investigate individual cases. Be that as it may, it would appear that while many commentators point to Freud's concept of repression as the chief mischief-maker in the recovered memory controversy (Ofshe & Watters, 1994), it is also possible to view it, troublesome or not, as a secondary inferential move. The primary move may have been the assumption of a connection between historical events and current clinical patterns held to be their representative effect (Tversky & Kahneman, 1982). In the absence of any memories of such events in patients who exhibit the patterns in question, the concept of repression rides piggy-back on the connection. The notion of repression evaporates when there is no warrant for positing the causal connection in question. For example, if it is not assumed that a patient with bulimia was sexually abused as a child, there is no need to attribute the lack of any memory of such abuse to an unconscious process responsible for the amnesia. Indeed, in a decade in which early sexual abuse has been regarded as tragically frequent, the *chance* association between it and any number of clinical syndromes may come to be perceived as causal, when it is only adventitious. Such vagaries of statistical association may result in suppositious connections between childhood abuse and clinical patterns thereafter held to be its markers.

It is clear that historical connections exist between diagnosing MPD and heightened public awareness of sexual abuse. Despite this, the existence of the disorder as a true nosological entity no more rises or falls on shifting conceptions of its etiology, than it does for any other condition. It is one thing to speculate about causation, and quite another to challenge the very reality of a phenomenon, whatever its origin (Victor, 1975, Hacking, 1986, Aldridge-Norris,1989, Braude, 1991, Macllwain, 1992 Merskey, 1992, Barton, 1993). If favored theories of etiology of the disorder proved to be false, the result may be an altered understanding of MPD, not its dismantling as a clinical reality. Were one irony not enough, McHugh's replacement for MPD, hysteria, was, as we all know, Freud's original candidate for the effects of early patterns of sexual abuse (Freud, 1896a, 1896b, 1896c), and McHugh's position on the unreality of MPD sounds at times like a Proustian nostalgia for the memorable albeit anachronistic pastries of yesteryear.

McHugh may be way off target in limiting psychiatric practice to the hard-nosed disciplines. How does the field embrace the problems of mind and behavior while remaining aloof from issues of the value sphere: ethics, law, ideology, social structure, and the like? Incursions into the domain of values of course run the risk of "trendiness": it comes with the territory. Contrary to McHugh however, the problem hardly stems from overextensions of a discipline all too eager to become mired in them. These issues are its life's blood. The value-free ideal of a profession dedicated to the relief of suffering is illusory. Psychiatry is vulnerable because many of the problems it engages are not the kind that can be adjudicated by "science," hard-nosed or otherwise. They are frequently resolved by quasi-legal or quasi-moral decisions and policies, putting them beyond the pale of scientific discourse in the strictest sense. To shrink from them is to abandon psychiatry altogether, but to pretend that grappling with them must be uniquely a scientific skill is either obscurantism or an expansionist plot against terms like "scientific."

Finally, McHugh's antidote for misdirection may well be an example of the condition it is supposed to cure when he advises the development of a medical discipline that delivers less to fashion and brings more to patients and their families (McHugh, 1992, pp. 509-510). The sentiment is noble, but the words are couched in commendatory terms quite bereft of practical, specific proposals. Certainly it would be grand to know how to avoid pursuing shibboleths before our enthusiasm for them drove us down corridors of cultural fancy. But perhaps the promise of securing any such moderation through the application of facile formulae is the true misdirection. Should we awaken a decade after our latest excursion only to find ourselves at the exhausted end of a mere fad, maybe such odysseys are what we must time to time expect from the progress of an enterprise so closely bound up with the care of souls.

Endnotes

1   The author wishes to express his thanks to Professor Stephen Braude for his timely feedback on certain arguments in the paper.

2   I say "variation" on a theme, because Weyer did not hold precisely to the view that witches had "delusions" in the flatfooted psychiatric sense of this term. For Weyer, witches were the victims of thought-insertion by a veridical source, the Devil. This contrasts with the Schneiderian notion of thought-insertion as stemming from endogenous processes. Weyer was a Catholic-basher whose "enlightened" approach to witches was actually a game of musical chairs with who should be persecuted. Weyer's choice was poisoners and magicians, especially Catholic exorcists. Whiggish medical historians, eager to claim progessive historical movements for medicine, tend to comb Weyer's treatise *De praestigiis daemonum*. for signs of embryonic modernity. With some exceptions, like the hardly earth-shattering discovery that Barbara Kremers, a ten year old malingerer supposedly surviving without eating, was being sneaked victuals by her older sister when no one was looking, they are bound to be disappointed. The treatise fairly abounds in demonology--for good reasons. Sixteenth century physicians were committed demonologists, like every other pundit of the day.

3   Freud, who sided with the conceptual shift, nevertheless attributed its authorship to Charcot. The shift resulted in manufacturing a "sickness" role for individuals who are thereby brought under a different social jurisdiction (Szasz, 1961). Simply because the shift in question did not represent an empirical discovery on a par with the discovery of the circulation of the blood or the discovery of the spirochete in neurosyphilis does not mean it was an *illicit* one. Moore (1975) and Pies (1979) have persuasively addressed themselves to the weakness of Szasz's argument that the tenn

"illness" in "mental illness" must be metaphorical when extended to evaluations of behavior, in contrast to deviations from standards of somatic integrity.

4   As far as I am concerned, the decision to rename MPD (Multiple Personality Disorder) DID (Dissociative Identity Disorder) is a puzzling one. Do its architects imagine something is gained by giving a clinical entity another name? Doesn't a rose by any other name smell as sweet? The terminological switch from MPD to DID was reportedly undertaken with the motive of reinforcing the idea that MPD must not be viewed as embodying any suggestion that separate "personalities" actually coexist. For those who believe they do, how can a mere linguistic revision dissuade them from adopting this point of view? Moreover, if separate personalities could actually coexist, what better proof of this conceptually elusive notion might be adduced than MPD? It is puzzling why a philosophical stance on individuation is put forth absenting the intelligibility of the claim it purports to supplant.

5   McHugh is somewhat inaccurate here, as is Lenore Terr (1994), when, in seeking to bolster her hastily manufactured theory of Type I and Type II traumatic histories, she references claims of the kidnapped Chowchilla children: "Nobody repressed. And nobody forgot... The Chowchilla children consistently remembered everything" (p. 11). Later on in the same chapter, Terr discloses: "When I interviewed twenty-five of the children four to five years after the kidnapping, half of them misdescribed, or remembered misperceiving, something originally connected with the ordeal. Three of the eight children who had initially reported misperceptions or hallucinations had given up their mistakes by this time. But another eight kids, seven of whom had reported things right in the first interview, now exhibited faulty memories, describing a new 'man with a long nose,' a 'man with a pillow stuffed into his pants,' an additional pair of 'girl kidnappers,' a brand new 'black man,' and a 'light blue van' "(p.28). Still later, in a chapter about James Ellroy,

she writes: "Distorted time sense adds inaccuracies to memory. Five years after the Chowchilla kidnapping, four of the youngsters said that the event had seemed to take a much shorter time than the twenty-seven hours it actually took. Two Chowchilla children confused day and night. Seven others skewed time, reordering their memories of events following the kidnapping into a time preceding it" (p.201). So much for the inerrant nature of Type I memories of trauma. Of course, in the effort to minimize counterexamples to McHugh's thesis or to Terr's theory of Type I memories that traumatic events are usually remembered, such discrepancies are customarily relegated to the category of "minor details." In fact, the entire recovered memory movement, in an exercise that can only be reckoned as exceedingly Talmudic, has distinguished between features of memory that are "minor details" and those of "central traumatic import"—without supplying operational definitions of either.

References

Acosta, F. (1975). Etiology and treatment of homosexuality: A review.

Archives of Sexual Behavior, 4, 9-30.

Aldridge-Morris, R (1989). Multiple personality disorder: An exercise in deception. London: Lawrence Erlbaum Associates.

Ankarloo, B. & Henningsen, G. (1993). Early modern witchcraft: Centres and peripheries.Oxford: Clarendon press.

Austin, J. L. (1961). Philosophical papers. Oxford: Oxford University Press.

Barton, C. (1993). A sociological examination of the multiple personality disorder controversy in psychiatry and allied professions: Rational skepticism or extremism? Unpublished paper.

Becker, H. (1963). Outsiders: Studies in the sociology of deviance. New York: The Free Press.

Begelman, D. A. (1971). The ethics of behavioral control and a new mythology. Psychotherapy: Theory, Research and Practice, 8, 165-169.

_______________ (1993). Possession: interdisciplinary roots. *Dissociation, 4,* 201-212.

_______________(1966). A taste of honey: Dr. Guttmacher on Dr. Szasz. *Psychological Reports, 18,* 531-534.

Boyer, P. & Nissenbaum, S. (1974).   Salem Possessed: The social origins of witchcraft. Cambridge: Harvard University Press.

Braude, S. E. (1991). First person plural: Multiple personality disorder and the philosophy of mind. London: Routledge.

Demos, J. P. (1982). Entertaining Satan: Witchcraft and the culture of early new England. Oxford: Oxford University Press.

Esterson, A. (1993). Seductive Mirage: An Exploration of the Work of Sigmund Freud. Chicago, Illinois: Open Court.

Freud, S. (1896a). Heredity and the aetiology of the neuroses. SE, 3, 143-146.

______________(1896b). Further remarks on the neuro-psychoses of defense. SE, 3, 162-185.

______________(1896c). The aetiology of hysteria. SE, 3, 191-221.

Godbeer, R. (1992). The devil's dominion: Magic and religion in early New England Cambridge: Cambridge University Press.

Goffman, E. (1961). Asylums. New York: Doubleday.

Guttmacher, M. (1964). Critique of the views of Thomas Szasz on legal psychiatry. Archives of General Psychiatry, 10, 238-245.

Hacking, I. (1986). The invention of split personalities. In A. Donagan, N. A. Perovick, Jr., & M. V. Wedlin (Eds.) Human nature and natural knowledge, (pp. 63-85). Dordreckt, the Netherlands: Reidel.

Karlsen, C. F. (1987). The devil in the shape of a woman. New York: Vintage Books.

Kittredge, G. L. (1929). Witchcraft in Old and New England. Cambridge: Harvard University Press.

Kors, A. C., and Peters, E. (Eds.) (1972).   Witchcraft in Europe 1100-1700: A documentary history.Philadelphia: University of Pennsylvania Press.

Leader, E. (1975). Transsexualism: A study of cross-gender identity disorder. Clinical Social Work Journal, 3, 155-156.

Lunbeck, E. (1994). The psychiatric persuasion: Knowledge, gender, and power in modern America. Princeton, New Jersey: Princeton university Press.

Macilwain, I. A. (1992). Multiple personality disorder. The British Journal of Psychiatry, 161, 863.

Macmillan, M. (1991). Freud Evaluated: The Completed Arc. New York: North-Holland.

Martin, R. (1975). Legal challenges to behavior modification: Trends in schools, corrections and mental health. Champaign, Illinois: Research Press.

Mather, C. (1693). The wonders of the invisible world Observations as well historical as theological, upon the nature, the number, and the operations of the Devil. London: (Publisher Unknown).

McGowan, J. (1991). Postmodernism and its critics. Ithaca, New York: Cornell University Press.

McHugh, P.R. (1992). Psychiatric misadventures. The American Scholar, 61, 49,

McHugh, P. R. (1994). Psychotherapy awry. The American Scholar, 63, 17-30.

Merskey, H. (1992). The manufacture of MPD. The British Journal of Psychiatry, 160, 327-340.

Moore, M. S. (1975). Some myths about "mental illness." Archives of General Psychiatry, 32, 1485-1490.

Mora, G. (1991). Witches, devils, and doctors in the Renaissance: Johann Weyer, De praestigiis daemonum. Binghamton, New. York: Medieval & Renaissance Texts and Studies.

North, C. S., Ryall, J. M., Ricci, D. A., and Wetzel, R. D. (1993). Multiple personalities, multiple disorders: Psychiatric classification and media influence. Oxford: Oxford University Press.

Ofshe, R. and Watters, E. (1994). Making monsters: False memories, psychotherapy, and sexual hysteria. New York: Charles Scribner's Sons.

Ohmer, E. (1988). Somatization disorder. Psychiatric Annals, 18, 330-331.

Pies, R. (1979). On myths and countermyths. Archives of General Psychiatry, 36, 140-

Robbins, R. H. (1959) The Encyclopedia of Witchcraft and Demonolgy. New York: Crown Publishers.

Ross, C. A. (1989). Multiple personality disorder: Diagnosis, clinical features, and treatment. New York: Wiley.

Ryan, A. (1993). Foucault's life and hard times. New York Review of Books, April, 12-17. Simons, R. C., & Hughes, C. C. (Eds.) (1985). The culture-bound syndromes: Folk Ilnesses of psychiatric and anthropological interest. Dirdrecht, Netherlands: D. Reidel.

Swartz: M., Landennan, R., George, LK, et. al. (1991). Somatization disorder. In Robins, L. N. and Regier, D. A. (Eds.), Psychiatric disorders in America: The epidemiologic catchment area study. (pp. 220-257). New York: Free Press.

Szasz, T. S. (1961). The myth of mental illness. New York: Harper & Row.

Terr, L. (1994). Unchained memories: True stories of traumatic memories, lost and found.New York: Basic Books.

Tversky, A. and Kahneman, D.(Eds.) (1982). Judgments under uncertainty: Heuristics and biases. London: Cambridge University Press.

Vatz, R E. and Weinberg, L. S. (Eds.) (1983). Thomas Szasz: Primary values and major contentions. Buffalo, New York: Prometheus Press..

Victor, G. (1975). Sybil: Grand hysteria or folie a deux. American Journal of Psychiatry, 132-202.

Waismann, F. (1963). Verifiability. In A. G. N. Flew (Ed.), Logic and language (first series), (pp. 117-144). Oxford: Basil Blackwell.

Yates, A. (1989). Current perspectives on the eating disorders: History, psychology and biological aspects. Journal of the American Academy of Child and Adolescent Psychiatry, 28, 813-828.

Vaillant, G. (1984). The disadvantages ofDSM-III outweigh its advantages. American Journal of Psychiatry, 141, 542-545.

Zilboorg, G. (1935). The medical man and the witch during the Renaissance. Baltimore: Johns Hopkins Press.

Zilboorg, G. and Henry, G. (1941). A history of medical psychology. New York: Norton.

The Art of Healing: Bernie
Siegel on a Roll

There's a crucial distinction between providing cancer patients with a better quality of life while they struggle with their illness vs. actually altering the course of their disease. Bernie sometimes fails to draw it. When he doesn't, he inevitably lags behind what informed sources tell us about the curative issue since the publication of studies seemingly favorable to his point of view (Spiegel, Bloom, Kramer & Gottheil, 1989; Fawzy et.al., 1993). They concluded that a course of psychotherapy prolonged life in comparison to the shorter life span of a group of patients who went without it. On a more systematic and quite different note cf. Coyne, Stefanek & Palmer, 2007.

Elsewhere in *The Art of Healing*, Bernie intimates he's not always up to curing disease, while backtracking on this two sentences later: "Even if I can't cure their disease, but can help people to live, I've done something for them. So I sent out letters to a hundred of our patients with cancer, saying, 'If you want to live and have a longer, better life, come to a meeting.' "(page 17). Well, if you can't cure a disease, why intimate you can, in promising a cancer patient a *longer* life?

When cancer patients are not randomly assigned to conditions—a research methodology that may be precluded on ethical grounds alone—the study is a correlational, not experimental one. That is, any effect of psychotherapy in comparison with a control group of untreated patients might well stem from variables other than treatment v. no treatment. In other words, the individual who opts for psychotherapy may represent a bundle of independent variables that favor increased longevity as a correlate of his or her population.

Before tackling the issue of Bernie's conclusions being shakier than he imagines, we should note the snippets of New Age musings that course through the first five pages of his book—and beyond. They have a way of diverting the reader from the hope fans place in his sometime promise that "…it is possible to prevent disease" (page 2). Of course, I would imagine that *curing*, not *preventing* disease would be the chief preoccupation of cancer patients, and it is barely noticeable that Bernie has smuggled in yet another vision of things to come in addition to curing disease and enhancing life: preventing disease. The problem with this third promise is that we'd never be able to decide if it was Bernie's methods that *prevented* cancer in a population of persons who might not have developed it without his ministrations. But nowhere in his book is there a discussion of a non-cancer patient population included in a treatment program as a specifically preventive measure.

The Art of Healing, subtitled *Uncovering Your Inner Wisdom and Potential for Self-Healing* begins by recounting an episode at a Connecticut DMV licensing center in which Bernie meets an official whose mother was a past patient of his. Radiating gratitude for the author's care, the official "…was talking about her mother's *life*. Imagine that. It wasn't about her physical body or the disease; it was about the things that made her mother's life meaningful." When Bernie left, he said he "felt so good." He then remarks, "Our meeting had not been by accident or by chance. It was a gift. There are no coincidences."

Where to begin? Bernie feels that the encounter didn't come about by either accident or chance, as though there were an important difference between "by accident" and "through chance" in ordinary parlance. (Usually the two both cover what can loosely be considered the opposite of *planned* or *contrived*.) He then goes on to declare that the encounter was a "gift," and that there are "no coincidences." Does he imply that the meeting was, after all, scheduled by someone or something other than the two persons who encounter each other? If so, who or what? We needn't tarry unduly over supplying an answer to the question, since the thinking is in all likelihood a residue of the Jungian notion of *synchronicity*, the idea that what appears to be coincidental is not really this, but a coming together with a difference. Bernie refers to himself elsewhere in his book as a "Jungian surgeon." This ostensible oxymoron combines his once being a Yale pediatric surgeon while currently appropriating the mind-set of a New Age guru.

He continues posing questions that would attract a spiritually minded elect. "How does the invisible become visible? What part of our being still sees when we leave our physical body in a near-death experience?…How do clairvoyants and psychics communicate with people and animals, whether distant or dead? How does the community of cells in the body speak to the conscious mind about its needs and health? And what is the language of creation and the soul?" Whoa! One at a time, doc, although it seems that the momentum behind these escalating interrogatives is, *inter alia*, a back-door plug for religious belief, the ever resurfacing theme of our pattern-seeking species. Some such subtext of Bernie's is confirmed in his reaction to the Wells Cathedral in England: "I felt I was in the presence of the hand of God" (page 22).

Bernie is only one spokesman for the widespread view that a sense of the numinous—shared also by committed Atheists—has to be confirmation of the existence of a transcendent being. Likewise, "signs of God's presence" are reminders "to have faith," a lesson for him driven home by the words "In God We trust" on pennies (page 26). Finally, his dreams contain the message that "…first, there was consciousness and consciousness was with God…and consciousness was God, because God speaks in dreams and images—the universal language" (page 42). What is evidently a riff on John 1:1 could as easily be seen by unnamed orthodoxies as lapsing into heresy, Spinoza-style.

In what can only be characterized as animism, Bernie elsewhere poses questions about plant life as though it were imbued with a human intelligence that escapes the notice of biologists who have a different take on tropisms. Bernie asks: "How do seeds know which way is up when light and warmth are blocked? And why don't they give up when they realize they have been paved over and are hitting a stone wall?… Plants possess a source of wisdom in their genes and a sense of gravity too. They don't give in to adversity when they run into obstacles; they push forward or find new ways to reach the light." And the seedlings that don't? Are they to be designated as contrarians, passive-aggressive life-forms, or—were we to take the anthropomorphism a bit further— sore losers?

Consider two of Bernie's overwhelming questions. "What part of our being still sees when we leave our physical body in a near-death experience?" Why suppose that a near-death experience involves "leaving our physical body"? Is this implied by *any* altered state of consciousness, including dreams? (e,g., "What part of my being still sees when I leave my physical body to dream of flying through the air? What part of my being still sees when I leave my physical body thinking of foreign investments?") On a less mystical note, no part of my being leaves my body when I dream, because my dream *is* part of me, albeit in transmuted form.

"How do clairvoyants and psychics communicate with people and animals, whether distant or dead?" Well, they don't; supposing they do is to fall for a File-Drawer effect broadcasting the special abilities of savants who inveterately fail all rigorous tests of their imagined talents!

Bernie tells us that once the lid is lifted "off our unconscious, we can be guided by a deeper knowing" so that we can be placed within "the healing realm of our inner wisdom" because "The same intelligence that allows cells to communicate inside the human body is inherent in all life-forms" (page 3). Bernie is here getting down to the molecular brass tacks of his metaphysics, at which point he starts to flesh out the business at hand: "Books such as *The Psychobiology of Gene Expression,* by [Ernest] Rossi, give insight to the process by which the universal mind works. Rossi refers to a form of intelligence that communicates through changes in our genes." (page 5).

Dr. Rossi might use a helping hand, if only to underscore what this pundit is essentially driving at. It's the notion that every psychological event has a neurophysiological substratum. This couches the matter more generally and in a more plausible way than the theory that relevant processes can in every case be attributed to genes. There are changes in human behavior that are independent of genetic incursions. But the revised formulation runs the risk of vacuity, if only for the reason that no one would deny that for every psychological event there is a cause or parallel representation in the physical substratum of the nervous system. To understand this is hardly equivalent to being on the brink of some novel psychotherapeutic or behavior-changing innovation. Even

Freud in his 1895 *Project for a Scientific Psychology* was partial to the idea that all his psychological concepts could ultimately be grounded in physiological processes. Were we to manipulate the substratum in ways ensuring favored psychological results, we'd be ahead of the game. But at the present time, such interventions are in the realm of fantasy—except when it comes to a restricted set of biomedical applications, like psychotropic medications affecting neurotransmitters. A more economical approach would be to change or manipulate psychological variables, guaranteeing corresponding alterations in the substrata underlying them. This approach has the advantage of a route to a Holy Grail that can side-step going in through a back door which beckons tantalizingly (if only speculatively) from the distant future.

There's more. The remainder of his tome is a virtual passage through New Age ramblings that starts with inferences based upon suspect projective testing techniques. In a reference to one of his famous predecessors, Bernie observes "Carl Jung interpreted a patient's dream and correctly diagnosed a brain tumor" (page 44). But this forecast by the darling of the New Age set is virtually worthless as it stands when taken as indication of a special talent or, as the case may be, the validity of that staple of psychoanalytic theorizing, dream interpretation. First, Jung was a physician, and nowhere in the reference to him is there any inkling about whether the prediction represented a cold reading. That is, there's no discussion of Jungian observations of medical symptoms of the patient prior to what appears to be a revelation based upon dreams solely. Did the patient report chronic nausea, memory loss, headaches, vomiting, paralysis, visual anomalies, or dysphasic problems in the context of the diagnosis? If so, the announcement that he had a brain tumor may not have been all that surprising, nor driven by a dream in contrast to unreported medical facts. Some such subtext appears to be implied by Bernie's comments about Jung in his *Love, Medicine and Miracles* (1986). In chapter 7 of that book, Bernie remarks that "Jung correctly diagnosed a damming-up of cerebrospinal fluid probably due to a tumor" (page 158). So there *were* medical findings contributing to a diagnosis ostensibly spun as dream-driven!

Second, how many times had Jung made *failed* predictions about diagnoses based on dreams? Unless those mistakes are configured in a case for prophetic dream interpretation, the example in question may have appeal based once more on the familiar "File Drawer effect." It's a standard ploy for assorted psychics and in sundry parlor games. Were I to broadcast only my successes in a game of randomly generated predictions, I too might cut a reputation as a seer extraordinaire! Of course, the New Age appetite for matters Jungian conveniently overlooks other of this psychoanalyst's pronouncements.

Jung had this to say: "There is no question but that Hitler belongs in the category of the truly mystic medicine man. As somebody commented about him at the last Nuremberg party congress, since the time of Mohammed nothing like it has been seen in this world. This markedly mystic characteristic of Hitler's is what makes him do things which seem to us illogical, inexplicable, curious, and unreasonable. . . . So you see, Hitler is a medicine man, a form of spiritual vessel, a demi-deity, or, even better, a myth." Suddenly Jung's visionary pronouncements here are less compelling, since history has long since turned in its verdict on Hitler. Obscuring Jung's take on the dictator and mass murderer is a way of cherry-picking nuggets of the psychoanalyst's wisdom to ensure he always comes up smiling.

In 1934, Jung authored *The State of Psychotherapy Today*, in which he alleged differences between "Aryan" and Jewish psychologies. He solemnly declared that "The Jewish race as a whole possesses an unconscious which can be compared with the 'Aryan' only with reserve…the average Jew is far too conscious and differentiated to go about pregnant with the tensions of unborn futures. The 'Aryan' unconscious has a higher potential than the Jewish; that is both the advantage and disadvantage of a youthfulness not yet fully weaned from barbarism." What is there to say? If Jung can mouth such twaddle, anything is possible for the mind-benders. Karl Kraus, the Austrian editor and savant, was closer to the truth when he announced that psychoanalysis is the disease for which it professes to be the only cure. He is also quoted as observing that when it comes to chauvinists and racists, he harbors no petty prejudices: they are all equal jackasses.

Chapters 5 and 6 of *The Art of Healing* are devoted to the analysis of cancer patients' drawings. Bernie's approach here bears all the signs of the failure to heed current trends in behavioral science about projective techniques. Yet even his conspicuous detour around the caveats issued in this literature (Anastasi, 1982; Gittelman-Klein, 1986; Lowenstein, 1987; Dawes, 1994; Lilienfeld, et. al. 2000; Wood et al., 2003; Crews, 2006) is a study in taking back with one hand what is offered by the other. For example, while extolling the presumed virtues of a treatment approach that involves analyzing patients' drawings, Bernie indicates he was introduced to "spontaneous drawings" in the 1970s, and at a workshop conducted by Elisabeth Kübler-Ross. In it, he learned that "images and symbols from dreams are a dialogue between our psychic or somatic intelligence and our conscious mind," making it "easy to see that drawings too may be a form of communication with the collective consciousness and our greater self" (page 55). In an apostrophe that is all too reminiscent of L. Ron Hubbard's Scientology, Bernie feels that when parents do not help children process traumas, the latter "…store the feelings and memories of events in their subconscious mind and body, to be dealt with at a later time or never resolved…It is then that these seeds can manifest into conditions such as cancer, heart disease, respiratory or digestive illness, allergies, and more. These potential illnesses are often revealed in patients' drawings—and not just their own potential illnesses but also those of other family members." (pp. 61-62). Moreover, the claim that conditions like cancer are the residue of unprocessed traumatic memories, when there is no research evidence whatsoever to support such a theory, has to be height of irresponsible commentary.

Bernie fleshes out the revelatory aspect of drawings by declaring that there are implicit guidelines for their interpretation. First, he supplies some modest equipment to patients. Paper and crayons or colored pencils are used with the understanding that "all the colors of the rainbow" are "available for use, plus black, white, and brown, since every color has meaning associated with it" (page 65). The color purple is a "spiritual" color (page 66), whereas "Green is the color of life" (page 67). Not to be outdone by a generation of Rorschachers for whom color has a prominent place in their diagnoses—despite the latter having little or no relationship to diagnoses in standard psychiatric manuals like DSM-V—Bernie insists that "yellow represents energy; green is growth and life force: black symbolizes sadness or despair, and so on" (page 69).

He goes on to emphasize the importance of spatial placement: "The center of the drawing represents what is centrally significant to the artist...The upper right quadrant of a picture represents the present, or the 'here and now'" (page 67)...The lower right quadrant represents either the near future or the recent past; the lower left represents the distant past; and either the far future or the death concept is shown in the upper left" (pp. 67-68).

Yet Bernie makes other statements about the foregoing parameters of analysis that leave the strong impression he is hedging his bets. To be sure, says he, color and placement have symbolic meaning; but we should not be constrained by overly rigid assumptions about these matters. After all, "...the placement of objects in quadrants should be used only as a guide, for there are no rules cast in stone when dealing with individuals' subconscious language. Quadrant placement is not a science but a theory based on common traits seen in hundreds of people's drawings, so it may not always be applicable" (page 68). Furthermore, he opines that evaluators may misconstrue things if they base interpretations on their "own understanding and beliefs," since "The drawing is not meant to be read like a horoscope" (page 66).

Apparently, there's much wiggle room between deciding what can be carved in stone and what lends itself to flexible interpretation when rules governing which is which are themselves shrouded in mystery. Does the color purple in the upper right quadrant guarantee something spiritual occurring in the present, or might this be the wrong slant for a patient when feedback from her betokens that an utterly different spin is the proper one? Here, Bernie dances between possibilities, as though any misconception about a drawing by an evaluator is little more than a trivial consideration that does little to invalidate the system under discussion. Because of this, it is something of a mystery as to whether Bernie's rules are at bottom flexible or non-existent: "Remember: you [the patient] are the only one who knows the truth behind the symbolism, so don't let others impose their incorrect interpretation on your inner wisdom and knowingness" (page 72). But if the patient hasn't the foggiest notion about understanding the symbolism in his or her drawing without the collaboration of the evaluator, and the latter's explanation may overstep permissible interpretation, how does one establish reality? Any answer Bernie would proffer only begs the critical question!

All of which may be beside the point. Bernie's fans, like most peddlers of holistic wisdom, keep their distance from—and barely suppressed antagonism to—empiricism. And that is why, despite all evidence to the contrary, they continue to be enthralled when gurus soapbox their wares. In the face of the best evidence-based studies about the Emperor's New Clothes, when you put your ear to the ground you can still hear them humming, "Do do that voodoo that you do so well." It's a Cole Porter ditty that spiffs up the most shoddy discourse.

References

Anastasi, A. (1982) *Psychological Testing.* New York: Macmillan.

Crews, F. C. (2006) Out, Damned Blot! In *Follies of the Wise.* Emeryville, California:

Abstract Shoemaker-Hoard, pp. 187-199.

Dawes, R. M. (1994) *House of Cards:Psychology and Psychotherapy Built on Myth.* New York: The Free Press.

Fawzy, F. I., Fawzy, N. W., Hyun, C. S., Elashoff, R., Guthrie, D., Fahey, J. L., et. al. (1993). Malignant melanoma: Effects of an early structured psychiatric intervention, coping and affective state on recurrence and survival 6 years later. *Archives of Genral Psychiatry*, 50, 681-689.

Gittelman-Klein, R. (1986) Questioning the clinical usefulness of psychological tests for children. *Developmental and Behavioral Pediatrics*, 7, 378-382.

Jung, C. G. & Jaffe, A. (1963) *Memories, Dreams, Reflections.* New York: Random House.

Lilienfeld, S. O., Wood, J. M. & Garb, H. N. (2000). *Psychological Science in the Public Interest*, 2, 27-66.

Lowenstein, L. F. (1987). Are projective techniques dead? *British Journal of Projective Psychology*, 32, 2-21.

Rossi, E. L. (2002) *The Psychobiology of Gene Expression.* New York: W. W. Norton.

Siegel, B. S. (1986) *Love, Medicine and Miracles: Lessons Learned About Self-Healing From A Surgeon's Experience With Exceptional Patients.* New York: Harper & Row.

Siegel, B. S. (2013) *The Art of Healing: Uncovering Your Inner Wisdom and Potential for Self-Healing.* Novato, California: New World Library.

Spiegel D., Bloom J.R., Kraemer, H. C., & Gottheil, E. (1989) Effect of psychosocial treatment on survival of patients with cancer. *Lancet,* October 14: *2,* 888-891

Wood, J. M., Nezworski, M. T., Lilienfeld, S. O., Garb, H. N. (2003) *What's Wrong with the Rorschach? Science Confronts the Controversial Inkblot Test.* San Francisco: Jossey-Bass.

Giving the Devil His Due:
M. Scott Peck's *People of the Lie:*
The Hope of Healing Human Evil
and *Glimpses of the Devil*

Where to begin? One surmises there is a subtext in M. Scott Peck's appeal to readers since the publication of his popular *The Road Less Traveled* (Peck, 1978). It is his view that "science" can vindicate "religion" with assistance from those who, like him, purport to have knowledge of both. For many in his readership, his having been a practicing psychiatrist added a certain luster to his religious views, enhancing a portfolio usually lacking in other inspirational authors. Hence, the attractiveness to his fans of such notions as "the psychology of evil," "a science of evil," or "evil as mental illness," ideas that hover tantalizingly between the spiritual and the prescription pad; between the City of God and the consulting room.

Although Peck makes no brief for Creation Science or Intelligent Design, the mating of science and religion is his continuing mantra. This troublesome aspect of his world view deserves more scrutiny than he is prepared to concede. He assumes that religious beliefs about demon possession are "hypotheses," subject to the same strategies of confirmation as scientific theories. The position is also articulated by some on the opposite side of a philosophical divide, like the atheist Richard Dawkins (Dawkins, 2006). Dawkins believes the existence of God is a "theory" about which science eventually has something telling to say. Despite this, the problem is surely more complicated than holding that science and religion differ only with respect to the mathematical likelihood of confirmation. For example, it is puzzling as to what data-base science might even hypothetically appeal in confirming the existence of the "soul," whatever the fancied improbability of so doing.

Other treatises likewise confuse logically independent strands of discourse. When medieval thought and tradition intersect with modernity, some religiously minded commentators may intimate that science and rational thought can be put aside, to be replaced by faith as its own form of spiritual truth. This vintage palaver is suspect, inasmuch as its spin on "faith" turns out to be tacitly dependent on science and reason in the first place. Thus, on occasion and before determining authentic possessions, "scientifically" oriented physicians, medical practitioners whose relationship to the Vatican is on the suspiciously chummy side, are polled in order to determine whether certain "possessions" fall within the scope of natural law. The paradox here is obvious: physicians, presumably specialists on natural diseases, are, in virtue of their exclusionary pronouncements thereby cast as self-styled experts on the compass of otherworldly phenomena lying wholly outside the purview of their expertise.

Exorcists and theologians, customarily bereft of scientific credentials, consequently rely on those secular conjectures to ascertain which possessions must be regarded as "authentic." The symbiosis seems to be a form of contrived reciprocity, designed, as one might well imagine, to validate the supernaturalistic mind-set. However, medical practitioners have no more business declaring which phenomena must be understood in supernaturalistic terms than entomologists have pontificating on Hindu scripture. (*Objection*: but physicians do not fashion supernaturalistic explanations; they only declare what phenomena can be covered by naturalistic formulations. *Response*: physicians have no authority to declare that any phenomenon is outside the purview of natural law; when they do, the implication is that the supernatural is authorized as agency. What other implication can the exclusionary emphasis possibly have?)

Peck's tendency to confuse disparate levels of discourse had him engaging "demonic" forces in exorcisms as though the challenge could be likened to a laboratory experiment, or an exercise well within the compass of a flatfooted empiricism. This is not the only problem of Peck's discourse, but it is seminal enough to cast a pall over almost everything else he discusses.

Peck believes he is an adept at discerning "evil" with a difference, unlike one atheist who accompanied him at an exorcism. The disbeliever perceived no such elemental stuff. Peck flirts momentarily with the plausible idea that exorcisms might be heavily influenced by suggestion, and, like Freud before him, dismissed any role for suggestibility without supplying the reasons for so doing. Evidently, personal premonitions were accorded the highest epistemological value in this psychiatrist's version of "science."

Peck was sure he personally confronted Satan during an exorcism. His account of the encounter with the fallen angel is as vivid as it is suspect. Taken aback by a facial expression "that could be described only as Satanic," he recoils from a "sense of a fifty-million-year-old heaviness I received from this serpentine being" (Peck, 1983, p.196).

If fifty million years ago marked the debut of the Evil One, he first appeared at the tertiary phase of the Cenozoic era. At that time, there were no humans to bedevil, unless Satan's modest aim was to work his wiles on the brainless creatures then slithering about on the planet. Since that era was not even close to the creation of the universe, the Devil, by Dr. Peck's calculations, was a late comer to the heaven from which he was later expelled because of his pride, envy, and incessant grumbling—to the din of trumpeting archangels.

Peck's description of his contact with the archfiend is doubtlessly inspired by centuries of iconography, and a rumor mill spruced up by the transports of fancy bequeathed us by the likes of Hieryonomos Bosch, Albrecht Dürer, Gustav Doré, William Blake, and numerous imaginative others. Even granting his theological premises, on what "scientific" basis does Peck distinguish the presence he experienced as Satan—as opposed to a lesser demon, a lesser demon imitating Satan, a patient simulating a lesser demon, a patient simulating Satan, or the group suggestibility of a team of exorcists who, with the notable exception of an atheist, seem enraptured by Peck's commanding presence? Moreover, Peck's identification of the evil one makes little sense absenting previously authenticated encounters with him. In Dr. Peck's proposed "science of evil" what are the empirically established rules by which a malevolent entity is accorded a greater or lesser stature in demonic hierarchies? And what uniquely "scientific" rules permit Dr. Peck to identify real demons in the first place?

Peck informs us with his trademark air of solemnity that true possessions are actually rare. The assertion flies in the face of other supposed "facts" about their prevalence. These include the spate of possessions reported in early modern European history, not to mention the current epidemic of possessions believed to be occurring within communities of American Charismatics, Fundamentalists, and Pentecostals. Even Wilkinson, as late as 2007, documents the increasing popularity of the rite of exorcism in and around such traditionally circumspect European vicinities as Rome. Dr. Peck not only throws caution to the winds on the basis of limited experience with the putatively demonic; he also implies that many believers have the wrong take on the phenomenon in question, and that, as we shall see, centuries of history can be summarily ignored.

Writers in this country, who like Peck promote the value of exorcism, celebrate the Christian version of the ritual. Like such early church fathers as Justin Martyr, Tertullian, and Cyprian, they evidently believe that the successful casting out of devils by Christian clergy, following the example of Jesus, suggests a proof of Christianity. The emphasis all but ignores those exorcisms documented across the wider transcultural landscape. Christian rites are in the slim minority when one considers the international panorama, especially rituals that are an ingredient form of cultural life in countless other societies. In addition, the efficacy of Christian exorcism, like the one undertaken on Anneliese Michel (Goodman, 1981; 1988), can be lengthy, traumatic, and unsuccessful, whereas others are remarkably successful. Failures are routinely explained by positing either the intransigence or enduring malevolence of the demonic presence involved, or some moral failure in the exorcized individual. However, if "science" is to be our bent, any fleshed out conception of what Peck calls a "science of evil" should also include carefully researched ratios of successful to unsuccessful American exorcisms (with suitable operational definitions of success and failure), lest the unwary appropriate a lopsided view of the power of the rite.

Even the unreported failures of American exorcisms are a comparatively minor problem for Christian practitioners when one considers successful exorcisms outside the Christian fold. For example, Giel, Gezahegn, and van Luijk (1968) and Torrey (1986) report the case of an Ethiopian exorcist, Abba Wolde Tensae, who kept records of brief and successful African exorcisms totaling a million over a fourteen year period. How does the Christian exorcist reconcile such heathen success stories with the religious convictions he draws from his own practices? By assuming that the power of his faith is such that its devils transmute into other forms in non-Christian cultures? In line with this, Peck avers in *People of the Lie*: "Would that same spirit be identifiable—under a different name—in the exorcisms of Hindus or Hottentots?" He goes on to question whether Satan is "merely a demon that attacks Judeo-Christians" or a cross-cultural enemy?" While granting the question to be an important one (Peck, 1983, p. 201), Peck supplies no hint about how it can be answered—even hypothetically.

Peck's hunch about the transmuted forms of the Devil parallels past attempts at extending the purview of the Christian gospel of salvation even to individuals who lived before Jesus. The doctrine of the "righteous pagan" was circulated by the second century missionary bishop of Lyons, Irenaeus, who sought to reconcile the idea that there is no salvation without acceptance of the gospel with the inconvenient fact that most of humanity had no knowledge of Christianity, much less an inspirational relationship with Jesus Christ. He accordingly fashioned a doctrine of *dispensationalism*, the idea that ethical pagans had a dim recognition of higher truths that God had arranged to disclose to them through dilatory instruction. This courtesy culminated with the possibility of salvation by accepting the gospel after death in whatever region of the after-life they happened to find themselves.

Irenaeus, no doubt a zealous purveyor of higher truths of his own devising, was a major player in cobbling a version of Christianity that thumbed its nose at second century competitors like Gnosticism. To this day, orthodoxy harbors the delusion that the religion it touts either lacks a piebald provenance or had been around forever in its present form.

The argument that the success of non-Christian exorcisms is illusory, and either does not involve real demonic entities or is a staged manipulation of the Devil to befuddle heathen sensibility, overlooks another possibility altogether. Perhaps the sword can cut both ways, and American exorcists tout the wrong religion! For consider: if successful Christian exorcisms are didactic illustrations of the truth of Christianity, why isn't the shoe on the other foot considering the even more impressive record of successful non-Christian exorcisms across the immense transcultural landscape?

Even within the Christian tradition itself, Dr. Peck makes no mention of the tortuous history of exorcist practice, especially in the early modern historical period, the sixteenth and seventeenth centuries. During that time frame, the number of exorcisms, reportedly far from rare, was influenced by era, geography, and socioreligious climate. Demonic possession, often attributed to witchcraft, increased in England and the central European nations at points at which antagonisms between Catholics and Protestants heated up. Barnett (1965) has pointed out that Catholic Ireland was virtually witchcraft free during periods that witch-panics and exorcisms abounded elsewhere. The same became true after a time in Spain, where Catholic hegemony and a preoccupation with rooting out infidels like Jews, Judaizers, and Moriscos held sway (Atkinson, 1960; Peters, 1989; Elliot, 1990; Netanyahu, 1995).

During the early modern period Catholic/Protestant antagonisms often took the form of clashes over the reality of demon possession. In the seventeenth century, for example, French exorcisms played a strategic role for Catholic orthodoxy. They were spectacular events, notorious for their theatrical flair, and often staged for numerous spectators. At Loudon, seven thousand were reportedly in attendance at one exorcism (Oesterreich, 1996). The propagandistic value of the spectacles was not lost on the Huguenots, or French Protestants. They had doctrinally renounced exorcism and the real presence of Christ in the Eucharist as remnants of Catholic superstition. "Successful" exorcisms effectively moved thousands into Catholic confessionals, after driving a partisan point home more speedily than lengthy treatises in defense of the true faith (Walker, 1981).

Nowadays the Catholic and Protestant approaches to exorcism are often reversals of the early modern picture. Catholicism, reeling from the history of fraudulence and pseudo-possessions in Europe (Robbins, 1959), has adopted a circumspect attitude toward the rite. The stance notwithstanding, there is the occasional priest who breaks ranks with his church to conduct maverick rituals out of the conviction he must personally rise to the occasion to save an endangered soul. Many Charismatics, Evangelicals, Pentecostals, and Born-Agains within the Heartland Deliverance Ministry nowadays embrace the ritual, often in huge gatherings supervised by itinerant preachers (Cuneo, 2001).

As a rule, Catholic exorcisms are allowable only after endorsement by such higher placed prelates like bishops, and only when a case meets stringent criteria of possession. Stringency was in part a historical outgrowth of the troublesome profusion of pseudo-possessions documented by the Church. In this atmosphere, the seventeenth century ecclesiastical landscape was peppered with the fulminations of bishops and archbishops, like Clement August of Cologne, who inveighed against a generation of venal exorcists whose avarice drove them to see devils everywhere. In a pastoral letter of 1669, the bishop of Pomerania, having grown incensed with the carnival atmosphere surrounding exorcism, threatened excommunication of priests initiating wildcat exorcisms prior to obtaining permission from him. Felix Joseph Huber de Wavrans, bishop of Ypres, likewise castigated the charlatanism of exorcists a century after the Loudon possessions (Lea, 1957, p. 1055). Unmasked pseudo-possessions were exposed in cases like those of John Darrell, a Protestant exorcist, who was convicted of rehearsing people how to act possessed (Thomas, 1971). Countless pseudo-possessions were investigated and exposed by James I of England, translator of the Bible, and himself a prominent demonologist of his day.

Pseudo-possessions, whether or not a result of charlatanism, increased in seventeenth century Europe to a point at which the rhetorical value of the rite to Catholicism was nearly overshadowed by a widespread atmosphere of mendacity and hucksterism. Today, the reticence of diocesan officials to approve exorcisms mirrors the skepticism of their forbears in whose age it was common knowledge that fools rushed in where angels feared to tread. Martin Antoine Del Rio's 1599 treatise *Disquisitionum Magicarum* summarized the pitfalls of exorcisms undertaken without proper authorization: "It is a device of the demon to pretend to be ejected by them in their public exorcisms," and "All are warned to place no faith in the father of lies" (Lea, 1957, p. 1051).

It is rarely noted in the popular literature on the subject that criteria of possession within the Christian tradition have run an inconsistent course down through the centuries. Older criteria tended to get stripped away from a presumptively authentic core when they became viewed as explainable in naturalistic terms, and with the advance of scientific understanding. A related phenomenon that challenged the appearance of legitimacy was that many exorcisms could drag on interminably— sometimes for years. In some cases, demons would reappear after presumably effective expulsions, deflating erstwhile triumphant exorcists.

The church formulated more stringent criteria of possession in the context of the foregoing concerns. Among those that survived the whittling down process were: revulsion to sacred objects, paranormal language, paranormal strength, and paranormal linguistic ability. The last named capability often manifested in a proficiency in a language presumably unknown to the host. Prior to the evolution of these four stigmata, the nature of demonic signs tended to shift over time, in accord with the thinking of the day. A Rouen treatise of 1644 listed eleven signs of possession, whereas Pere Esprit de Bosroger and Michael Dalton in his 1627 *Guide to Jurymen* listed seven. Francesco-Maria Guazzo, in his *Compendium Maleficarum*, developed a group of forty-seven signs (Robbins, 1959).

There are, of course, other dramatic signs of possession that, while not classical, were often understood to meet an unwritten test of stringency. Some examples include: several basso voices emerging from a teenager who was not visibly articulating the words (Vogel, 1935), mysterious stenches that came from nowhere (Goodman, 1988), spinning on one's back like a top (Summers, 1956), and levitating

(Fielding-Ould, 1919; Thurston, 1952; Rogo, 1982; Crabtree, 1985; Noll, 1990).

In criticizing the Catholic Church's traditional criteria of possession—although Peck is not above using its *Rituale Romanum* in his exorcisms—he begs a critical question. He states, that his belief, "based on experience, is that these [Roman Catholic] criteria are so unealistically strict" they would preclude exorcisms in a majority of cases in which victims are "genuinely possessed by the demonic" (Peck, 2005, p. 104). Yet Peck's "experience" of the demonic is limited to but two rituals, neither of them successful. The record is not only dismal; it is a paltry basis for glib generalizations about the restrictive nature of Catholic criteria. Furthermore, the latter were historically formulated to sharpen differences between real and pseudo-possessions. Peck cannot, without begging the question, maintain that phenomena excluded by traditional criteria are nonetheless authentic possessions, with nothing to back up his claim other than personal conviction.

In yesteryear, belief in the malevolent power of spirits and demons increased as the social impetus to discover them gained momentum. The number of reported possessions soared in periods of religious strife and factionalism. Yet in any such periods of crisis, inconsistent strands in the theology of demonic possession developed concurrently. The Christian tradition today and in yesteryear was not of one mind in its approach to the subject. In the distant past it harbored trends that were at cross purposes. Among these was a skeptical approach that still acknowledged the reality of spiritual intrusions. In 1749, Tartarotti, a theologian, insisted that barely one out of a thousand energumens (individuals possessed by evil spirits) was truly possessed. That the preponderance of these pseudo-possessions was relieved through exorcism only proved for him that fictional states could be remedied by "imaginary nostrums" (Lea, 1957, p. 1455). Tartarotti was not only aware that criteria of possession had run a tortuous, rather than smooth, ecclesiastical course; he saw little connection between successful exorcisms and the underlying condition of the allegedly possessed host.

Other theologians contributed to the wary, or skeptical tradition of demonology. Essentially, it held that any trafficking with or "fix" on demonic agency was fraught with pitfalls. This circumspect tradition coexisted with more ardent ones during eras in which a demonological mind-set went unquestioned. Hence, it was hardly secularization of oultook or radical disbelief that created opposition to a seamless tradition of demonological practice, including exorcism.

Clergymen with more than a nodding acquaintance with possession and exorcism have contributed to this wary or circumspect tradition. Their overriding premise, suggested in the remarks of Del Rio already cited, was that it was impossible to beat the Devil at his own game. The circumspect brand of theology was not only manifested by Catholic commentators; in one of its Protestant forms, avoiding snares laid by the Devil meant repudiation of all demonic invocation—even those like exorcism with a cherished place in church ritual. One of its principal spokesmen was a physician, Johann Weyer, sometimes considered the father of modern psychiatry (Zilboorg, 1935; Zilboorg & Henry, 1941).

Ironically, psychiatric historians laud Weyer as a pathfinder out of a superstitious age. The designation is problematic, since the thrust of Weyer's *De Praesitgiis Daemonum* (Mora, 1991), was not the renunciation of demonology, but rather the reordering of the ways Satan makes his influence manifest. Weyer's vindication of witches, so praised by psychiatric historians as the beginning of a scientific/medical approach to the oppressed women of the sixteenth century, was never intended as undermining demonology. On the contrary, while humanitarian in effect, Weyer's slant was laced with the customary misogyny of the day. Since women were inferior to men, declared Weyer, they were as "witches" more vulnerable to the deceits of the Devil. Their belief about their presumed prowess—that they were empowered by Satan to cast spells of possession—was merely a delusion installed by him. When it came to befuddling old women, Weyer argued, the Devil enjoyed an easy victory. The message was less "medical" than it was demonological with a difference. Psychiatric historians would do well to scrutinize *De Praestigiis Demonum* more searchingly before fashioning their version of a psychiatric poster-child of modernity; Weyer's work fairly brims with demonological speculation.

For Weyer, there was no effective defense against the Devil other than reliance on the fortress of a simple faith. That faith had to be uncluttered by the contrivances of the Catholic Church—including its exorcisms. Weyer's world view involved no less than a game of musical chairs over which real Satanic ally deserved persecution. The older villains in the Catholic panoply, the witches, were, *pace* Weyer, replaced by male magicians, and, not surprisingly, Catholic exorcists. Thomas Erastus, perceiving what he took to be the arbitrariness of Weyer's recasting of operative demonic minions, subjected the physician's arguments to withering criticism (Monter, 1969).

The intricacy of demonic guile was not a Weyerian innovation. The theme was also discernable in the writings of the early Church fathers. In the third century C. E., heresiologists like Origen cautioned wariness in dealing with occult powers, an admonition that became woven into the fabric of later demonology. Early Church fathers like Hippolytus in his *Philosophoumena* anathematized involvement in such black arts as sortilege and conjuration. Although the latter in acceptable form, exorcism, was widely advertised as evidence of the superiority of the orthodox faith, no evidence exists for exorcisms having converted disbelievers between the Apostolic Age and the fourth century C. E. (Fox, 1986, p.329). As one might expect from constituencies on the other side of the fence, exorcisms resulting in dramatic personality transformations in the possessed were often greeted with contempt, as they were by Protestants in later centuries. For them, the transformations might well have seemed a false simulacrum of change, or, alternatively, a riddle whose challenge merely taxed explanation in terms of more familiar paradigms. The emperor Marcus, dismissive of the Christian rite, classified exorcisms along with cockfighting (Fox, 1986, p. 329).

Dr. Peck, much like others before him, may harbor a distorted picture of the inherent problems of demonology, even within the Christian tradition. Tabling for now the challenge to faith posed by disbelief in a secularist society, the complications for the doctrinaire Christian exorcist only begin—even within orthodox traditions. There appear to be several implicit premises of understanding driving exorcist practice, many of which have not been given the searching attention they deserve. In examining them, we shall assume for the sake of argument that the Devil exists and Christianity is true.

There are indisputable signs of true possession. The assumption has two complications. First, what is "indisputable" during certain eras later accommodated to explanation along naturalistic, not paranormal lines. For example, forms of epilepsy and conversion disorder were once classified as possession phenomena before medical advances brought them under the purview of naturalistic explanation. Accordingly, what is an "indisputable" sign of spirit intrusion in one epoch may in time become something less than this, depending upon the thinking of an age. However, there is no way to predict such future explanatory accommodations, whatever the direction of classification. This means that any particular formulation about the paranormality of demonic signs is always at best tentative or speculative.

Second, a so-called indisputable sign of possession must have an unquestionable connection to raw demonhood in order to be a valid indication of it. Yet "raw demonhood" cannot amount to merely another batch of signs of dubious validity without incurring a charge of circularity. Even if an actual devil in the flesh produced a "sign" of his presence, its recurrence on future occasions would be impossible to interpret for a variety of reasons, not the least of which might be an energumen's deliberate or unconscious simulation.

As was mentioned, Church history is in part the story of how pseudo-possession can be carefully distinguished from true possession. The problem with any premise about "true signs" is that it is on a collision course with the assumption, emphasized by Weyer, that Satan is the "father of lies." The conundrum here is that the arch liar, depending upon momentary whim or strategy, may be the kind of creature given to producing misleading signs of his presence—or absence. The possibility found its way into Descartes' speculations in the service of establishing true knowledge. A so-called "pseudo-possession" may therefore be a true Satanic presence contrived to mislead exorcists. Accordingly, time-honored indices of pseudo-possession cannot be disambiguated. The issue has been engaged before, and is not without historical importance.

In the episcopate of French Angers in 1599, Marther Brossier, a girl who exhibited signs of possession a year before, became the focus of ecclesiastical inquiry. Her case was a prominent one, sparking divisions of opinion between prelates imbued with a mounting spirit of rationalism, and a more credulous group. The former constituency was represented by Bishop Miron, Cardinal de Gondi, Archbishop of Paris, and prominent physicians (White, 1955; Robbins, 1959). The latter constituency was composed of Capuchin Monks, led by Father Seraphin (Walker & Dickerman, 1991).

Demons were supposedly detected through the water and linguistic tests, both of which were administered to Marthe by Bishop Miron. The first of these crucibles involved being able to discriminate in single blind trials between holy water and ordinary (i.e., unblessed) well water. The second test involved being able to discriminate between Latin passages extracted from St. Jerome's Vulgate Bible and pagan poetry in the same language. Marthe failed the discriminations miserably, whereupon the Bishop declared her pseudo-possessed.

The Capuchins demurred over the Bishop's verdict. Their conviction Marthe was truly possessed was not gainsaid by failures to pass time-honored tests of diabolical possession. Failures on the tests for them were precisely how one should expect demons to behave when wishing to remain undetected: as if there were no demons at all, as indicated by test failures! (Although why they should contrive signs of pseudo-possession in the first place if their diabolical aim was to elude discovery is another issue.)

For the Capuchins, Marthe's demons could pass the tests readily if they so desired. According to the monks, demonic depravity and slyness were even more imposing than the other team of exorcists had imagined. They were manifested by simulating failure on acid tests of possession in order to convince the team the case was innocuous, one of mere pseudo-possession. (We should note that the Capuchin argument in effect amounts to a partiality to one set of signs—those that had them convinced Marthe was possessed in the first place—over another set, construed by the rationalist team to be positive results on the water and linguistic tests.)

History has accorded little attention to the Capuchin thesis of runaway demonic guile. Theologically, it deserves more. It implies the necessity of reappraisals of classical tests of possession. Be that as it may, the monks were probably unaware at the time of how far their position in Marthe's case could be pushed to advance a radical skepticism about their own traditions. After all, any test of possession was credited by theologians who also posited the preternatural cunning of the Devil. Yet they expected the latter to accommodate nicely to ecclesiastical strategies contrived for battle with him! Perhaps the Devil's reputation for "preternatural cunning" means having no expectations of victory when locking horns with him.

Even here, Peck hedges his bets about the craftiness of the evil one. He concurs with his mentor Malachi Martin, author of *Hostage to the Devil* (1977), that exorcism, even given the malevolence of Satan, reveals his "extraordinary demonic stupidity," as well as his "extraordinary demonic brilliance" (Peck, 1983, p. 208). Peck offers as evidence of the former speculation the bizarre notion that Satan does not understand science, a "theory" confounded by the possibility he is only faking ignorance of it.

Be that as it may, the Devil's fancied incapacity may be shared by American fundamentalists. Their tedious iteration of the shibboleth "Evolution is only a theory" belies their ignorance of what science is all about, not to mention its technical deployment of the term "theory." Heliocentricity, the structure of the solar system, gravitation, and the atomic structure of matter are also "theories," although ones associated with a high degree of certainty. Alternatively, in reviewing imputed endowments among the spirits peopling demonic hierarchies, if the archfiend must be identified exclusively in terms of brilliance (as many of Peck's medieval forbears maintained), an obtuse devil hardly qualifies as Satan.

Not content with risible characterizations of the diabolic host, Peck continues his zany polemic by announcing that angels are inferior to humankind in some respects. Of course, such exercises in altering the received wisdom about transcendental character traits are free for the asking, and have been attempted before. Mark Twain's demon in his

Mysterious Stranger was drenched in cynicism, disillusionment, and irony—a sort of Holden Caulfield with horns. The French novelist, Anatole France, in a Gnostic mood, sketched a view of the world at the mercy of an evil, not beneficent, godhead. We can envision confirmation of such a horrific being as everywhere in sight, from inquisitions and epidemics to tsunamis, gulags, and genocides. Madame Helena Blavatsky, the Theosophist, saw the Devil (as did Jung in his doctrine of the unity of opposites) possessing a modicum of goodness as a necessary tincture in the homeopathy of godhead. (They were both anticipated by Shakespeare, who in *Henry V* had his royal hero conjecture, "There is a soul of goodness in things evil would men observingly distill it out.") As in the Gnostic scriptures, Blavatsky's theosophical demon was the light-bearer, or agent of enlightenment, a deity whose worldly influence was in stark contrast to a godhead somewhat removed from human affairs—as he was in the deistic beliefs of the Founding Fathers. Snakes did not always receive a bad press in the early, albeit discarded, scriptures of dualistic theology.

Skepticism about the actual existence of the Devil is thematic in liberal Protestant theology, whereas the mythological character of good and evil gods were principal themes in the works of Nietzsche and Freud. Jeffery Burton Russell, a religiously inspired historian of the theology of Satan, feels that there is more at stake in dismissing the existence of the Devil. To do so, Russell avers, means dismissing: "...the resurrection, the incarnation, and indeed the whole idea of revelation,"—in which case the entire New Testament is riddled with enough misconception "as to be altogether dismissed" (Russell, 1986, pp.217-218). Do Russell's comments constitute an argument in favor of the Devil's existence or merely one in favor of what the writers of the Gospels believed about it? The latter shades into the former if one assumes that what Gospel authorities believed cannot possibly be doubted.

Let us take the aforementioned Capuchin case about demonic possession a step further. Negative signs of possession, as on the water and linguistic tests, ultimately require validation against raw demonhood. Otherwise, there is no way to assess whether subterfuges even in relation to acid tests of diabolical presence become another aspect of the demon's attack. As was already mentioned, however, it is hard to formulate what raw demonhood amounts to other than yet another batch of demonic "signs," as revealed by tests. Obviously, the Capuchins felt one slew of symptoms was critical in establishing Marthe's possession, whereas Bishop Miron's team was partial to another group of signs. In short, it is impossible to ascertain the significance of test failures without creating a warped circle of reasoning. Nor can we take time-honored ecclesiastical assumptions as a guide. If hosts like Marthe were truly possessed, failures on the water and linguistic tests would simply mean these were poor crucibles for detection. Demons, crafty infernals that they are, might always manufacture test reactions devised cunningly to throw exorcists off the track. As we well might sense, the inadequacy of a "classical test" can be generalized to all procedures by which exorcists rule out diabolical agency. Theologically, this renders negative tests of possession problematic. Accordingly, the Capuchin arguments undermine a favored strategy of exorcists, since they imply that test failures cannot be disambiguated. If the Capuchins were correct, there is no way to differentiate pseudo-possession from demonic simulation of same, unless the validity of classical signs was guaranteed. But we cannot grant this without conceding assumptions such tests were devised to establish in the first place.

————*The failure of naturalistic explanation for a phenomenon is sufficient to prove it is in the paranormal or supernaturalistic sphere.* The term "failure" here is ambiguous. It may mean a failure of naturalistic explanation relative to an understanding of physical law in a given era, or it may pertain to its failure *sub specie aeternitatis.* However, the latter sense of "failure" cannot be deduced from any contemporary strain on natural law to embrace a phenomenon. This means that the possibility of naturalistic explanation is not forever precluded by its current difficulty in accommodating an exceptional event. Accordingly, present failures of naturalistic explanation augur nothing about which of the two magisteria embraces a particular phenomenon.

————*There is an incontrovertible connection between a paranormal phenomenon and the truth of a particular religion.* Even if paranormal explanation was appropriate in a given case of possession, the truth of a particular creed like Christianity would need to be reconciled with the success of rituals practiced by alternative creeds. For example, if a hypothetical levitation of a host were documented in an African, Indonesian, or Oceanic ritual, this would not for a Christian document the truth of a non-Christian polytheism. Therefore, an analogous levitation during a Christian ritual cannot similarly document the truth of the Christian religion for a believer outside the fold. Should the Christian apologist argue that his own deity simply transmutes its form in connection with the rituals of tribal cultures, the non-Christian can fashion an analogous argument in favor of the transmuted influence of pagan deities in Christian exorcisms.

Ordinarily, investigative efforts to document psychokinesis, or the psychic ability to move objects around is a talent with a pathetic showing under controlled conditions (Girden, 1962; Gardner, 1988). Usually, the reported instances of the phenomenon are shorn of efforts to attribute this presumably paranormal ability to demonic forces. Accordingly, this and countless other explanations of certain unusual effects compete with parochial religious explanations. In the famous case of Bridey Murphy, a woman whom parapsychologists believed could not have possibly known about the events she recalled of a past life, "past memories" served to bolster a belief in reincarnation, a very un-Christian notion indeed, according to St. Augustine. In cases of unusual and seemingly paranormal events, it is always possible to generate endless possibilities of explanation that compete with particular religious belief systems.

——*The success of exorcism confirms the truth of a particular religious creed.* The success of an exorcism, as the theologian Tartarotti has observed, bears little logical connection to the reality of demonic possession, much less to the truth of any religious creed. Successful exorcisms may only reflect a belief on the part of a host that an entity has been expelled. However, contrary to the majority view in secular medicine, the sometime efficacy of exorcism may be a rational basis for recommending its use as a therapeutic strategy in select cases where the cultural loading is strong enough to maximize success.

——*Satan's cleverest trick is to convince us he doesn't exist.* The view is an older one, having been articulated by, among others, Baudelaire, the French poet and author of *Les Fleurs du Mal* (Russell, 1986, p. 206). There is something to be said for the contrary thesis. If the Devil's actual existence is independent of framing moral judgments, then Baudelaire might have been dead wrong. We do not feel compelled to resolve the ontological issue about Satan in advance of deciding moral issues (although the metaphysical grounding of Evil might be perceived by some as dependent on such a resolution). The cleverest trick the Devil can pull off is to convince us he does exist—if he does. Belief in him cannot be a bulwark against fending off evil if such a belief sidetracks the arduous task of developing insight into actions enshrouded in moral ambiguity and lack of transparency. Belief in the Devil may be an artifice of the morally lackadaisical: it short-circuits the complexity of moral argument in favor of a diversion of finding the Devil's mark or sign. The latter trivializes the problem of evil by transforming the tragic nature of the moral challenge into a charade, a game of hide and seek by which evil is identified through manuals of signs, rather than through a complex faculty of discernment. The true moral agent cannot depend upon codicils in diagnosing evil.

Whether or not an act is evil or morally wrong—and therefore, in the mind-set of believers, the handiwork of the Devil—already presupposes a judgment encumbered by moral indeterminacy. It cannot be a determination established by extracting a signifier of the Evil One from a batch of casuistically ordained signs. If the Devil can convince us he exists, we have already capitulated to the notion of abandoning moral indeterminacy in favor of a gambol in which his mark, an entry in some time-honored codification, only has to be revealed or uncovered— like the patch of anesthesia on a witch's body, the rejection by water, the revulsion to sacred objects, and other artifacts of morally indolent belief systems. But the moral enterprise cannot be likened to an affair of uncovering the hidden sign; is more akin to judging the nature of things from a distinctively moral perspective that repudiates facile formulae. Because of this, the moral agent is always out at sea—he cannot rely on anything as simplistic as a manual of signs assuring him of a roadmap to goodness. *Lord, lord, why hast thou forsaken me?* exclaimed Jesus on the Cross. In the crowning moment of moral agony, there is nothing to hold on to in defining moral choice.

To many believers, it may be evident that Satan is the author of all worldly evil. But to the truly engaged moral agent the problem is precisely the challenge of determining which of one's acts can be rightly perceived as morally wrong, as leading to evil consequences in the world. This is not usually a matter of complete moral transparency, and the alibi "Satan made me do it" most of the time represents conjecture after the fact, retrospective wisdom. The moral enterprise is essentially bound up with deciding whether a particular decision is right or wrong, not whether an indisputably wrong act is resistible as a temptation of the Devil. To fault the Devil for one's actions is in addition a way of passing the buck in relation to deeds that are our own responsibility, not someone else's—least of all an infernal being we improvise in order to ensure someone else is left holding the bag for our own moral failings.

* * *

Dr. Peck's allusions to psychiatric "science" are sprinkled liberally throughout his two books. Yet he harbors an old-fashioned, if not addled, conception of the discipline. He is particularly unsympathetic to the "prevailing secularism" of modern psychiatry, holding that its evaluations would have hastened Joan of Arc's being burned at the stake. But Joan was burned as a heretic because of the theology of clerics imbued with the same metaphysics to which Peck, in a more or less modernized (some Born-Agains would say bastardized) form, subscribes.

A review of Dr. Peck's psychiatric assumptions betokens outdated views on the discipline. In both *People of the Lie* and *Glimpses of the Devil*, his segues from clinical experiences with troubled patients to allegedly "evil" people to exorcisms of demons are gratuitous ones. By admission, he is a newcomer to the exorcist arena, having had only two ritual encounters with those dark forces he is confident are more ominous than the nastiness of patients whose distinguishing trait is their "narcissism." Sometimes, however, he is unsure of what scenario is unfolding, as in the case of his patient "Charlene." Her driving perversity not to be helped—not to mention her wish to bed her psychiatrist—has Peck perplexed over whether the patient was an ordinary evil doer without demonic underpinnings, or whether infernal agency was playing a key role in her pathology. He admits to being confused about the case within a month of initiating treatment with the patient, and owns up to still being befuddled after seeing her two to four times a week for three years! (This frequency of visits for a solo practitioner is a dead giveaway of the theoretical psychiatric perspective Dr. Peck finds compelling, albeit one, as we shall see, that is fast becoming a museum relic in recent years.)

Peck felt that Charlene defied ordinary psychodynamic understanding, prompting one to question whether his grasp of the compass of "ordinary psychodynamic understanding" is as keen as he intimates. With the possible exception of psychoanalysts and other like-minded clinicians who feel that the explanatory capabilities of a purely motivational psychology are inconceivably wide, and who ply their trade irrespective of the current state of psychological knowledge, there is no "ordinary psychodynamic understanding" of many of the diagnostic entities listed in the DSM-V, or Diagnostic and Statistical Manual of the American Psychiatric Association, Fifth Revision. Rather, practitioners like Peck are addicted to freewheeling speculation about "psychodynamics" without a jot of experimental evidence for their flights of fancy. As in Charlene's case, failing such understanding is hardly surprising when it is the lot of many other textbook patterns. Just short of the four hundred and twenty first session with the patient, Peck is left still pondering what she is all about. His hunch is "autistic," a diagnostic stretch for a patient with an advanced verbal repertoire, a genius for head-games, a relatively independent life-style, and "a capacity for humor and obvious high intelligence," according to her bemused psychiatrist.

Peck also had a faulty grasp of the compass of the DSM, a manual not only designed to include all diagnostic categories of psychiatric disability, but to cover, as it were, all possible bets. Those familiar with its diagnostic categories appreciate how difficult it is to imagine a pattern of deviant behavior that is *not* encompassed by them. The inclusiveness is as much a characteristic of personality disorder diagnoses as it is of major clinical diagnoses. The former cover personality styles or trends, like the borderline, narcissistic, or antisocial patterns, whereas the latter cover symptom pictures like schizophrenia, bipolar disorder, or substance abuse patterns.

In *Glimpses of the Devil,* Peck diagnosed "possession" in one case because he felt a schizophrenic episode was too brief for meeting criteria for this diagnosis. The patient's "instantaneous entrance into and departure from a state of classical schizophrenia" could only mean that "…faking a somewhat unusual, even esoteric, form of behavior by a person who had no history of ever being previously exposed to such behavior is as paranormal as fluently speaking a foreign language one has never learned" (2005, p. 105).

On the contrary, the brevity of a psychotic phase in a woman whose first break is somewhat later in her chronology than would be expected for an onset of schizophrenia is a good reason for suspecting it was not schizophrenia that Peck observed, but some other psychiatric condition. The DSM-V provides for such episodes under the heading "Brief Psychotic Disorder," whether or not an etiology is known. Moreover, forms of depression, bipolar disorder, or toxic conditions can give rise to temporary psychotic phases often confused with schizophrenia. Peck concludes that the patient's episode defies psychiatric classification when this is hardly the case: "I have never heard of such a schizophrenic episode that was anywhere near as brief as Jersey's" (2005, p. 105). If paranormality is one's bias, then Peck should not suspect possession on the basis of a badly simulated schizophrenia, but on the basis of an aptly emulated brief psychotic disorder. However, if the latter condition is already included in standard diagnostic nomenclature, why suspect paranormality in the first place? A hypothetical case of a pattern that evades all extant psychiatric classification—and what kind of pattern could that conceivably be?—only calls for a new psychiatric classification, not a cue for switching metaphysical gears.

Furthermore, if the demon shows his hand by a botched up simulation of schizophrenia, perhaps he is as "stupid" as Peck conjectures. On the other hand, if he is capable of a flawless emulation of schizophrenia, why not turn in such a performance—if only to escape detection that would result in expulsion during exorcism? That would show, contrary to Peck's intuitions, that the demon is really smart. However, what is the difference between a smart Devil who is so clever he can ape a perfect schizophrenia, and a textbook case of schizophrenia without tell-tale paranormal stigmata? In a sense, Peck is driven to a theory of the Devil's stupidity, since to grant him high intelligence would be to concede the possibility of paranormal manifestations that are materially no different from phenomena comfortably classified by secular medicine.

While we are at it, why not classify *any* human trait or idiosyncrasy as the work of a smart Devil, as opposed to a happenstance denuded of paranormality? (The logic demands a natural segue on yet another controversial front: why restrict Creation Science or Intelligent Design to biology classes solely? Why not teach it in physics and chemistry classes also? Is there not an "irreducible complexity" to atomic structures and their multifarious combinatory forms, if such complexity is held to characterize their resultant macrostructures, like the eye? The suggestion means either expanding the conceptual playing field of religious imperialism or else a *reductio ad absurdum* of vainglorious efforts to do so.)

Time and again in *People of the Lie* and *Glimpses of the Devil*, Peck maintains he must go otherworldly because of a patient's unique pattern. For example, in the case of his patient "Jersey," Peck avers that it is clear he would be able to exclude the possibility she was demonically possessed if she "was suffering from a standard, well-recognized psychiatric illness" (2005, p. 100). Of course, Peck here stacks the deck in favor of demonic influence since there are patterns embraced by the DSM-V that are neither "standard" nor "well-recognized." This is because they are rare, disputed, or may straddle separate diagnostic categories. Despite this, Jersey's pattern is quite standard, psychiatrically classified, although disputed by some as a true condition. Peck's clinical unfamiliarity with Dissociative Identity Disorder or Other Specified or Unspecified Dissociative Disorder has him convinced that Jersey is demonically possessed because her behavior defies any psychiatric classification when the opposite is the case.

While DID (a.k.a. Multiple Personality Disorder) has been the subject of controversy in recent years, the dispute revolves around whether the condition is an epiphenomenon of the treatment process or suggestibility, not over whether the patterns it purports to cover have ever been observed. "Jersey" has all the earmarks of a DID case, whether or not one of her alters is "Satan." Clinicians who treat these patients are familiar with the unusual cast of characters alters can embody, iatrogenically created (i.e., by the treatment process itself) or otherwise. One red flag among several others is that Jersey remembers being incested by her father, a marker for patients with DID, *irrespective of the truth or falsity of the allegation*. Peck also perceives Jersey as highly "suggestible," his access to the demonic presence facilitated through hypnosis, another marker. Finally, he remarks that the patient is still bothered by "voices" six years after her exorcism, a finding Peck refused to regard as an indication he had been barking up the wrong diagnostic tree from the outset.

On another note, Peck was certain that Jersey's feeling of sympathy for her demons was an initial sign her pattern did not square with standard psychopathology. Untrue. It did not, perhaps, fit most cases of schizophrenia, in which an acute symptom is "voices," usually one in number, persecutory in nature, and condemning the patient or commanding her to do violence to herself or, more rarely (as possibly in the case of the Virginia Tech tragedy of 2007 or the Sandy Hook tragedy of 2012), others. In DID, on the other hand, "voices," often more than one in number, and frequently differentiated as to age or sex, can have a consoling, admonishing, or protective aspect, as well as a conflicting, or self-condemnatory one. The alter who emerges as the ISH or "Inner Self-Helper," as this alter is on occasion identified, is routinely a moderate, rational, or nurturing personality in relation to the host. In DID, the more the number of alters, the more the likelihood of their representing different ages or sexes, according to reports from the field. A routine cast would be a depressed host and/or alter, a seductive alter, a vulnerable child alter, and an aggressive alter which may double as a child protector. Again, actual observations of such role enactments are separate from considering iatrogenesis (Fine, 1989; Kluft, 1989; Torem, 1989; Ross, Norton & Fraser, 1989).

Peck also errs in characterizing DID. He has defined it as a condition in which the host personality is not aware of the existence of its "alters," a generalization that is often mistaken. The attribute of "co-consciousness" is a shifting affair among patients diagnosed with DID, and one diagnostic sign of the disorder is auditory hallucinations, or the awareness of "voices" within the head that represent alters who issue instructions to the host, to one another, or are otherwise in various stages of conflict with each other. It is hard to see how a host can experience such voices yet be "unaware" of the existence of alters. More often than not, there is awareness of some alters, but not others who emerge—iatrogenically or otherwise—later in the treatment process.

In general, Peck's approach was to suspect possession when a pattern of behavior defies DSM-V categorization, a somewhat disingenuous standard, since in a footnote in *Glimpses of the Devil* he avers that while some clinicians suspect his cases of assumed possession are actually cases of MPD, he suspects the possibility that their MPD cases "might actually be cases of possession" (Peck, 2005, p. 102). So patterns of behavior Peck designates as "possession" because they defy psychiatric classification *can* be covered by DSM-V criteria for certain conditions after all!

Some authors partial to supernaturalistic explanations of clinical phenomena (Friesen, 1991) have maintained that they are able to discriminate DID-type alters from true demonic presences, thus challenging the assumption that all such phenomena can be subsumed under psychiatric categories purely. Their arguments hinge on the observation that putative demonic presences share different characteristics from psychiatric alters. The argument begs the question, since it depends upon the questionable assumption that there cannot be essential or qualitative differences among alters nonetheless psychiatric in nature.

In *People of the Lie*, authored as late as 1983, the author asserted that many parents of schizophrenic children "seem to be ambulatory schizophrenics or evil or both." He goes on to reference the so-called "schizophrenogenic parent." (pp. 128-129). Much of what has been written about such parents is wrongheaded (Sperling, 1954; Hill, 1955), and represents the backwash of older psychoanalytic theorizing predicated on blaming family dynamics for everything. Its propagandists failed to consider the possibility that parental pathology might often be the effect, not the cause, of having a schizophrenic child, and that there is no evidence whatsoever that parental attitudes play a causal role in the genesis of the disorder.

On an additional note, Peck is guilty of a *lapsus linguae*. It is not the schizophrenic *parent*, but the schizophrenogenic *mother* who has been viewed as the pathogenic agent, a theory that would be consigned unremarkably to the annals of "science fiction" were it not for the fact that faulting the woman for worldly evil is a theme as ancient as the Book of Genesis. Even at that, Peck mischaracterizes the etiological picture, which is not that schizophrenia is usually mirrored in parents, but only that a higher incidence of the pathology occurs in extended family histories. A genetic transmission is also suggested (McGue, et. al., 1981; 1984)—albeit inconsistently—by higher concordance rates in identical twins in comparison to fraternal twins and control groups of unrelated siblings.

Peck's outdated psychiatry is sprinkled not too sparingly throughout both his books. His theories about obsessive-compulsive disorder are a case in point. In relation to his patient "George" in *People of the Lie*, Peck states that OCD is curable but the cure—psychoanalytic psychotherapy— will take a long time" (1983, p. 20). Actually, psychoanalytic therapy, long term or otherwise, is an ineffectual nostrum, whereas research has indicated the disorder is alleviated by a combination of antidepressant medication—Luvox (generically, Fluoxamine Maleate) is the FDA-approved agent in its treatment (Goodman, et. al.,1989—together with a cognitive-behavioral therapeutic approach (CBT) incorporating exposure, response-prevention, or flooding strategies (March & Mulle, 1998).

When it comes to the etiology of OCD, Peck is likewise in the antediluvian mode. In *People of the Lie* he states that Obsessive Compulsive Disorder originates in early childhood, and is caused by "less than an ideal toilet-training situation" (1983, p. 36). There is no research evidence indicating that OCD has anything to do with early bowel training. Even most psychoanalysts nowadays have repudiated this mythology about the delayed effects of early psychosexual stages of fixation, as propounded in the orthodox Freudian canon. Of course, the etiology of OCD in the canon meandered across the theoretical landscape, as if were angling to find a comfortable niche within the depredations of sexuality. Around 1896 it was recruited as a companion piece to hysteria during Freud's "Seduction Theory" phase. At that time, it figured as the alleged aftermath of sexually abusing pre-adolescent girls, transforming them later into "hysterics." The theory is falsified by the fact that OCD has an equal distribution among males and females, although there are probably more male than female molesters (Rasmusssen & Eisen, 1990; 1992).

After Freud repudiated the seduction hypothesis, based as it was on the reality of external trauma, he beat a retreat back into the head to emphasize purely intrapsychic mechanisms. As a result, OCD was construed as the effect of anal fixation. Since memory is usually lacking for the first three years of life during which most toilet training is accomplished, Freud could not have established a connection between the training and later character traits on the basis of reliable patient information. And it is questionable how much of his practice included collecting patient information from parents and other family members. The conclusion is that Freud had a bad case of serving up "data" that were theory-driven, and seldom based upon a sound methodology in establishing clinical knowledge. Nowadays, investigators are pursuing promising, albeit speculative leads about the physiological basis for OCD, including the possibility of an autoimmune deficiency or damage to the basal ganglia of brain centers (Belkin, 2005).

In *People of the Lie*, Peck promotes unsubstantiated notions about the origins of specific fears, or phobias, declaring that "Phobias are the result of displacement," occurring when a normal revulsion "is displaced onto something else" (1983, p. 146). Once again, the analysis is borrowed from the anachronistic Freudian template, specifically the "Little Hans" case. The theory is largely rejected nowadays both by theorists and clinical practitioners. It was critiqued effectively by Wolpe and Rachman (1960) over a half century ago, while working clinicians have long known that they were—to use an apt metaphor—beating a dead horse in fashioning effective treatment regimens based upon a suppositious process of "displacement." Considering the fact that snakes and spiders are universally high on the list of feared creatures, it seems odd that "displacement" as formulated in the canon takes on such a stereotyped form in phobic patterns. What Freud once insisted were the unconscious underpinnings of phobias has a surprisingly narrow band of displacement. Neonate monkeys, hardly a species prone to unconscious displacement—or, as McGinn (1999) has indicated, unconscious anything—have an innate fear of snakes, whereas snakes and spiders top the list of animal phobias in the human species. Peck's patient "Billie" was probably less prone to displacement than she was to a mammalian evolutionary heritage.

Peck's genuflections at the Freudian shrine are seldom nuanced. In *People of the Lie* he declares that his patient Charlene's amorous designs on him could be traced to her failing to overcome the "Oedipal dilemma," since "All healthy children experience sexual desire for the parent of the opposite sex," a Victorian tall-tale instilled in an ever diminishing number of students in psychoanalytic training programs, not to mention receiving little serious regard in the austere corridors of experimental psychology or within the ranks of humanities scholars who have awakened from their dogmatic slumbers (Cioffi, 1974; Wallace, 1983; Daly and Wilson, 1990; Degler, 1991; Erickson, 1993; Crews 1995; 1998; McGinn, 1999). The holdovers are the select few who cannot bring themselves to admit that the snows of yesteryear have long since melted away.

Peck's preference for the routine administrative procedures of psychiatric practice seem oddly out of place when it comes to the possessed: Before exorcisms "patients should sign not simple but elaborate authorization forms" (1983, p. 187). Evidently, Peck believes demonic influence over the possessed evaporates while signing consent forms, since his assumption is that it is the *patient* who signs the form, not the entity whose reputation for assuming executive control is advertised widely throughout Peck's two books. True, a demon that usurps executive control when consent forms are signed may be perversely sealing its own fate should the exorcism be successful. But the ploy still negates the possibility of the *patient* being the true signatory, thereby undermining any legal/administrative rationale for adopting the procedure.

* * *

There is something in Peck's religious stance that smacks of a certain one-sidedness verging on arrogance. His commentary on the unsuccessful exorcism of his patient Beccah Armitage is noteworthy for its failure to discuss the significance of an essential feature of her case: her Jewish heritage. This fact appears to be less significant to Dr. Peck than his musings on her depression, the "evilness" of her mother and husband, her family enmities, features of her "shadowy childhood" (2005, p. 134), and of course, her "possession." But it is also possible that he has overlooked an auspicious strand in his approach to the patient, whatever her true diagnosis. At one point, Peck admits there was much he never learned about Beccah, neé Rebecca Weintraub.

Peck's virtual recruitment of Beccah for Christianity is a not so invisible undercurrent in light of the Christian "deliverance" he administered to rescue her endangered soul. The effort is reminiscent of older scandalous scenarios, like the kidnapping of a six-year old Jewish boy, Edgardo Mortara, by Pope Pius IX, on the pretext that Edgardo became the spiritual property of the true faith because he was secretly baptized by a Catholic servant in his parents' household. This pontiff attributed the international furor drummed up by the case to troublemaking "freethinkers" in the thrall of Rousseau and Malthus. The latter secular pundit, in the opinion of Pius, was an agent of dark forces, having foisted birth control on an innocent laity (Will, 2000).

Peck lays the foundation for his not so subtle attempt at conversion by disclosing Beccah's former flirtation with the Episcopal faith, an interest fomented by her husband, and only temporarily thwarted by the turmoil generated over the proposed revision of its Book of Common Prayer. Later demands by the husband to convert to the Greek Orthodox faith resulted in the patient's capitulation to the denominational arm-twisting, although Beccah found the second retread "bizarre" (2005, p. 142). Despite what the reader may sense as Peck's undercover hard sell for Christianity, other indications of the patient's true identification as Jewish are unmistakable: "Beccah had only one pleasant memory of her childhood. It was of her father on the Sabbath, the only day he was home" (2005, p. 136). In what can only be described as trivial in the light of her husband's manipulation of the patient's faith, Peck announces that he "took Beccah's side against her husband in the matter of her clothing, and with me as her therapeutic ally she started fighting back" (2005, p. 142). Not even an aside from Peck about the possibility of the patient's tacit identification as a Jew as a component in her spiritual crisis.

Other blind spots over the problem of religious identification cry out for commentary. For example, Peck registers surprise that Beccah called Satan "Lucifer." Lucifer is the term for the devil in the Old Testament, but "Satan" is the term used in the New Testament (2005, p. 162). The substitution is hardly surprising at all if, unlike Peck, a psychiatrist were sensitive to signs of confusion or conflict over religious identification, like the patient's rejection of Christian symbology with verbal obscenities perhaps misattributed to Satanic malevolence. In line with this, Peck reports that Beccah had a "violent response" to Christian symbols (2005, p. 174). In all of this, Peck's slant is that there is something in Beccah that is not really her and which repudiates Christianity, when it is more likely that there is a natural part of her that rejects Christianity. A divided self need not embody two beings, but one in conflict over warring inclinations.

On a final note, Peck avers in *Glimpses of the Devil* that "psychiatrists are trained to doubt themselves" (2005, p.152). The virtue is seldom in sight in M. Scott Peck's writings. Its neglect may be the real demon he should have exorcised before he passed from us.

References

Atkinson, W. C. (1960). *A history of Spain and Portugal.* Middlesex, England: Penguin Books.

Barnett, R. (1965). Witchcraft, psychopathology, and hallucinations. *British Journal of Psychiatry,* 3, 439-445.

Belkin, L. (2005). Can you catch obsessive-compulsive disorder? *New York Times Magazine,* May 22, pp. 64-69.

Cioffi, F. (1974). Was Freud a liar? *The Listener,* February 7, 172-174.

Crabtree, A. (1985). *Multiple man: Explorations in possession and multiple personality.* London: Grafton Books.

Crews, F.C. (1995). *The memory wars: Freud's legacy in dispute.* New York: A New York Review Book.

Crews, F.C. (1998). *Unauthorized Freud: Doubters confront a legend.* New York: Viking Penguin.

Cuneo, M.W. (2001). *American exorcism: Expelling demons in the land of plenty.* New York: Doubleday.

Daly, M & Wilson, M. (1990). Is parent-offspring conflict sex linked? Freudian and Darwinian models. *Journal of Personality.* 58: 163-189.

Dawkins, R. (2006). *The god delusion.* New York: Houghton Mifflin Company.

Degler, C. N. (1991). Has sociobiology cracked the riddle of the incest taboo? *Contention,* 1: 109-130.

Elliott, J. H. (1990). *Imperial Spain.* London: Penguin Books.

Erickson, M. T. (1993). Rethinking Oedipus: An evolutionary perspective of incest avoidance. *American Journal of Psychiatry*, 150: 411-416.

Fielding-Ould (1919). *The wonders of the saints.* London: Watkins.

Fine, C. G. (1989). Treatment errors and iatrogenesis across therapeutic modalities in MPD allied dissociative disorders. *Dissociation*, II, 2, 77-82.

Fox, R. L. (1986). *Pagans and Christians*, New York: Harper & Row.

Friesen, J. G. (1991). *Uncovering the Mystery of MPD.* Nashville, Tennessee: Thomas Nelson

Gardner, M. (1988). *The New Age: Notes of a Fringe Watcher.* Buffalo, New York.

Giel, R., Gezahegn, Y. & van Lujik, J. N. (1968). Faith-healing and spirit possession in Ghion, Ethiopia. *Social Science and Medicine*, 2, 63-79.

Girden, E. (1962). A review of psychokinesis. *Psychological Bulletin*, 59, 353-388.

Goodman, F. D. (1981). *The exorcism of Anneliese Michel.* New York: Doubleday.

Goodman, F. D. (1988). *How about Demons? Exorcism and possession in the modern world.* Bloomington, Indiana: University of Indiana Press.

Goodman, W. K., Price, L. H., Rasmussen, S. A., Delgado, P. L., Heniger, G. R. & Charney, D. S. (1989. Efficacy of fluvoxamine in obsessive-compulsive disorder. A double-blind comparison with placebo. *Archives of General Psychiatry.* 46 (1), 36-41.

Hill, L. B. (1955). *Psychotherapeutic intervention in schizophrenia.* Chicago: University of Chicago Press.

Kluft, R. P. (1989). Iatrogenic creation of new alter personalities. *Dissociation*, II, 2, 83-91.

Lea, H. C. (1957). *Materials toward a history of witchcraft* (3 Vols.) New York: Thomas Yoseloff.

March, J. S. & Mulle, K. (1998) *OCD in children and adolescents: A cognitive-behavioral treatment manual.* New York: The Guilford Press.

Martin, M. (1977). *Hostage to the Devil.* New York, N.Y.: Bantam Books.

McGinn, C. (1999). Freud under analysis. *New York Review of Books*, 56, No. 17, 20-24.

McGue, Gottesman, I. I. and Rao, D. C. (1981). The transmission of schizophrenia under a multifactorial threshold model. *American Journal of Human Genetics*, 65, 280-286.

McGue, M. Gottesman, I. I. and Rao, D. C. (1985). Resolving genetic models for the transmission of schizophrenia. *Genetic Epidemiology*, 2, 99-110.

Monter, E. W. (1969). *European witchcraft.* New York: Wiley.

Mora, G. (1991). *Witches, devils, and doctors in the Renaissance: Johann weyer, De Praestigiis Daemomum.* Binghamton, New York: Medieval and Renaissance Studies.

Netanyahu, B. (1995). *The origins of the Inquisition in fifteenth century Spain*. New York: Random House.

Noll, R. (1990). *Bizarre diseases of the mind*. New York: Berkley Books.

Oesterreich, T. K. (1966). *Possession: Demoniacal and other*. New Hyde Paris, New York: University Books.

Peck, M. S. (1978). *The road less traveled: A new psychology of love, traditional values and spiritual growth*. New York: Simon & Shuster.

Peck, M. S. (1983). *People of the lie: The hope for healing human evil*. New York: Simon & Shuster.

Peck, M. S. (2005). *Glimpses of the devil: A psychiatrist's personal accounts of possession, exorcism, and redemption*. New York: Free Press.

Peters, E. (1980). *Inquisition*. Berkeley, California: University of California Press.

Rassmussen, S. A. & Eisen, J. L. (1990). Epidemiology of obsessive compulsive disorder. *Journal of Clinical Psychiatry*, 53 (Suppl.), 10-14.

Rassmussen, S. A. & Eisen, J. L. (1992). The epidemiology and differential diagnosis of obsessive compulsive disorder. *Journal of Clinical Psychiatry*, 55, 4-10.

Robbins, R. H. (1959). *The encyclopedia of witchcraft and demonology*. New York: Crown.

Rogo, D. S. (1982). *Miracles: A parascientific inquiry into wondrous phenomena*. New York: Dial Press.

Ross, C. A., Norton, G. R. and Fraser, G. A. (1989). Evidence against the iatrogenesis of multiple personality disorder. *Dissociation*, II, 2, 61-65.

Russell, J. B. (1986). *Mephistopheles: The devil in the modern world.* Ithaca, N.Y.: Cornell University Press.

Sperling, M. (1954). Reactive schizophrenia in children. *American Journal of Orthopsychiatry.* 24, 506-512.

Summers, M. (1956). *The history of witchcraft and demonology.* Secaucus, New Jersey: University Books.

Thomas, K. (1971). *Religion and the decline of magic.* New York: Scribner's.

Thurston, H. (1952). *The physician phenomena of mysticism.* Chicago: H. Regnery Company

Torem, M. (1989). Iatrogenic factors in the perpetuation of splitting and multiplicity. *Dissociation*, II, 2, 92-98.

Torrey, E. F. (1986). *Witchdoctors and psychiatrists: The common roots of psychotherapy and its future.* Northvale, New Jersey: Jason Aronson.

Vogel, C. (1935). *Begone Satan!* Collegeville, Minnesota: Celestine Kapsner, St. John's Abbey.

Walker, D. P. (1981). *Unclean spirits: Possession and exorcism in France and England in the late sixteenth and seventeenth centuries.* Philadelphia: University of Pennsylvania Press.

Walker, A. M. & Dickerman, E. H. (1991). "A woman under the influence": A case of alleged possession in sixteenth-century France. *Sixteenth Century Journal*, 22, 535-556.

Wallace, E. R. (1983). *Freud and anthropology: A history and reappraisal.* New York: International Universities Press.

White, A. D. (1955), *A history of warfare of science and theology.* New York: George Braziller.

Wills, G. (2000). *Papal sin: Structures of deceit.* New York: Doubleday.

Wolpe, J. and Rachman, S. (1960). Psychoanalytic evidence: A critique based on Freud's case of Little Hans. In *Critical Essays on Psychoanalysis.* S. Rachman (Ed.), Oxford, England: Pergamon Press.

Zilboorg, G.. (1935). *The medical man and the witch during the Renaissance.* Baltimore: The Johns Hopkins University Press.

Zilboorg, G. & Henry, A. (1941). *A history of medical psychology.* New York: W. W. Norton.

Wilkinson, T. (2007). *The Vatican's exorcists: Driving out the devil in the 21st century.* New York, N. Y.: Warner Books.

The Three Faces of Psychotherapy

Despite the assumptions of many of its practitioners, ignorance about psychotherapy is at very fundamental levels, and perhaps will be for the foreseeable future. One issue pertains to what it is; another to why we don't know more about it at this juncture in history. The two may be connected. What we know about psychotherapy at any given point in time might depend in great part about what we take it generally to be. An arena of discourse should be defined before one vets it: taxonomy before inquiry. A provisional classification might be something like the foregoing.

Psychotherapy is compositionally threefold. It encompasses *behavior-changing*, *meaning-providing*, and *status-affecting* aspects. Zilbergeld (1982) has distinguished between the first and second functions. I propose to add a third, the status-affecting function, expanding his dichotomy. The three categories seem broad enough to embrace all the reputed functions of the psychotherapist, and if there are others, we have the option of adding categories to include them.

The *behavior-changing* aspects of psychotherapy pertain to the most widely publicized functions of the trade: the amelioration of a specific problem or problems. The function is often, but not always, construed to be the removal of symptoms, or the facilitation of a behavioral or psychological goal through the application of certain techniques or interactions, however circumscribed or non-specific. For example, a patient (1) is referred to a psychotherapist because he or she has a drinking, marital, sexual, affective, or cognitive problem. However, the upset in question need not be as well defined as these conditions. A person may seek help for feelings he or she cannot quite define. In such cases, an individual has a presentiment that something is wrong—even terribly wrong—although difficult or impossible to pin down. The complaints sometimes may be indications of an diagnosis like depression or a condition which has a familiar place in diagnostic manuals like the DSM-V. Sometimes, however, the problem posed by a patient is another kind of condition, one that may or may not run a chronic course, or one a patient cannot quite encapsulate, as in an "existential neurosis." The latter is accompanied by an experience of anomie, alienation, or aimlessness (Frankl, 1963; 1967; Ledermann. 1972).

We might even imagine behavior-changing services geared toward patients who are uncertain as to whether they have a problem at all. They feel all right, to be sure, but have doubts about whether they ought to be more worried about themselves than they actually are. Far from being an unusual complaint, I suspect such self-doubts are more widespread in eras in which a drive toward conformity leaves few stones unturned in encouraging everyone to accommodate to a conventional or preordained mold. Be that as it may, professional help may be sought for all of the foregoing types of problems, with the aim of changing something. Hence, the behavior-changing aspect of the psychotherapist's role.

Eradicating the unwanted aspects of a clinical problem often involves replacing it with a more desirable pattern, as in a marital or substance-abuse problem. Accordingly, behavior-changing not only presumes remediation; facilitation of desirable replacement patterns is likewise a goal. It may also be an inevitable one. After all, the reduction of symptomatic behavior means substituting patterns that may have more to recommend them than simply the absence of what they replace. A pattern of sobriety in career drinkers is more than merely the termination of ongoing inebriation; the absence of acute symptoms like auditory hallucinations in a young adult is more than merely an end to mental destabilization, and the relief from post-partum depression in a young mother means more than merely the end of her dysphoria. Getting rid of the unwanted automatically guarantees a desideratum, although the latter is not necessarily an additional step to be contemplated in a multi-dimensional treatment process.

"Behavior-change" as herein discussed is not restricted to overt behavioral patterns exclusively. Such factors as thoughts, feelings, wishes, desires, intentions, a subclass of which has perhaps been mischaracterized as "private events" by psychologists (Skinner, 1945; Ryle, 1949;) are also included within this realm of consideration.

A narrower definition of the term "behavior" may be at the bottom of some misinterpretations of the therapeutic compass of practitioners in the cognitive-behavioral or radical behavioristic tradition by their psychodynamic colleagues. Practitioners of the former traditions use the term "behavior" in a wider way than the one attributed to them by their critics. It is used to cover any dependent variable, including those typically designated as "mental," or "private" by those of psychodynamic or psychoanalytic persuasion. Accordingly, as I understand its applications, the behavioral approach is one its advocates insist may be adapted for any human problem, not merely the distress of individuals who don't know what to do with fidgety hands.

As we define the behavior-changing services of psychotherapy, they include what Wolff (1971) has distinguished as its therapeutic and developmental functions. In this author's dichotomy, the former are fairly circumscribed modalities, described by psychoanalysts like Winnicott (1963) and Guntrip (1961; 1968) as the "doing to" techniques of psychotherapy. The latter, or the "being with" functions of the profession cover a more complex level of therapist-patient interaction, the earmark of which are caring, acceptance, empathic understanding, and involvement with the total person.

I do not wish to obscure the differences between the two aforementioned functions of behavior-changing service; yet behavior-changing they indisputably are, as intangible as the "being-with" function may prove to be. We lump them together uncontroversially as elements in the treatment process assumed to be causally related to outcome—when this transpires. There is no guarantee that any component in such a process is causally efficacious, and the insistence that it is in the absence of proof has to be one of the most glaring wish-fulfillments of a professional elite discharging a mandate it assumes works precisely as advertized (Zilbergeld, 1983; Myers, 2002; Arkowitz & Lilienfeld, 2008).

The distinction between the "doing to" and "being with" functions of behavior-changing services seems apt when we consider that while one may be teachable as a part of a training curriculum, the other seems to be a knack of a therapist's personality, deriving from his or her natural talents as a caring human being. If the "being with" function is teachable at all—we take no position on this possibility one way or the other—the training in question would probably be exceedingly more complex and prolonged than that requisite for administering any specialized technique. The latter can be appropriated in medical or graduate schools or workshops, but "being with" someone can currently only be facetiously characterized as the upshot of curricular coursework.

On the other hand, it is possible that being a decent human being won't guarantee that a practitioner is fully capable of discharging either "doing to" or "being with" aspects of psychotherapy, although certain caveats are in order here. There are over 500 research studies confirming the finding that caring human beings without a history of professional training can do as well treating patients as a cadre of experienced psychotherapists with degrees after their names (Dawes, 2008). The finding is undoubtedly a chastening (if not traumatic) one for seasoned professionals, although its implications may be several. Some may consider it to dampen claims of a special expertise on the part of a professional class. Others may feel it testifies to surprising or unforeseen abilities in the untrained. Another might be what the finding tells us about the inherent characteristics of phenomena responding equally well to the ministrations of quite different levels of treatment constituency.

Other possibilities exist. A person can be incandescent with patient-friendly virtue, yet bomb out as a treatment specialist in the consulting room. But I suspect that without the "being with" knack a practitioner is at a serious disadvantage as a psychotherapist with certain populations of patients. On yet another level, it may be a mistake to assume that the "being with" function is the only one making psychotherapy effective, although I daresay there are those who believe this. Accordingly, there may be some who have perpetuated a mythology about treatment: that its positive outcome in every case is a non-specific factor deriving from the "being with" function. However, just as the "how to" function avails little with certain patient populations when the therapist is short on "being with" capabilities, so too might the "being with" component come to naught in relation to the problems of other clinical populations. There are still "how to" techniques research indicates are superior to "being with" abilities in bringing about positive therapeutic outcome. Among these might be classified those developed for the treatment of phobias, types of sexual dysfunction, and obsessive-compulsive disorder. Treatment programmed for specific clinical populations and administered in future by a sophisticated robot might, from the standpoint of actual amelioration of symptoms, be superior to a live therapist palpitating with holistic wisdom, albeit clueless about the advantage of such techniques as exposure, flooding, or response prevention in the treatment of obsessive-compulsive disorder. So it may be a mistake to insist that the essential variable in any form of therapy is the personality of the therapist. There is in all likelihood no common denominator, personality or otherwise, that can be identified as a common thread in the successful treatment of troubled persons. Those of us who believe otherwise should be wary of fashioning mythologies about treatment that will not survive a litmus test of efficacy across such a diverse range of problems remanded to the care of a professional cadre.

The mythology is already flourishing in the media, where all manner of gratuitous assumptions about psychotherapy seem to enliven presentations of the subject. Moreover, it is hardly compelling to insist that the personality of the therapist is the crucial determinant of efficacy when the characteristics of this factor are routinely left unspecified. Moreover, therapists run a gamut of personality styles that are quite striking. There have been practitioners with a soft-edge personality, like Carl Rogers and Rollo May, therapists with a hard-edge, like Albert Ellis or Fritz Perls, therapists who emphasize the structured approach, like Joseph Wolpe or Ivor Lovaas, and those who radiate nurturance, like Frieda Fromm-Reichman, There are combative therapists like John Rosen, those dedicated to body work, like Wilhelm Reich and Alexander Lowen, those who prize freedom of choice and contractual obligations like Thomas Szasz, low-profilers like Charles Brenner, and those who are in the tradition of left-wing chic, like R. D. Laing. Some emphasize cognitions, some unconscious motives, some biological factors, some group or family emphases, some contingencies of reinforcement, some nutrition, some synchronicity, mysticism, or spirituality; some the past, including former lives, others the future, and some a smorgasbord of several of these. If practitioners who promote these sundry forms of treatment share anything in common, it is apparently the unyielding belief that their approach is not only beneficial, it is more so than any other one. Unfortunately, research does not seem to back up their claims to sovereignty over treatment results. Furthermore, those offering therapeutic services comprise a panoply of temperaments bewilderingly diverse for an enterprise some of whose spokespersons insist require indispensible characteristics of personality style. If "personality" style is critical for the practice, evidently any will do, a lesson to be drawn from but a brief glance at the passing parade (3).

Psychotherapists also perform "status-affecting" services, among which are overt or covert diagnostic, classificatory, acts or assessments, the most popular of which are the diagnoses listed in manuals like DSM-V. Is the patient paranoid, or is his hostility fleeting, more situational? Is this parent a child-abuser? Is he or she capable of bonding properly with children? Is a pattern a neurological one presenting as a psychological one purely, or a psychological one with quasi-neurological signs? Is this youngster learning-disabled?

Status-affecting services may, of course, have implications for a chosen direction of positive behavior-change, but not always. Alzheimer's Disease, Tay-Sachs Disease, or Huntington's Chorea, may prompt decisions about future clinical care without a corresponding hope of symptom amelioration. On the other hand, we feel that removing a sexually abusive parent from the home situation has behavior-changing implications for both victim and victimizer.

"Meaning-imparting" services represent yet a third aspect of psychotherapy. Yet it is an elusive one, because "meaning" can be defined in many ways. What psychotherapy "means" to a patient may be far from what it "means" to his or her therapist. And what "Meaning" (with a capital "M") means to an existential therapist is yet another story (Sartre, 1957; 2007; Deurzen, 2002). Viktor Frankl (1959), for example, developed a system of psychotherapy called Logotherapy, the aim of which is to restore or originate "Meaning" in a patient's life. Frankl's system was inspired by his experiences as a concentration camp victim during World war II. In his system, "Meaning" is construed as a sense of personal fulfillment created by engaging life in an action-oriented, problem-solving way. The formulation is close in spirit to the goal of existential psychotherapy as formulated by Sartre (1957; 2007). For this existentialist thinker, a similar idea of "Meaning" refers to action patterns we undertake in a world which defines our "Being." For Sartre, the other side of action-oriented decision making is "Nothingness" or "Non-Being," ideas not identifiable with death, but the plight of individuals who have fundamental problems of action and decision-making serving to define them.

When I speak of the meaning-imparting function of psychotherapy, I refer to a sense of the term "meaning" in a somewhat broader way than does the existential psychotherapist. I wish to focus on it as a dimension of life—psychotherapy being another aspect of a life—pertaining to such admittedly nebulous things as the significance of the therapeutic encounter independent of behavior-change. In this sense of "meaning," I use the term to refer to a patient's perceived or experiential world that can be separated, as it were, from his or her decision-making, how symptomatic patterns are changed or affected, or how status-affecting services impact on individuals receiving services. "Meaning" as herewith understood, is what is left over after behavior-changing or status-affecting components of the therapeutic process are subtracted out.

It is difficult to dwell on the meaning-imparting function of psychotherapy without sounding trendy. Perhaps this is because we associate such terminology with the work of a generation of treatment practitioners many of us feel have defaulted on the promise to develop demonstrably effective behavior change modalities, or because they confuse change with the trappings of counter-culture sensibility, like those reminiscent of the sixties. Indeed, many of us partial to more hard-nosed traditions of clinical theory and practice feel that Third Force Psychology—at least in many of its forms—is a hodge-podge of wacky techniques administered by dotty gurus to flakey disciples. Some of us feel that so-called Humanistic Psychology fairly bulges with self-styled prophets, diets, communes, holistic health, oriental philosophies like Zen, weekends at mountain retreats, curious forms of body massage, marathon sessions at which hundreds take the "training" before taking "responsibility," and "Temple Dances" choreographed by the avatars of insular societies touting them as requisite disciplines for attaining higher levels of consciousness. Whatever personal associations are mustered over the term "meaning," we should not construe the latter to be a particular route to treatment, goal- seeking or finding, fulfillment, or self-actualization, but as something cutting across all types of treatment approach. In short, something big! Let me illustrate what I mean through several examples.

Those of us who in the profession who have worked extensively with patients whose problems run a chronic course, or those who have been the recipients of state and federal entitlement programs like Medicaid, Medicare or Social Security Disability, are familiar with their remaining in treatment long after status and immediate behavior-change have ceased to be compelling issues. In many, (if not a majority) of such cases, longer-term treatment is felt to be justified if only to prevent further regression or to monitor patients for premonitory signs of such over an indefinite period of time. In this respect, the reason for the protracted time-frame for treatment is unrelated to the Freudian claim that considers analysis to be "interminable" (Freud, 1937). It is related to a deeper, reality that a patient's world—his or her perceived and experienced one—is different in therapy than it would be without it. However, this understanding should not be misconstrued; in a trivial sense to have the benefit of a therapeutic encounter is to frame a life of "meaning" different than one experienced without it. The same might be said for *any* experience one might have—patient or otherwise, treatment context or otherwise. For the patient, psychotherapy structures his or her life in a way utterly different from the one led without it. And I mean by "different" fundamentally different, and in ways that do not boil down to achieving this or that insight, facet of behavior-change, or a change with bells and whistles. For such patients, psychotherapy is not the glue to "fix" a life; it is essentially another form of life. Moreover, as long as treatment practitioners themselves are in the grip of a picture of psychotherapy as nothing more than a vehicle to rectify problematic behavior, it may escape notice altogether that it functions often (although not invariably) as a way of life itself coloring, as it were, a patient's world experience. This is especially true for patients in psychotherapy over extended periods of time. Behavior-changing capabilities aside, psychotherapy is for many an invisible package of "meanings"—cognitions, if you will—about the nature of the world and one's place in it.

It is not a stretch to conjecture that psychoanalysis, particularly in the heyday of its popularity in Europe and America, functioned as much as a way of life for its patients and analysts as it did as a vehicle for behavior change. Just like a civilization within a larger society, it had its shamans and high priests who ruled on matters of holy writ and interpretation, permissible boundaries of technique and procedure, rites of passage, and the like. It had its coterie of zealots who received the mantle of the true faith, guarding it against heretics, reformers, and revisionists, and amassed a retinue of idolators and groupies (always more heavily represented in the humanities, arts, philosophy, and the entertainment business than the hard-nosed sciences), and, above all, its vocabulary of discourse.

Manifestly, psychoanalysis involves a shared world of meaning for its followers—including patients, practitioners, and historians of the subject. Their perceived world might have as its cornerstone the tenets of Freud's theory, classical or revised, although the ideological underpinnings of its belief system constitute but a small part of what may be designated as its "meaning" in the sense herein discussed. The "meaning" of which we speak patterns a life, conferring upon it a special kind of significance. The chronic patient who attends group psychotherapy meetings each week for an extended period of time may, in so doing, alter a stream of ongoing experience the importance of which cannot be gainsaid. "Meaning" here is independent of specific and shifting levels of anxiety or destabilization, decision-making or the absence of it, the truth or falsity of some theory, or the efficacy of particular treatment regimens. What overrides all these considerations is the "meaning" of the therapeutic experience itself against the backdrop of what a personal world would be without it.

Another distinguishing feature of the "meaning" we refer to may be contrasted with parochial senses of the term within given treatment approaches. In systems like Frankl's Logotherapy, the relevant sense of the concept of meaning—called Nöoetic Meaning—is the developmental aftermath or goal of the therapeutic process. In other words, existential psychotherapy creates or restores Meaning as a desirable product of treatment. In this respect, it is an experience of fulfillment Frankl's approach attempts to cultivate. In the sense of meaning about which I speak, it is already provided within the treatment experience itself, and independently of whether circumscribed treatment goals are or are not realized. In this sense of "meaning," the path *is* the goal, not merely a chosen route to it. In other words, the vehicle is the fulfillment—although, indeed, such terms as "goal" and "fulfillment" can be misleading, suggesting as they do an aura of impending behavior change in the flatfooted sense.

Other examples might be helpful here. On a level of the spiritual or religious life, we may contrast two views of church attendance that are roughly the analogues of contrasting senses of "meaning" we have been discussing. On the one hand, we might say that religiosity is fostered or cultivated by church attendance if we construe the latter to be a chosen vehicle for the realization of higher spiritual goals, like salvation. On the other hand, we might say that the meaning of religion on another level of consideration is in part the actual church attendance itself, not its import for eschatological ends, rapturous or otherwise. On this view, the spiritual life is a package deal, of which church attendance is an integral part. In this sense of spiritual meaning, the scientific question originally posed by Francis Galton, "What empirical evidence is there for the efficacy of prayer?" might be regarded as a senseless one (not to unbelievers, of course!). It's not what church attendance or prayer guarantees in the after-life that justifies it, but the meaning imparted to the spiritual life such participation ensures. In an important sense, you cannot ungum a world of religious meaning from its constituent elements like church attendance or prayer, anymore than you can have a triangle without one of its three sides. The meaning created by the structure of a given experience has it own grammar or interrelationship of parts, arranged or governed by an implicit set of rules.

The Catholic parishioner who objects to the de-Latinization of the mass may be considered to be "old-fashioned," "bound by tradition," or some such dismissive judgment. On the other hand, to be thus accused of preferring religious form over substance is, from the subjective perspective of the parishioner in question, the dismantling of a valued aspect of one's religious world of meaning, irrespective of the pronouncements of refashioned dogma or newer ecclesiastical tradition. In this respect, the world of meaning adumbrated by dogma is simply one that differs from the one in which the Latin mass is a cherished component.

There is a rough analogy between the argument that psychotherapy should be judged (or justified) solely by its behavior-changing capabilities, and the proper aim of patterns in other walks of life. Take the example of the performing artist. It is often taken as axiomatic that the *raison d'etre* of rehearsal is the final stage performance before a public. However, our economy is not one that creates opportunities for the pool of available talent. Accordingly, the life of the performing artist—at least as far as some of the most significant aspects of the creative process is concerned—*is* the life he or she leads in rehearsal rooms or workshops. Often these endeavors are undertaken with an eye toward public performance—but not always. Not every event of the creative type derives its value as a dry-run for public exposure. There are many instances in which there is no anticipation of a public staging to justify performing. Moreover, there are countless cases in the arts in which the most significant events realized are those precisely envisioned without an audience. The contrast between a gig a musician routinely gets paid for and the caliber of the music he produces at a private jamming session is more marked for the progressive jazz musician than it is for other categories of performing artists like dancers. In fact, many such musicians regard the public gig (in which the paid performer has to accommodate to the tastes of invited guests at weddings, roasts, and other ceremonial occasions) as one the only redeeming feature of which is the remuneration. Creatively speaking, the private jamming session allows for the improvisation of musical forms out of place in such settings as weddings and bar-mitzvahs. The attitude of the contemporary musician to what he does for an audience, paid gig, or rock concerts teeming with teen agers showered with laser beams, is often one of veiled contempt.

In the sphere of psychotherapy, the meaning-imparting aspect of the enterprise is, for better or worse, that dimension of it complicating efforts to focus exclusively on behavior-change from a scientific point of view. Historically, investigations of therapeutic outcome are conducted by technocrats trained in the use of research methodology. When we hear, as we do from time to time, that psychotherapy is an "art" not a "science," the technocrats wince. Perhaps they should—but only if their view of the enterprise is appropriated. Given the prevalence of the world-view they seek to deconstuct, they feel such a science is thwarted more often than not.

The hunch that psychotherapy is more art than science is an intriguing one. It appears to be the expression of sentiment that would be view as alarming were it extended to "treatment" in unrelated venues. It is hardly comforting to patients with brain tumors, diabetes, or epilepsy to remind them that medicine is, after all, more "art" than "science." And at the risk of outraging sensibilities in that invisible empire of power, the Humanities, let me insist that there are areas of treatment where art is not only inappropriate, but to be avoided at all costs, as when it comes to the proper diagnosis of neurodegenerative disease, the most advisable surgical procedure, or the preferred regimen of medication to allay a downward course of systemic illness.

Endnotes

[1]   There is a widespread preference for the term "client" in contrast to "patient" among some professional constituencies, presumably reflecting the wish to avoid the pitfalls of the so-called "medical model" of psychopathology. Whatever the merits of the proposal, it should be noted that "client" has an ambiguity not shared by "patient." For example, an industrial psychologist evaluating prospective employees for a corporation may harbor reservations about which "client" he represents. On the other hand, a military psychiatrist evaluating the fitness of servicemen and women for combat after they presented with symptoms of acute stress disorder would have little doubt about identifying who the "patient" is—whatever misgivings may be harbored about who the "client" is.

[2]   A conceptual issue thus arises about the character of the relationship between remediation and replacement strategies. In line with this, is the removal of an undesirable pattern *conceptually* independent of the one installed as a consequence of this change, so that the therapeutic maneuver cannot be said to necessitate two distinct enterprises? Is the removal of the offending symptomatic pattern a guarantee of achieving all implicit psychotherapeutic goals? Or does the answer hinge on the nature of the particular problem under scrutiny? Under what conditions do we need to facilitate a second profile after ameliorating the target problem? Example: a depressed person is successfully treated in a course of psychotherapy. Should the therapist in question pose a question about a second stage of treatment focused on the development of replacement behaviors, should we elect to say: (a) this proves that the treatment of this case of depression involves separate therapeutic goals and strategies, or (b) the case represents an *incomplete* resolution of a unitary problem of depression?

[3]   Years ago, that formidable trouper, Sophie Tucker, admonished a television audience that she didn't care what church her viewers went to, as long as they went to church. What wisdom would old Sophie have imparted to candidates for careers in psychotherapy had she been sidetracked into the profession? That she wouldn't care what personalities they had—just so long as they had one?

References

American Psychiatric Association (2013). *Diagnostic and statistical manual of mental disorders, fifth edition.* Washington, D.C.: American Psychiatric Association.

Arkowitz, H., and Lilienfeld, S. O. (2008) Psychotherapy on Trial. In Lilienfeld, S. O., Ruscio, J., and Lynn, S. J. (Eds.) *Navigating the Mindfield: A Guide to Separating Science from Pseudoscience in Mental Health.* Amherst, N.Y.: Prometheus Books, pp. 103-110.

Dawes, R. M. (2008). Psychotherapy: The Myth of Expertise. In Lilienfeld, S. O., Ruscio, J., and Lynn, S. J. (Eds.) *Navigating the Mindfield: A Guide to Separating Science from Pseudoscience in Mental Health.* Amherst, N.Y.: Prometheus Books, pp. 311-344.

Deurzen, E. van. (2002). *Existential Counseling and Psychotherapy In Practice.* London: sage Publications.

Frankl, V. E. (1959). *Man's Search for Meaning: An Introduction to Logotherapy.* New York: Beacon Press.

Frankl, V. E. (1967). *Psychotherapy and Existentialism: Selected papers on Logotherapy.* New York: Simon & Shuster.

Freud, S. (1937). Analysis Terminable and Interminable. *The International Journal of Psychoanalysis, 18,* 373-405.

Guntrip, H. (1961). *Personality, Structure, and Human Interaction.* London: Hogarth Press.

Guntrip, H. (1968). *Schizoid Phenomena, Object Relations and the Self.* London: Hogarth Press.

Ledermann, E. K. (1972). *Existential Neurosis*. London: Butterworths.

Myers, D. (2002). *Intuition: Its Powers and Perils*. New Haven, CT: Yale University Press.

Ryle, G. (1949). *The concept of mind*. New York: Barnes &Noble.

Sartre, J. P. (1957). *Existentialsm and Humanism*. New York: Philosophical Library.

Sartre, J. P (2007). *Existentialism Is A Humanism*. New Haven: Yale University Press.

Skinner, B. F. (1945) The operational analysis of psychological terms. *Psychological Review*, 52, 270-294.

Winnicott, D. W. (1963). Psychiatric disorder in terms of infantile maturational processes. In *The Maturational Processes and the Facilitating Environment*. London: Hogarth Press.

Wolff, H. H. (1971). The therapeutic and developmental functions of psychotherapy. *British Journal of Medical Psychology*, *44*, 117-130.

Zilbergeld, B. (1983). *The shrinking of America: Myths of psychological change*. Boston: Little Brown & Company

B. F. Skinner on Private Events

J. L. Austin once remarked that the current state of philosophy is like the surface of the sun: a pretty fair mess. United efforts by philosophers to resolve the other minds problem (Ayer, 1946; Wisdom, 1956: Thomson, 1951; Sellars, 1953; Putnam, 1957; Austin, 1961; Aune, 1961; Kirby, 1966), or its offshoots, like the private language problem (Wittgenstein, 1958), have likewise kept pace with the spirit of disorder. They sometimes appear to be on the verge of abandoning interest in the issue altogether, in the hopes of tackling problems distinguished by at least an occasional sense of achievement. It is surprising in the light of their frustrations that radical behaviorists like Skinner believe they can resolve the problem by ingenious—if questionable—adjustments in their wider account of how variables come to control behavior. They appear to believe that privacy can be packaged in ways uniquely suited to relieving the subject of any tendency to become as worrisome for them as it is for philosophers. Accordingly, a question arises over whether Skinner's analysis of private events illuminates something new or insightful in speculation on the subject. In the opinion of the present author, the truth is quite the opposite: the radical behavioristic approach to private events enshrouds the topic in paradox and counterintuitive implications.

Any discussion of Skinner's contribution to our understanding of private events—not to mention his psychological approach in general—tends to run up against a disconcerting road block. While there may be ambiguity about what he explicitly believed about the topics he discussed, confusion is often attributed to those outside the fold. If one were to poll his sympathizers in psychology about what they felt was a distinguishing feature of his contribution to psychology, an answer might be its misunderstanding by critics. The conviction among his followers that his thought has been misconstrued regularly is everywhere in evidence. For example, in a commemorative issue on Skinner in the November, 1992 issue of *American Psychologist*, a majority of the contributors cite routine misinterpretations of the psychologist's writings. Among the culprits referenced were nativists like Chomsky (Palmer and Donahoe, 1992), cognitivists like Mahoney (Rakos, 1992; Todd & Morris, 1992), literary critics like Krutch, Koestler, Jessup, and Hacker (Dinsmoor, 1992), and philosophers like Dennett (Baum & Heath, 1992) Taylor and Dretske (Rachlin, 1992), and Scriven and Malcolm. Todd and Morris (1992) in the same issue of the magazine draw attention to what they have called a tradition of "academic folklore" ostensibly manifesting a "steady misrepresentation" of Skinner's views. As if to document what appears to be a contrarian tradition, two loyalists referred to the article by Skinner in an issue of *Brain and Behavior Sciences* in which he was finally driven to lament: "I am sorry if so many of my replies must consist of a series of corrections, but nothing else seems to serve" (Todd & Morris, 1992, p. 1441).

Few contributors in the same issue of *American Psychologist* considered the possibility that a problem arises from ambiguities in the published writings of Skinner himself. There are, however, notable exceptions to this. Lee (1992) argued that Skinner's concept of behavior is problematic, and Glenn, Ellis, & Greenspoon (1992) averred that Skinner's definition of an operant as a class of responses fails to distinguish it relative to other salient categories. Despite these exceptions, the response to criticisms of Skinner on the part of those sympathetic to his point of view has been stalwart. It has also over time exhibited signs of parochialism. Day has referenced what he calls a "messianic commitment" to radical behaviorism on the part of its proponents (Day, 1980, p. 169). The complacency does a disservice to the issues Skinner addressed. Those are momentous ones, and not the kind a thinker however celebrated should be expected to resolve—even during the course of a lifetime. It is imperative, therefore, that inquiry into them remain unencumbered by a response-set wedded to the conviction that disagreeing with Skinner necessarily involves misunderstanding him. In the spirit of the kind of debate he himself would have endorsed, the following is intended as a tentative contribution to the rubric of private events in a science of behavior.

Radical Behaviorism and Private Events

Skinner has been forthright in his insistence that a scientific account of private events is the "heart of behaviorism" (Skinner, 1974, p.212). The characterization was meant to emphasize the focus as not only a legitimate area of inquiry, but an enterprise distinguishing radical behaviorism from other behavioristic approaches. The latter presumably have either rejected the study of private events altogether, or posit intervening variables eschewed by Skinner as either redundant way-stations or mentalistic fictions. There is little reason to suppose, however, that the relatively exclusive focus on public events would shift appreciably under radical behaviorism or behavior analysis, even if the interest in private events within its ranks were to undergo an unparalleled surge of activity. What form this might take is difficult to envision. Radical behaviorists, despite their commitment to the analysis of events under the skin, have in the past dealt with the subject in largely ceremonial ways, or as place-holders in broader discussions about the proper purview of scientific scrutiny. Despite their commitment to the study of private events, ostensibly dictated by a philosophy of science, there has been little indication of notable contributions to the subject on their part. It is as though those who proclaim no fear of water are reluctant to get their feet wet.

Causal Efficacy

It might be conjectured Skinner's analysis takes back with the left hand what it grants with the right. On one level, it seeks to compensate for the neglect of private events in "methodological behaviorism" (Skinner, 1945; Moore, 2001) by reestablishing the rightful place of the topic in a complete scientific formulation. Yet Skinner's *contretemps* is the relegation of private events to a limbo of causal inefficacy as the mere by-products of behavior (Martin, 1978; Schnaitter, 1978). The move seems to clash dramatically with the spirit of philosophical largesse enshrined in the Skinnerian conviction that events under the skin are no different metaphysically from public behaviors. If cut from the same ontological cloth, wherefore the causal disenfranchisement? In this connection, Skinner has declared that private events are no more than links in a causal chain—and ordinarily, not even that. As an example, he insists that when one man strikes another due to anger, the latter is still left unexplained. Going on, he states that once relevant causal variables are identified the feeling of anger is "much less important by way of explanation" (Skinner, 1953, p. 279).

Despite the fact that the foregoing remarks seem to reflect a philosophical allegiance to a form of epiphenomenalism (Creel, 1980)—usually identified as the doctrine that "mental" events have no efficacy in causal chains—its ambiguity is evident. We cannot be sure whether "the feeling of anger" is causally disenfranchised by Skinner because it is a sheer "mentalism" defying a scientific approach as a presumed event in a mysterious, hence elusive medium, *or*, as a covert physical response, it lacks causal status because the independent variables of which it is a function remain to be explained. The two slants are quite different ones. The former is sometimes suggested by Skinner's allusions to the mentalistic trappings into which talk of private events is conventionally cast, as in his remark: "One is still free, of course, to assume that there are events of a nonphysical nature accessible to the experiencing organism and therefore wholly private" (Skinner, 1953, pp. 279-280).

Infinite Regress

The second interpretation, that causality is lacking because independent variables of which the covert physical event is a function have not been explicated, is an argument that would appear to establish a set of double standards for covert and overt behaviors. If the covert event does not enjoy parity of causal status with external independent variables because its determining conditions have not been specified, the same can be said for any independent variable, public or private. Thus, a physical blow to the head cannot explain the covert sensation of pain in the victim because the independent variables that in turn control the blow have not been analyzed (i.e., supplied with a functional analysis). Skinner's argument actually courts a problem of the infinite regress of causal relations, in which no independent variable or set of them counts as explanatory because it too is a function of some prior set of conditions. Thus, if Smith's environment, not Smith, is responsible for his creative achievements, what is responsible for the environment that created the environment that created Smith's achievement? Likewise, if Smith's private sensations (even as covert physical events) are causally disenfranchised, so is the environment construed as puppet master of his private life!

Skinner's colloquies on the illusion of "freedom" in other of his writings (Skinner, 1971) may also court the same difficulty. If Smith cannot be said to be "free" or to personally achieve anything because his actions are environmentally determined, then neither are environments causally responsible for anything, since they too cannot be explained without recourse to the preexisting independent variables of which they too are a function. Ironically, Skinner himself seems to have appreciated the point. Yet he demurred from denying that an infinite regress penalizes physical causation. Mentalistic explanations, he avers, "block further inquiry," and that their "force" has declined as understanding the role of the environment steadily replaces them (Skinner, 1974, p.210).

Skinner assumes that the rationale for stopping an infinite regress is the point at which "effective action" can be taken—although he does not explain why the idea of "explanatory force" is necessarily linked to effective action. The latter, on its face, would appear to be an advantage in any approach aimed at controlling, predicting, or modifying behavior, although it is not exactly clear why this capacity should be a *criterion* of explanatory power. Even so, it remains a mystery why Skinner should assume that mentalistic explanations lack the capacity to promote effective action. For example, a Cartesian dualist who witnesses a colleague having an accident occasions his rushing to the victim's side in order to provide assistance. His action is focused on relieving his friend's pain, although his philosophical persuasion has him believing the friend is in a state of mental anguish (as evidenced by his groans), and is, in fact, a human being with a purely and inseparably mental and physical side to his nature. The dualist may harbor a philosophically questionable account of the mind-body quandary, but how does such a philosophy prevent effective action in any sense endorsed by Skinner? Why would a radical behaviorist have an edge on effective action in the context under discussion? Is there some cryptic sense of "effective action" coming into play in behavior analysis noticeably lacking in mentalistic accounts of behavior?

In a similar vein, Skinner has declared throughout his writings that inner events construed as mentalistic cannot be affected (i.e., controlled) directly: "No one has ever directly modified any of the *mental* activities or traits...There is no way in which one can make contact with them" (Skinner, 1974, p. 208). Among traits that cannot presumably be modified directly Skinner lists, *inter alia*, "ideas" and "beliefs." Anyone other than a radical behaviorist might find the claim that ideas and beliefs cannot be modified directly counterintuitive, if only for the reason that he or she believes they are so modified all the time. If they weren't, it is thought, experience could teach us nothing, while education, even in the broad sense of the term, would be a waste of time.

However, there may be another reason for Skinner's claim. It is possible that ideas and beliefs, on the mentalistic assumption they are occurrences in an immaterial medium, cannot because of this be directly modified, because we cannot, as it were, "get our hands" on such elusive stuff. It is as though the challenge were akin to trying to tangle with a ghost. The problem is: if an immaterialistic medium is a scientific fiction, what is the allegedly "scientific" basis for assuming beliefs and ideas couldn't be modified if it weren't?

Canonical Exposition

Unquestionably, the analysis of private events within the behavior-analytic tradition held a special meaning for Skinner. His most detailed discussion of the subject can be found in his essay *On the Operational*

Analysis of Psychological Terms (1945). Subsequent, although shorter expositions may be found in chapter seventeen of *Science and Human Behavior* (1953), *Verbal Behavior* (1957), *Contingencies of Reinforcement* (1969), *Beyond Freedom and Dignity* (1971), and *About Behaviorism* (1974). Briefly, Skinner's treatment of the problem confronts the issue of how we come to discriminate among events occurring under the skin, since we must learn such an achievement, and the resultant personal knowledge depends upon how we are "reinforced" by the verbal community for describing our private lives accurately. However, according to Skinner external reinforcement cannot be made contingent on the property of privacy. Reliance by others on observable or public events (presumably the correlates of our internal states) is the route by which they are able to reinforce our accurate self-descriptions. While Skinner outlines several distinguishable ways private events may come to control behavior, the thrust of his analysis is that the verbal community relies on the public accompaniments of private states to reinforce what he terms "tacts," or descriptive statements about them (Skinner, 1957). For example, I am reinforced for saying *I am in pain* when the verbal community notices I wince or grab my jaw while experiencing a toothache.

In *Verbal Behavior*, Skinner distinguishes between *tacts* and *mands*. The former are verbal responses evoked by external events or certain descriptive properties of them, whereas the latter are operants which correspond to verbal responses reinforced by a characteristic consequence when the speaker is in a state of deprivation or under aversive control. There is nothing about the distinction that prohibits given verbal operants sharing characteristics of both types of response. For example, *I am in pain* is a tact under the control of a private event, although it is routinely emitted in contexts in which the speaker is manding reinforcement from an internally aversive state of affairs. Consequently, there would appear to be a place in the verbal repertoire for *tands* and *macts*, since many of us who mand reinforcement need not be completely *tact*less!

Skinner's writings about privacy have two principal emphases: (1) how radical behaviorism, unlike other philosophies of science, provides for the study of private events, and (2) how his treatment of privacy addresses itself to and resolves certain paradoxes in the acquisition of self-descriptive verbal repertoires. The second of these emphases is the more intriguing one. The first seems to have been repeated so often, it probably represents little more than a reminder to those who got the point decades ago.

Radical Behaviorism and Philosophy

There are, generally speaking, several areas of Skinner's treatment of private events which can be contrasted with positions in contemporary philosophy. One of these concerns what mental predicates can be properly construed as actually referring to private events or events under the skin. Another area involves the analysis of concepts thus localized. Radical behaviorists on occasion suggest that Skinner's approach is (1) confused with older forms of behaviorism denying that private events are a proper subject matter for psychology; (2) confused with logical positivism, which in its earlier Carnapian form provided for the translation of mentalistic concepts into physicalistic reduction sentences (Carnap, 1932/1933; 1953); (3) confused with logical behaviorism which declares that references to seemingly private events are in reality references to behavioral dispositions of a predominantly public kind; (4) confused as to the causal role of private events in public behavior; and (5) similar to Wittgenstein's analysis of privacy.

Wittgenstein and Skinner

With respect to (5), Day (1959) and Costall (1980) have drawn attention to the alleged affinities between Wittgenstein and Skinner. However, the disparities are also noteworthy, and speak to fundamental differences between the views of both men. The similarity of viewpoint has been stressed because both were skeptical about the possibility of first-person knowledge of private events like sensations. But Wittgenstein's skepticism sprang from his view that that the concept of "knowledge"—entailing as it does the possibility of being wrong—was not applicable to one's experiencing sensations like pains. In the case of my sensations, claiming that I *know* I am in pain is tantamount to forcing the verb to "go on holiday" from its accustomed usage in utterly different linguistic contexts, since the grammar of first-person sensation statements is different than it is for statements about public objects.

Skinner, on the other hand, felt that self-knowledge about sensations was indeed achievable, but only as a by-product of the way the verbal community reinforced self-descriptive repertoires in the presence of the requisite private event. The handicap here is that the verbal community is in a disadvantaged position with respect to determining whether the covert event is actually occurring, because it cannot make reinforcement contingent upon the property of privacy. For Skinner, skepticism about private events was born of the shakiness of first-person "knowledge" about them *before* the verbal community created the relevant discriminations; for Wittgenstein, the concept of first-person "knowledge" of one's sensations was *always* a misnomer because the notion of knowledge is inapplicable in relation to one's private sensations. Skinner felt that "knowledge" of another's private sensations was always inferential; Wittgenstein felt otherwise.

I hear something in the other room that sounds like a groan—but I cannot be sure. In such a context, I *infer* someone is in pain. But when the victim of an industrial accident is howling and writhing on the floor in plain sight of co-workers, his arm mangled and bloody, I am no longer *inferring* his being in pain: I know this, according to Wittgenstein (i.e., knowing others are in pain is often not merely a surmise, a.k.a. "inferential"):

If for Skinner knowledge about private events in others is always *inferential,* what data would be sufficient under his formulation to satisfy requirements for certainty about such states? Here, we face a conundrum. According to Skinner, first-person "knowledge" about private events is dependent upon reinforcement by the verbal community, which in turn is saddled with an inferential mode in assessing private states in others. If neither the verbal community nor the individual in question possesses certain knowledge about the latter's private states (because the latter under the formulation is dependent upon the former for its discriminative powers), what hypothetical information would clinch a case for certainty? Since the very concept of *inference* entails the possibility of being mistaken should it prove false, does radical behaviorism imply that beliefs about private states always fall short of certainty? Is this tantamount to implying that there is a possibility, however remote, that private states in others may be totally misconstrued, or, in a worst case scenario, that there may not be private events at all—because the verbal community and, *a fortiori*, the individual who comes to know himself precisely because of its tutelage, have both been led down the wrong epistemic path?

Far from sharing affinities, the views of both Wittgenstein and Skinner about private events contrast sharply. To summarize: the former felt that I cannot "know" I have a toothache because the concept of self-knowledge is inapplicable to private sensations; Skinner felt that I can make a mistake about my sensations in the same way I can about other physical events, especially when I have not been taught to discriminate them properly by a verbal community.

Wittgenstein's discussions of privacy at Cambridge University— dutifully attended by such enraptured students as G. E. Moore—were accorded the title "the Toothache Club." Toothaches are a convenient springboard for discussions of private events to this day. The opinion of a celebrated contemporary academic addressing the problem from a radical behavioristic perspective illustrates the point. Catania (1992), for example, insists that dentists and patients have different "accesses" to toothaches in the latter. He goes on to declare that the dentist is a better judge of "where the pain really is" in cases of referred pain. He concludes that if we can be mistaken about the location of a toothache, how can we be sure that *any* of our reports of private sensations are trustworthy? (Catania, 1992, p. 1526). But his argument is fallacious.

Skepticism and Certainty

Where to begin? The author avers that a dentist can be a better judge of where my pain is than I when I have a toothache, and goes on to broaden skepticism about first-person reports of sensations by indicating that any doubts I should have about the location of my toothache has implications for my certainty about other of my private sensations. On the contrary, my dentist is *not* a better judge of where my pain is than I am, only a better judge of the location of the decay in the troublesome tooth in question. In fact, if, after inspecting my mouth to probe the toothsome event, he were to suddenly announce I could not be experiencing the pain where I (truthfully) said I was experiencing it, I could well challenge his understanding of the grammar of sensation reports (Wittgenstein, 1958). I might point out, for example, that the very concept of *referred* pain contradicts the claim that it is the dentist, not I, who is the ultimate arbiter of where my pain is—whatever the physical location of the decay giving rise to it. For consider: if my dentist were the final authority on where I feel my pain—presumably because my pain is a physical event, and he is the expert on localizing this— then the very idea of referred pain is incoherent. That is, if, according to the radical behaviorist, the locus of the pain had to be the same as the physical event giving rise to it, how does the notion of referred pain get a foothold in any account of what was going on in the dentist's office? In other words, how can I have any such thing as "referred pain," implying as it does a sensation localized some distance away from the physical event giving rise to it, when the radical behaviorist insists that I can make a mistake about the location of my pain when it does not jibe with where my dentist claims I must be feeling it? For referred pain is precisely that: a sensation localized away from the relevant physical event, a logical impossibility on the radical behavioristic account of private events. The meaningfulness of the very concept of referred pain is parasitic on a perceived location of a sensation differing from the location of the physical toothsome event. This means that an instrumental invasion of the organism—a future technology Skinner has envisioned as pinning down the actual physical characteristics of the private event—would still have to come to terms with any paradox occasioned by the perceived, or experienced location of the sensation in question. This may become a complicated affair, but the complication would not eventuate in *correcting* one's impression of where he or she actually feels the sensation.

The same logic holds for the phenomenon of phantom limb in amputees. In these cases, a patient may feel a pain that is experienced outside his body; he may feel it, for example, in the region of toes that no longer exist. Yet it would be absurd to suggest that he must be mistaking the perceived location of the pain because neurologists inform us that the physical event giving rise to it occurs elsewhere under the skin. That it does—and it surely does—hardly precludes an amputee's experience of pain outside his body. We can, of course, undertake to convince such a patient that he is mistaking the location of perceived pain, although we do so at the risk of engaging in mere language reform, not engineering an insight more in accord with the supposed reality of the physical world.

The foregoing argument may not conclusively confound the Skinnerian thesis that if a private event like a toothache is ultimately a physical one, and that the sensation of ache must be localized in the same place as the physical event it is. A radical behaviorist may go on to insist that his thesis can be salvaged by denying that the physical event in question is actually the decaying tooth. He could hold, for example, that the relevant physical event is a happening within the organism mediating between the ache and the decaying tooth that meets a requirement of identity of locus with the sensation. But arguments aimed at establishing such spatial harmonies can at best serve to bolster a plausible case for Identity Theory (Place, 1956; Feigl, 1967; Smart, 1959). They cannot be used to defend the counterintuitive notion that when the physicalistic cards are on the table, dentists are in a better position to localize *my* sensations than I am.

What could have led the author of the above passage to make the claim that there are others who might instruct me how to correct my impression of where I feel my pain, because they have a better take on the physical picture of things, as dentists do? The answer is not hard to find, and some of the blame is traceable to equivocation in many of Skinner's pronouncements about the subject. For example, in his 1945 essay *Operational Analysis of Psychological Terms*, he states that consciousness is a social product, a form of reacting to one's own behavior. The upshot of this analysis is that an individual becomes aware of himself only when he is reinforced by an outside verbal community for being so. In other words, we "enlarge the possibilities of awareness of ourselves" only to the extent this is facilitated by others! (Skinner, 1945, p. 593).

Skinner seems to imply—although in a somewhat murky way—that "self-awareness" is something more than merely learning to speak correctly about oneself. He seems to suggest that the "possibilities of awareness" created for me by the verbal community encompass a broader achievement than correct naming. This is also implied by Catania's assertion that one's perception of pain may stand in need of correction. Other of Skinner's remarks on private events smack of similar equivocations. For example, in About Behaviorism he remarked that teaching individuals to "classify objects correctly" follows in some way from teaching him or her "to notice very small differences in his sensations" (Skinner, 1974, p.13)

It is difficult to envision how being trained to "see" differences among one's sensations amounts to nothing more than a species of linguistic skill (i.e., attaching the right terms to certain sensations). As if to emphasize the idea that Skinner's externally derived notion of self-awareness encompasses more than merely a species of linguistic achievement, he remarks in *Beyond Freedom and Dignity* that without assistance from the verbal community "all behavior would be unconscious…Consciousness is a social product" (Skinner, 1971, p. 192).

Consciousness—at least in the ordinary sense of the use of this term—means something more than being able to attach the term *pain* to the appropriate sensation; it also means being aware (having, experiencing, perceiving, discriminating, harboring, sensing) the sensation when I have it, irrespective of whether or not I deploy the term *pain* correctly or in accordance with whatever linguistic conventions have been established by a verbal community.

Hidden Equivocations

When a radical behaviorist uses terms like "discriminate," the *picture* he may have of the term is that of a linguistic token in a set of verbal practices from which the vagaries of ordinary language have been pruned. He may even come to believe his verbal behavior permits more precision, being less vulnerable to the ambiguities of ordinary parlance. Perhaps this is true—some of the time. However, in the present context, it would appear that the "discriminations" trained by the verbal community in shaping self-awareness may encompass at least two achievements not systematically distinguished in the Skinnerian canon. For what is the precise nature of the alleged discrimination? If the verbal community is ultimately responsible for my awareness of my own private states, is this tantamount to *training me to become aware of or distinguish experientially among my sensations*, or *training me to describe myself accurately when I have them*, or both? The distinctions here are weighty ones, and they tend to get obscured underneath jargon about "discrimination." Furthermore, to the extent this jargon detracts from the ability to differentiate clearly between two rather different claims, it is the language of obfuscation, not clarity.

We are not born knowing how to use certain terms, so our dependence upon a verbal community to teach us the language of self-ascription is hardly a bold or challengeable claim. That on some basic level we must rely on others to learn how to speak about ourselves—or anything else for that matter—is a common assumption that tends to get pawned off as an epiphany when encased in terms like "discrimination," "collateral responses," and "reinforcement." That we need the assistance of others to *feel* a sensation, or otherwise "discriminate" among certain of our sensations is a patently absurd claim—for several reasons. Lower mammals experience pain without a trace of anything akin to a verbal community to enable this ability. Accordingly, to dispute this on the human level would appear to represent a break with the best informed Darwinian extrapolations. In addition, if we are dependent on others to accomplish such a feat, this implies we can be taught to "discriminate" our sensations improperly should the verbal community perversely decide to corrupt its instruction. On the contrary, mismanaging the task of verbal reinforcement is just that: attaching the wrong terms to whatever private states are under discussion; it is hardly akin to reordering or otherwise altering the private sensations of individuals acquiring language skills.

Imagine that as a developing and non-verbal organism I experience a toothache, and the verbal community decides to play a trick on me. It elects to reinforce me for saying *I feel euphoric* whenever I emit a collateral response ordinarily associated with toothache. Does the radical behaviorist imply I subsequently experience a mania in contexts in which others experience pain; or, alternatively, experience toothache but use the wrong words to describe it? Calling the effects of improper outside reinforcement breakdowns in "self-awareness" would appear to be a rather overblown way of characterizing bungled linguistic training about my vocabulary of self-description—*if* this is all "self-awareness" amounts to. After all, if I claim to be euphoric when I am actually in pain, my disadvantage is only that I have not mastered English well, not that I need an opiate.

The upshot of one interpretation of the radical behavioristic thesis about private events—that "self-awareness" encompasses considerably more than teaching the proper vocabulary of self-ascription—is that there are no collateral responses to pain indelibly stamped as such. In this connection, if the verbal community on occasion gets it wrong or botches up its tutelage, then the character of the private event will shift as a function of the net improper reinforcement. On this interpretation, if I experience euphoria where another experiences pain because of an incompatible history of reinforcement by the verbal community, what entitles the latter to assume there is any such thing as a reliable connection between a particular class of collateral physical responses and the name or identity of the private event that should be verbally reinforced? In this context, "collateral" responses cannot occasion characteristic reinforcements by the verbal community, since such reinforcement itself creates the character of the private event in question! It becomes, as it were, its own self-fulfilling prophecy. Even if instrumental invasion of the organism were to reveal the same physiological events underpinning *pain* and *euphoria*, the conclusion might be that dissimilar sensations are mediated by the same physical correlate, not that the wrong term has entered into the language of self-ascription. I take this to be a *reductio ad absurdum* of the claim that verbal communities train individuals to "discriminate" their private states in the sense of perceiving differences among them on other than a naming, or linguistic, level.

The radical behaviorist is on the horns of a dilemma. Either his approach to private events on one interpretation entails counterintuitive consequences, or else embodies a theory of verbal acquisition which, underneath the technical terminology, seems actually quite trivial, boiling down to the common wisdom that others teach us how to speak about ourselves. And that this interpretation is not always the chosen one is made amply clear in Catania's assertion that a dentist knows better than I do about the perceived location of my toothache. If I can make a mistake about where I locate a pain, why not the possibility of error about whether I actually have one or not? I can only make a mistake about this on the theory that my discriminatory abilities are out of keeping with what others know about the matter because of the initial epistemological edge they enjoy about events under my skin. All the same, one wonders whether the skepticism about first-person knowledge of private events prior to reinforcement by the verbal community is a deduction from a strained theory, and not in keeping with the natural history of the species.

Mistrusting Verbal Behavior

Skinner has in the past expressed views that seem to derive from a concocted way of looking at a problem, and one that is heedless of the realities of cultural practice. For example, in *Science and Human Behavior* he remarked that there is a "lack of a reliable subjective vocabulary" and that "Everyone mistrusts verbal responses" that describe private events within the organism. As an example, he cites the case of someone who pleads headache faced with an onerous task, a person who cannot be "successfully challenged" (Skinner, 1953, p. 260).

What set of actual cultural practices do such remarks portray? Laymen are not bereft of reliable subjective vocabularies, nor does everyone mistrust verbal responses describing private events. Great emphasis is placed upon first-person reports about the location, quality, and intensity of pain in standard medical and dental examinations, and skepticism about them on the part of clinical practitioners, with the exception of factitious phenomena, is virtually non-existent. The same is true for reports of various kinds of sensations outside of clinical contexts. Skinner has overgeneralized a skepticism about verbal reports of private events from special cases like those in which, for example, liars report headaches in order to avoid onerous obligations. He has, in effect, portrayed a fictional picture of cultural practice, possibly because of deductions from his view about how private events come to control behavior. Who distrusts the private experience of pain as reported by an ingenuous youth who starts to yelp after an anvil is accidentally dropped on his foot? Who mistrusts the scream of pain from a dental patient who is having a wisdom tooth extracted without anesthesia? What cardiologist mistrusts the report of chest pain from a patient suddenly experiencing such a symptom? Negative results on an EKG or stress tests do not ordinarily occasion doubts about subjective reports of pain in such cases. At best, they only eventuate in a different diagnosis: reflux disorder or muscle strain, perhaps.

Skinner has in effect recast scenarios common to cultural practices, taking skepticism about the statements of liars as exemplifying the standard response to reports of private states. Even here, however, his depiction is faulty. We often distrust the statements of those who plead headache in the context of unpleasant tasks, not because their statements are about private events, but because we have reason to believe that they may be dissembling—especially when they have a past record of this. Moreover, we do, as a matter of cultural practice, challenge the claims of other people reporting private states or otherwise. When liars aver that they were not accomplices in vandalism or at a break-in at someone's home, do we disbelieve them because what they report was a *public* event?

Metaphors and Metonymical Extension

Another example of a questionable theory of verbal acquisition is Skinner's remarks about metaphorical extension in *Verbal Behavior*. In enumerating the several ways he feels verbal control over the private event is instituted, he stated that the verbal community can reinforce a statement about a private event by having it "transferred" from the public event through the process of "metaphorical and metonymical extension." (Skinner, 1957, p. 132).

Skinner saw no problem in his notion of "metaphorical extension," although his analysis may represent the putative confusion of drawing parallels between features of private and public stimuli and providing a plausible account about the transformative processes under discussion. For example, to show that the metaphor *a stabbing pain* mirrors the physical properties of knives or their effects on us when we are stabbed is hardly a satisfactory explanation of why I am able to exclaim *I have a stabbing pain*. Skinner goes on to say that *I have a stabbing pain* is instituted when it "shares some of the properties of the stimuli produced by sharp objects" (Skinner, 1957, p. 133). What if an individual were never stabbed, or never experienced the private events on the basis of which the transference supposedly takes place; could such an individual never emit *I have a stabbing pain*? What knives do to paper or cloth will not provide the necessary basis for transference; in such cases there has to be a history of private stimulation to afford a basis for a transfer from a public feature to the private event.

The point may be better illustrated in connection with *I have butterflies in my stomach*. What public event is at the basis for such a metaphorical extension to a private event—especially since having actual butterflies in the gastrointestinal tract has little or no relation to the either the metaphor or the private event it purportedly describes.

Skinner's reliance on metaphorical extension is seemingly in the service of relying on public stimuli to sharpen awareness of the inchoate or dubious world of private stimulation. Thus, we learn to discriminate private states by relying on external exemplars: the *piercing* pain, the *bubbling up* sensation, the *hot* flash, the *burning* feeling, and so on. Doesn't the process also go in the other direction? Do not individuals illuminate something about public stimuli or the external world by characterizing it through metaphors based upon private states? For example: the world is a *depressing* place, his remarks were *painful*, her boyfriend is "*hot*," her words were *cold*, life is like a *dream*, he brought *ill* tidings, she's a *dizzy* blonde, he writes *nervous* prose, politicians are a *headache*, mothers-in-law are *pains in the neck*, he makes one's *flesh crawl*, he was *itching* to debate the point, *glum* news, *languid* prose, *anxious* times, a *heartfelt* exchange, a *sullen* invitation, a *soulful* poem, a *raging* sea, a *manic* exchange, a *dour* message, a *hurtful* announcement, a *boring* speech, a *thoughtful* letter, *disappointing* news, a *downbeat* day, a *sentimental* journey, an *insane* choice, an *angry* ocean, a *disgusting* remark, a *consuming* hobby, a *reflective* stance, a *nauseating* speech, and so on—ad infinitum, it would seem. If publicity gives privacy its discriminative character, isn't the reverse also true?

Finally, it should be noted that Skinner's analysis frequently begs the question. In the metaphor *the tempest in my mind*, the internal event is not somehow clarified by reference to the public event that shares characteristics with it on the metaphoric level. The explanatory challenge is showing precisely why the metaphoric extension in this case is apt. The description *tempestuous feelings* does not enter the verbal repertoire because a feeling is like a gale *simpliciter*. Why the feeling is like a gale in the first place is the explanatory challenge for radical behaviorism. One cannot, as it were, point to the "similarity" between feelings and storms to prove Skinner's point since the "similarity" may exist only because of the existence of the metaphor.

Stimulus Similarity

I have the same pain I had an hour ago depends upon the notion of stimulus similarity between past and present pains. The radical behavioristic treatment of private events should prompt its proponents to raise the disquieting question: "How does one know two sensations are identical or similar if it is possible to be mistaken about it?" There a problem here that cannot be dispatched by relegating it to a process of generalization or what Skinner has called "induction." For how do I assess the *similarity* of pains unless "sameness" is reinforced like every other feature of my private experience? In other words, how, under radical behaviorism, can I ever learn that the pain I had today is the same as the one I had yesterday when I must learn to discriminate them as such with the assistance of a verbal community that reinforces verbal expressions of "sameness?" After all, if self-awareness of private events is shaped by the verbal community, my ability to tell whether consecutive events under my skin are experienced as the same or different from each other likewise ought to be subject to outside tutelage. However, the collateral responses associated with reports of similar sensations may differ considerably, not to mention the fact that private sensations can be experienced without any collateral behavior serving to occasion outside verbal reinforcement. For example, my reaction to a pain I experience today may be muted—or non-existent: a dramatically different response than the reaction to the same pain I had yesterday when I howled and grimaced. Today, I stoically brace up as I experience the same sensation. If I must learn to detect "sameness"—or "differences" among my sensations on the basis of how the verbal community enables me to discriminate them, how is this conceivably accomplished? Something about the behavior-analytic explanation of the entire process appears to be viciously circular.

In *Verbal Behavior* Skinner addresses the possibility of metaphorical extension by noting, "…in expressions like *ebullient* or *dampened spirits*, however, we must search for possible similarities between public and private events to explain the metaphorical extension. Something within the skin must 'bubble up' or 'grow limp or cold' in some sense (Skinner, 1957, p. 133). His example, however, begs a critical question. The problem is only stated, not resolved, by hypothesizing similarity between public and private events by way of metaphor. Clinching a solution to the problem would amount to explaining how the metaphor comes to be apt in the first place. In other words, how does one learn to attach the phrase "bubbling up" to the event it purports to describe, even by way of metaphor? What instruction has the individual received in his or her past history of reinforcement that enables the emission of "bubbling up" or "dampening down" in contrast, maybe, to "drowning" or "heating up"? In addition, claiming that the private event must share in some sense with a "bubbling up" characteristic of the covert occurrence implies an isomorphism between the metaphor and the physical event it delineates. Yet instrumental invasion of the organism might not reveal any such isomorphism. The latter, if anything, would seem to characterize the relationship between a *sensation* or *raw feel* (i. e., *qualia*) and a metaphor solely, not between the covert physical event identified with the sensation. A neurophysiologist from a third-person perspective could conceivably isolate an α-process that is the physical aspect or underpinning of a β-type sensation, whereas a metaphor only captures a β-aspect of the event in question. As an identity theorist, Skinner has claimed that so-called private "mental" events like sensations are physical events under the skin. He also feels that physiologists who conduct instrumental invasions of the organism are nonetheless debarred from access to that aspect of the private event experienced by the individual whose event it is. Thus, the physiologist can hypothetically observe the underlying physical event, but not its sensational "quality," in the individual he investigates (Creel, 1980). Accordingly, the neurophysiologist who locates the physical event which is the underpinning of the sensation experienced by an individual without, however, knowing anything about the felt character of the sensation in question, could not determine what metaphorical extension would be appropriate in such a case. It is the experienced aspect of the private event, not its physicality from a third-person perspective that establishes the sympathetic connection between it and a metaphor.

Radical Behaviorism vs. Mentalism

Skinner's radical behaviorism is presumably an approach that seeks to avoid the pitfalls of "mentalism." The latter type of philosophical theory is said to be one that has characterized most psychological systems prior to radical behaviorism. The trend, according to Skinner, included reliance on cognitive way-stations, introspection, mediating, or indefinable variables owing their provenance to Cartesian dualism, or the theory that private states take place in a metaphysical order or medium differing from the physical world Skinner believes is the proper arena of a scientific focus. Mentalistic terms and concepts according to him thus need to be shorn from the behavioristic approach to analyzing behavior. The proposal may be hasty for two reasons: (1) the assault on mentalism is in part based upon negative existential propositions, and (2) there are mentalistic concepts which are not only not redundant in a scientific approach to behavior; they may be indispensable to it, as Hempel decades ago came to realize (Hempel, 1980; Rey, 1997).

(1) Skinner's criticism of mentalistic explanations takes the bull by the horns: events under the skin are *physical*, not *immaterial* ones in a mentalistic medium, as advertised by dualism. How is such a philosophical position to be understood?—surely not as an empirical thesis, since Skinner has never specified what data would instantiate ghosts in the machine. In short, the proposition that private events are ultimately physical in nature loses some of its meaning when the falsifiability (Popper, 1959) of the alternative theory remains unspecifiable, unclear, or shrouded in mystery.

(2) In his animal laboratory, an experimenter places a pigeon on a fixed ratio schedule of reinforcement under which the latter is delivered every third response (FR3 scheduling). There nonetheless exists an undetermined—not undeterminable, only unverbalized—interval schedule necessarily coinciding with the FR3 schedule already specified. This is because for every ratio (R) schedule there exists an interval schedule of reinforcement (I) coinciding with it. Interval schedules are those programmed to deliver reinforcement based upon the time elapsing between responses. Every R-schedule is extensionally equivalent to an overlapping I-schedule and vice-versa, implying that differing R-and I-schedules are denotatively the same. (This is not to claim that all interval and ratio schedules of reinforcement are coextensive; only that for any one of them there is an extensionally identical twin of the other type in the parallel universe of denotation.) Thus, the pigeon placed on the FR3 schedule is also placed on a variable interval schedule (VI) coinciding with it. If the pigeon takes ten minutes to emit the first three responses before reinforcement, five minutes to emit the next three responses before reinforcement and two minutes to emit the next three responses before reinforcement, it is thereby also subject to a VI schedule of reinforcement. In the improbable event that the

time elapsing between the three reinforcements was always the same, say, five minutes, an FR3 schedule coincides with a FI5 schedule. The question for the radical behaviorist is: what is the operative schedule programmed by the E? The answer is seldom "both," and for good reason. The radical behaviorist must assume it is the E's *intention*—a mentalism—that ordinarily determines schedule type. At least this is the implication, since what other criterion of schedule-type is relied on to explain an E's selective verbal behavior when differing schedule types describe the same events?

In the manner of a distinction drawn by W. V. Quine (Quine, 1972), we might wish to say that both types of scheduling *fit* the facts, but the E's arrangement *guides* the FR3 scheduling. However, "guiding" in Quine's sense involves a causal relationship, and unless we assume that the E's intention has causal force—a hunch that would be anathema to a radical behaviorist—we cannot restrict stimulus control to one schedule when two different ones fit the facts. True, the E is aware of *intending* to program the FR3 schedule, rather than the VI schedule, but "awareness" and "intention" are presumably dethroned as causally relevant in radical behavioristic formulations. Awareness is supposed to be a by-product of the training by the verbal community, while intention is a mere mentalism to be extruded from scientific accounts. Unfortunately, it will tend to rear its banished head even in relation to boilerplate distinctions of the experimental lab.

References

Armstrong, D. M. (1968). *A materialist theory of the mind*. New York: Humanities Press.

Aune, B. (1961). The problem of other minds. *Philosophical Review, 70*, 320-339.

Austin, J. L. (1961). *Philosophical papers*. London: Oxford University Press.

Ayer, A. J. (1946). Other minds. *Aristotelian Society Supplementary Volume, 28*, 188-197.

Baum, W. M. and Heath, J. I. (1992). Behavioral explanations and intentional explanations in psychology. *American Psychologist, 47*, No. 11, 1312-1317.

Catania, A. C. (1992). B. F. Skinner, organism. *American Psychologist, 47*, No. 11, 1521-1530.

Carnap, R. (1932/33). Psychology in physical language. *Erkenntnis, 3*, 107-142.

Carnap, R. (1953). Testability and meaning. In H. Feigl and M. Brodbeck, *Readings in the philosophy of science*, (Pp. 47-92), New York: Appleton-Century-Crofts.

Costall, A. (1980). The limits of language: Wittgenstein's later philosophy and Skinner's radical behaviorism. *Behaviorism: A Forum for Critical Discussion, 8*, 123-131.

Creel, R. (1980). Radical epiphenomenalism: B. F. Skinner's account of private events. *Behaviorism: A Forum for Critical Discussion, 8*, 31-53.

Day, W. F. (1969). On certain similarities between The Philosophical Investigations of Ludwig Wittgenstein and the operationism of B. F. Skinner. *Journal of the Experimental Analysis of Behavior, 12*, 489-506.

Day, W. F. (1980). Some comments on the book "Verbal Behavior." *Behaviorism; A Forum for Critical Discussion, 8*, 165-173.

Dinsmoor, J. A. (1992). Setting the record straight: The social views of B. F. Skinner. *American Psychologist, 47*, No. 11, 1454-1463.

Feigl, H. (1967). *The mental and the physical.* Minneapolis, Minnesota: Univerity of Minnesota Press.

Glenn, S. S., Ellis, J., and Greenspoon, J. (1992). On the revolutionary nature of the operant as a unit of behavioral selsction. *American Psychologist, 47*, No. 11, 1329-1336.

Hempel, C. (1980). The logical status of psychology. In N. Block (Ed.), *readings in the philosophy of psychology,* (Pp. 14-33), Vol I, Cambridge, Massachusetts: Harvard University Press.

Kirby, R. V. (1956). The other minds quandary. Ph.D. thesis. Berkeley, California: University of California.

Lee, V. I. (1992). Transdermal interpretation of the subject matter of behavior analysis. *American Psychologist, 47*, 1337-1343.

Martin, M. (1978). Interpreting Skinner. *Behaviorism: A Forum For Critical Discussion, 6*, 129-138.

Moore, J. (2001). On psychological terms that appeal to the mental. *Behavior and Philosophy, 29*, 167-186.

Palmer, D. C. and Donahoe, J. W. (1992). Essentialism and selectionism in cognitive science and behavior analysis. *American Psychologist, 47*, No. 11, 1344-1358.

Place, U. T. (1956). Is consciousness a brain process? *British Journal of Psychology, 57,* 44-50.

Popper, K. (1959). *The logic of scientific discovery.* London: Hutchinson.

Putnam, H. (1957). Psychological concepts, explication, and ordinary language. *Journal of Philosophy, 54,* 94-100.

Rachlin, H. (1992). Teleological behaviorism. *American Psychologist, 47,* No. 11, 1371-1382.

Rakos, R. F. (1992). Achieving the just society in the 21st century: What can Skinner contribute? *American psychologist, 47,* No. 11, 1499-1506.

Rey, G. *Contemporary philosophy of mind: A contentiously classical approach.* Oxford: Basil Blackwell.

Schnaitter, R. (1978). Private causes. *Behaviorism: A Forum For Critical Discussion, 6,* 1-12.

Sellars, W. (1953). A semantical solution of the mind-body problem, *Methods, 5,* 45-82.

Skinner, B. F. (1945) The operational analysis of psychological terms. *Psychological Review, 52,* 270-294.

Skinner, B. F. (1957). *Verbal behavior.* New York: Appleton-Century-Crofts.

Skinner, B. F. (1969). *Contingencies of reinforcement.* New York: Appleton-Century-Crofts.

Skinner, B. F. (1974). *About behaviorism.* New york: Alfred A. Knopf.

Skinner, B. F. (1971). *Beyond freedom and dignity.* New York: Alfred A. Knopf.

Smart, J. C. C. (1959). Sensations and brain processes. *Philosophical Review*, *68*,141-156.

Thomson, J. F. (1951). The argument from analogy and our knowledge of other minds. *Mind*, *40*, 336-350.

Todd, J. T. and Morris, E. K. (1992). Case histories in the steady power of misrepresentatation. *American Psychologist*, *47*, No. 11, 1441-1453.

Quine, W. V. (1972). Methodological reflections on current linguistic theory. In D. Davidson and G. Harman (Eds.), *Semantics of natural language*, (Pp. 442-454), Dordrecht, Netherlands: D. Reidel.

Wisdom, J. (1956). *Other minds.* Oxford: Basil Blackwell.

B. F. Skinner on Walden II and Other Utopian Visions

Everywhere they plan to bring in Utopia by turning this gang out and putting that gang in. Everywhere they believe in wizards and messiahs.

—H. L. Mencken, *Forum*, September, 1930.

Several questions arise about the design of utopian communities like B. F. Skinner's *Walden II* (Skinner, 1976). One pertains to whether their creation is desirable; a second to whether they can succeed on a continuing or indefinite basis. Another is a question about what demarcates a "utopian" community from groups of individuals who are culturally segregated, albeit products of naturally evolving social structures based upon ethnic, economic, or religious insularities. What, after all, qualifies as a utopian community—over and above other categories of segregated groups who intentionally or otherwise develop their uniquely styled group life?

The first issue, the desirability of a planned community, may sometimes depend upon the resolution of the second, the issue of longevity. In a practical sense, it is redundant to ask whether a given social design is a desirable goal to achieve if its creation or continuation is not possible in the first place. On the other hand, some defenders of particular social designs might hold that there is something worthwhile about the creation of a utopia even if its existence is brief. For them, the prospect of being short-lived may not be a satisfactory yardstick by which to judge a social vision, however disappointing its permanence.

Reasons for the shortened life of such schemes may vary. A particular planned community may not be feasible because it does not stand the test of time, eventually foundering on unforeseen consequences in the engineering, interpersonal, or economic spheres. Such a society may contain internal complications that are unexpected, and fated to affect its survival. Skinner's *Walden II* utopia is no different in this regard, and were it not a fictional depiction of a planned community, it would likewise be subject to whatever factors ensure or negate its continuation over time. Perhaps most designed communities from the outset lack transparency when it comes to these determinations.

In the past, utopian efforts in this country have often faltered because of the vagaries of time, place, and history. For example, a decade after its development in the Wabash Valley of Indiana, the experimental community of Rappists decided to relocate back to Pennsylvania, in part because of the antagonism of outsiders in the Midwest region. The community was sold to Robert Owen in 1825. Like Skinner, Owen was committed to the belief that human patterns were almost entirely a product of environmental influences, and his enormous influence on nineteenth century ideas about cultural design drew the interest of such notables as President James Monroe. Like Karl Marx, Owen held that provisional governing bodies of the experimental polity would eventually wither away into a leaderless communism. However, Owen's lecture tours took him to Europe, leaving a less than charismatic governance back home in its wake. This led to a deterioration of his New Harmony community, a decline not halted by his return to America to take charge. Despite several reorganizations of his society—including the expulsion of freeloaders and citizens who took advantage of commutarian largesse—its inherent complications eventually lead to Owens' farewell to New Harmony in 1827.

In contrast to secularist societies like Owen's and the Zoar Separatist Society founded in 1817 by Joseph Bimeler (Hinds, 1908), the New York Oneida colony of Perfectionists founded by John Humphrey Noyes in 1848 was inspired by religious and theological concepts, albeit radical ones when it came to sexual morality. Noyes held that monogamous liaisons were contrary to the will of God, and that pentagamy, or the communal sharing of sexual favors and liaisons was a necessary aspect of perfectability, as was education under the control of commutarian, not parental, regulation. However, after thirty-five years of Noyes's social experiment, the Oneida Community broke up after Noyes fled to Canada in the face of charges of sexual immorality (Hayden, 1976).

While most utopian communities in this country were founded in the eighteenth and nineteenth centuries, there were also societies that started in the seventeenth century, possibly because the promise of the New Land was one associated with throwing off the yoke of religious oppression common to emigrés from the European scene. The Pietist community of "Woman in the Wilderness" was founded in 1694, the Moravian community of "Irenia" in 1695, and "Bohemian Manor," created by Labadists in 1683.

Another issue arises for *Walden II*. This is the nature of the relationship between it and radical behaviorism, the underlying secular philosophy of science Skinner believed guided its development. The two are widely regarded as intertwined, the design of the utopia thought to spring from the application of principles enshrined in his philosophy of science. However, the necessary connection between the two is rarely examined as an issue in its own right. The same holds for alternative utopias based upon religious principles or philosophies. The present essay seeks to review this issue, since the concept of "deriving" behavioral applications like community design as well as therapeutic and educational modalities from alleged overriding philosophies is an unexplored area of inquiry.

Skinner himself imagined that a society modeled along behavioristic principles would be very different from one modeled along more traditional lines. The conjecture is speculative and subject to empirical confirmation. Its falsification would amount to the development of a utopia just like *Walden II*, only constructed on the basis of an alternative system of concepts. Since *Walden II* is a fictional depiction of a utopian community, an immediate test of Skinner's proposition about the dissimilarity of social structures inspired by contrasting philosophies cannot be made. We can at present only speak of future possibilities.

Another way of framing the issue is to imagine a society precisely like *Walden II*, with the exception that its architects believe it to be inspired by religious principles. Is such a society nonetheless still modeled along behavioristic lines, despite the fact that no one consciously relied on them in developing it? Is it possible to apply behavioral principles *unintentionally*? Here, we might imagine the development of a community inspired by religious concepts, but whose architects go about setting up institutional structures and patterns that can be explained using the alternative concepts of behavior-theory. In what sense would such a hypothetical community *not* be classifiable as an application of behavioristic principles? When behaviorists design the same community relying self-consciously on principles like *positive reinforcement, extinction, consequences of behavior, discriminative stimuli, operants,* and so forth, what would such a group of applied scientists be doing that their counterparts in the parallel religious community were not doing? Or is a behavioral "derivation" more than just a matter of what individuals, behavioral engineers or otherwise, actually do?

If it is held that the hypothetical religious community, one incorporating mentalistic concepts as a feature of its guiding principles, could never approximate the structure of a utopia created through the application of behavioristic principles, imagine the following possibility. A group of behavioral engineers pledging allegiance to radical behaviorism designs a utopia modeled along Skinnerian lines. The society is set up and flourishes. Unexpectedly, all the citizens of this community suddenly undergo a conversion to a religious system of belief. The conversion is fairly sudden and dramatic, as in the case of St. Paul on the road to Damascus. The question is: in what sense would the converted citizenry be logically compelled to change the design of their utopia in order that it conform to a new driving philosophy? Here, we will ignore for the moment how the citizens alter their verbal behavior—in effect no longer paying lip-service to the aforementioned behavioristic concepts. Such argot obviously involves a rather different set of verbal practices than a newly appropriated lingo involving terms like *salvation*, the *soul, good* works, the *after-life*, or *God's work on earth*. We are interested only in the structure of daily activities and patterns of societal behavior other than those in a verbal repertoire. What would be the necessary alterations of life-style the converted citizenry would be obliged to undertake in virtue of the conversion?

The use of mentalistic concepts is an aspect of the natural evolution of all world cultures. Yet one implication of B. F. Skinner's ideas on the design of cultures as instanced in his novel or in briefer essays (Skinner,

1972a, 1981) is that a society constructed by applying principles of his philosophy of science would be an improvement over systems highjacked by mentalistic concepts. In Skinner's view, such projects are inefficient at best, since their conceptual baggage would thwart the realization of professed social goals of whatever stripe. A reason he gives for this are the impediments imposed on effective action through reliance on notions of "freedom" or "autonomous man" in contrast to a functional analysis with a focus on the independent environmental variables of which behavior is a function. "Inefficient" here implies stumbling blocks to goals chartered by architects of whatever alternative philosophical persuasion prevails. Many of the latter have not been exempt from searching criticism by spokespersons of alternative creeds and persuasions. Historically, sundry philosophies have embraced utopian ideals that met with disapproval by other constituencies, depending upon the philosophical persuasion in question. Some disparaged versions of social engineering they felt approximated Orwellian nightmares, whereas others were critical of any kind of social engineering, holding that such efforts compromise ideals renouncing totalitarian control implicit in them. Others may deem social redesign as worthwhile pursuing, albeit difficult or impossible to achieve, while still others may be critical of designs they feel inferior to the ones they propose.

The issue of divergent social ideals aside, Skinner has been less than clear about precisely how traditional perspectives on social planning are diversions from an optimal path. Clarifying how behaviorism represents an improvement in the real world—as opposed to its depiction in a fictional work like *Walden Two*—involves revealing the actual differences between naturally evolving social structures and those inspired by his philosophy of science, radical behaviorism.

Skinner seems to have wavered between two separate lines of argument in his critique of preexisting social structures. On the one hand, he has faulted social planning not inspired by radical behavioristic principles, whereas on the other he felt the problem involves a traditional opposition to social engineering *simpliciter*. On the latter assumption, he indicated that a cultural antipathy to undertaking large-scale social design springs from a misplaced distrust of enterprises viewed as contrary to the "freedom" celebrated in "democratic" ideals or the notion of "autonomous man." There is quite a difference between holding that the house that Jack built was a white elephant because he was ignorant of architectural principles, and insisting that the effort was misplaced because the house in question is not the kind of place Jack should inhabit in the first place. Let us explore the first of these two alternatives, namely, that past social planning is deficient because it has been disadvantaged by not appropriating the proper philosophy of science.

Conceive of the following hypothetical situation. Suppose mentalistic language and concepts, like those that are infiltrated by causal references to *intentions, motives, desires, pleasures, feelings, hopes, aspirations,* and the like were traditionally coupled with effective social planning in the realization of cultural goals. As a matter of historical fact, the majority of actual utopian communities flourishing in the past not only relied on mentalistic concepts inspiring their respective planners; they relied on *spiritualistic* or religious premises, to boot. Examples of such communities on the American scene have been created and continue to be developed, some standing the test of time, others disappearing for a variety of reasons.

Skinner's work has been widely regarded within psychology as the basis for a wide range of "applications" affecting the lives of particular target populations. Among these are techniques to change the plight of psychiatric and developmentally disabled populations, innovations in educational curricula of normal and disabled populations, and applications as far removed from human improvement as guided missiles of war (Skinner, 1972b). Contemporary research on compromised clinical populations has revealed a degree of overlap when it comes to the therapeutic efficacy of treatment procedures inspired by different theoretical orientations in psychology. Despite this, there are indications of the superiority of behavioral approaches when it comes to intellectually compromised individuals, pervasive developmental disorders and broad-spectrum autistic conditions, learning disabilities, depression, specific fears, panic disorder, speech dysfluencies, obsessive-compulsive disorder, and types of sexual dysfunction. All the same, the nature of the connection between behavior theory and its presumed applications—just like the connection between radical behaviorism and *Walden II*—has received little attention. Behavior therapists or applied behavior analysts often speak about their clinical armamentaria as "experimentally derived treatment techniques." What sense of the term *derived* is operative here? The low visibility query underlying the rhetorical question is "What set of conceivable techniques would *not* be derivable from behavior theory if the latter is taken to be a set of principles explaining human behavior in the most general sense?"

In a study authored by Truax (1966), it was discovered that Rogerian therapy, in contrast to representing "unconditional positive regard," was actually selectively reinforcing clients' verbal behavior. An impartial observer might conclude that what he or she was privy to was not Rogers' professed approach, that of client-centered therapy, but another form of behavior therapy. One might elect to describe the therapeutic transaction as "disguised or unintended behavior therapy," since the Rogerian psychotherapist was unaware of the selective nature of the approach. Had the therapeutic ministration been effective, its success could therefore be explained in behavioristic terms.

The epiphany is that the success of all forms of psychotherapy can be explained—or at least analyzed—in behavioristic terms. And no wonder. If the latter is presumed to explain or otherwise account for human behavior in general, professional therapeutic patterns naturally fall within its compass as a subclass of a subject matter. Since behavior-theory has a wide explanatory compass, is *any* therapeutic approach "derivations" of this framework if the latter can explain their success? The answer, it seems to the present author, is a simple one. "Derivations" are simply those applications practiced by professionals who self-consciously use a special vocabulary and inventory of concepts to explain their efficacy.

Considering the wide compass of behavior-theory, it is difficult, if not impossible, to envision how it might fail to "explain" the success of all treatment techniques. Ironically, it can also explain their failures. In the Truax sudy, the client-centered interventions turned out to be the selective reinforcements of verbal behavior. Yet if "unconditional positive regard" remained true to form, it could be analyzed as "non-contingent reinforcement of verbal behavior." This insight should prompt us to recast our previous formulation. Is not as though Rogers' client-centered therapy was ineffective because it was not as a modality derivable from behavioristic principles; it was ineffective because it was employing the technique of non-contingent, rather than contingent, reinforcement of verbal operants. In other words, Rogers' techniques can as easily be recast as a mismanaged behavioristic approach, were it not for the fact that the Rogerian therapist did not play the behavioristic language-game. Because of this, client-centered therapy is routinely conceived as an approach that is a theoretical alternative to one inspired by behavioristic principles!

The alleged failure of behavioristically oriented experiments like *Walden II,* or actual utopias in Virginia and Mexico hardly documents a failure of applied behaviorism or its philosophy of science, radical behaviorism; it only documents at best a misappropriation or misapplication of concepts like *positive reinforcement, aversive control, stimulus control,* or *extinction.* These concepts are more advantageously viewed as explanatory principles embracing the widest categories of human behavior, rather than as names for specific and particularized interventions in parochial armamentaria. Theoretical orientations in psychology, including radical behaviorism, are not roadmaps and blueprints for discrete therapeutic techniques deducible from them, but only inventories of protean concepts and principles embracing whatever applications are in fact developed. That the opposite viewpoint has enjoyed popularity is more a matter of antiquarian interest than it is of logical significance.

References

Alcott, A. B. (1938). *The journals of Bronson Alcott.* Boston: Little, Brown & Company.

Alcott, A. B. (1991). *How like an angel came I down: Conversations with children on the gospels.* Hudson, New York: Lindisfarne Press.

Alcott, B. A. (2007). *Notes of conversations 1848-1875.* Teaneck, New Jersey: Fairleigh Dickinson University Press.

Bestor, A. (1970). *Backwoods utopias: The sectarian origins and the Owenite phase of commutarian socialism in America: 1663-1829.* Philadelphia: University of Pennsylvania Press.

Harrison, J. F. C. (1969). *Robert Owen and the Owenites in Britain and America: The quest for the new moral world.* London: Routledge& Kegan Paul.

Hayden, D. (1976). *Seven American utopias: The architecture of commutarian socialism, 1790-1975.* Cambridge, Massachusetts: The M.I.T. Press.

Hinds, W. A. (1908). *American communities and co-operative colonies.* Chicago, Illinois: Charles H. Kerr & Company.

Holloway, M. (1966). *Heavens on earth: Utopian communities in America, 1680-1880.* New York: Dover Publications.

Kern, L. J. (1981). *An ordered love: Sex roles and sexuality in Victorian utopias—The Shakers, the Mormons, and the Oneida Community.* Chapel Hill, North Carolina: University of North Carolina Press.

Kuhlmann, H. (2005). *Living Walden II: B. F. Skinner's utopia and experimental communities.* Urbana and Chicago, Illinois: University of Illinois Press.

Nordhoff, C. (1875). *The communistic societies of the United States: From personal visit and observation.* London: John Murray.

Owen, R. (1927). *A new view of society and other writings.* London: Everyman's Library.

Rexroth, K. (1974). *Communalism: From its origins to the twentieth century.* New York: The Seabury Press.

Sears, C. E. (1915). *Bronson Alcott's Fruitlands.* New York: Houghton Mifflin Company.

Shepard, O. (1937). *Pedlar's progess: The life of Bronson Alcott.* Boston: Little, brown and Company.

Shepard, O. (1938). *The Journals of Bronson Alcott.* Boston: Little, Brown and Company.

Skinner, B. F. (1972a). The design of cultures. In *Cumulative record: A selection of papers.* New York: Appleton-Century-Crofts, pp. 39-50.

Skinner, B. F. (1972b). Pigeons in a pelican. In *Cumulative record: A selection of papers.* New York: Appleton-century Crofts, pp. 574-591.

Skinner, B. F. (1976). *Walden two.* New York: Macmillan.

Skinner, B. F. (1981). The design of experimental communities. In K. Roemer (Ed.), *America as utopia.* New York: Burt Franklin, pp. 28-42.

www.ingramcontent.com/pod-product-compliance
Lightning Source LLC
Chambersburg PA
CBHW051435250726
48655CB00001B/73